Supervision in the

ONE WEEK LOAN

Helping professions

Second edition

SUPERVISION IN CONTEXT

Series editors:
Dr Peter Hawkins, Bath Consultancy Group
Robin Shohet, Centre for Staff Team Development, London and Scotland

---

Staff in all the helping professions are working under increasing amounts of pressure. They are having to balance growing levels of distress, disease and disturbance, while at the same time managing an increasing speed of change in the financing and organizational structures of their employing organizations. Staff will only stay effective at their important work if they are supported and well supervised. Often their supervisors move straight from being a skilled practitioner into a management and supervisory position, with no training in the skills that staff supervision requires.

This series is aimed at the increasing number of people who act as trainers, tutors, mentors and supervisors in the helping professions. It is also designed for those who are studying to become a trainer or supervisor and for supervisees, who can use the books to reflect on the many complex issues in their work.

The series is designed to follow on from the success of the bestselling title *Supervision in the Helping Professions* by Peter Hawkins and Robin Shohet. Each book explores the key issues, models and skills for trainers and supervisors in the main areas of the helping professions: social work and community care, the medical and nursing professions, psychotherapy, counselling and mentoring for managers.

Current and forthcoming titles:
Meg Bond and Stevie Holland: *Skills of Clinical Supervision for Nurses*
Allan Brown and Iain Bourne: *The Social Work Supervisor*
Maria Gilbert and Ken Evans: *Psychotherapy Supervision*
Peter Hawkins and Robin Shohet: *Supervision in the Helping Professions*
    (2nd edn)

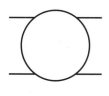

Supervision in the helping professions

An individual, group and organizational approach

Second edition

PETER HAWKINS and ROBIN SHOHET

Open University Press
Buckingham · Philadelphia

Open University Press
Celtic Court
22 Ballmoor
Buckingham
MK18 1XW

email: enquiries@openup.co.uk
world wide web: www.openup.co.uk

and
325 Chestnut Street
Philadelphia, PA 19106, USA

First Published 2000

A catalogue record of this book is available from the British Library

ISBN   0 335 20117 2 (pb)   0 335 20118 0 (hb)

Library of Congress Cataloging-in-Publication Data
Hawkins, Peter.
    Supervision in the helping professions: an individual, group and organizational approach / Peter Hawkins and Robin Shohet. – New enl. 2nd ed.
        p. cm. – (Supervision in context)
    Includes bibliographical references and index.
    ISBN 0-335-20118-0 – ISBN 0-335-20117-2 (pbk.)
    1. Counselors–Supervision of. 2. Psychotherapists–Supervision of. 3. Social workers–Supervision of. I. Shohet, Robin. II. Title. III. Series.

BF637.C6 H365 2000
361′.006′3–dc21   00-035989

Typeset by Graphicraft Limited, Hong Kong
Printed in Great Britain by Biddles Ltd, Guildford and King's Lynn

To all our supervisors and supervisees, especially those who were with us in our formative years at St Charles House Therapeutic Community of the Richmond Fellowship

Sed quis custodiet ipsos custodes?
(But who will care and protect the carers?)
Juvenal, *Satires*, 6, 1: 347

Contents

6   A process model of supervision

Part Three: Supervising groups, teams and networks 125

14 Conclusion: the wounded helper 191

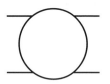# Notes on the authors

Peter Hawkins is Chairman of Bath Consultancy Group through which he works with a wide variety of organizations throughout the world on managing complex change. He writes and lectures in the field of organizational learning and culture, and strategic change. He is co-editor with Robin Shohet of the 'Supervision in Context' series published by Open University Press. Peter lives in Bath with his wife and three children.

Robin Shohet has been an individual and couple psychotherapist for over 20 years. He runs supervisor training courses through the Centre for Staff Team Development in the UK and abroad. Currently he combines this work with research and writing in the field of forgiveness and reconciliation. He is co-editor with Peter Hawkins of the 'Supervision in Context' series published by Open University Press. Robin lives in a spiritual community in the North of Scotland with his partner and two sons.

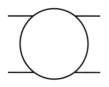

Preface to the second edition

It is now many years since we spent numerous weeks away together writing *Supervision in the Helping Professions*. The book was published in 1989 and we have been gratified by both the number of copies sold and the letters and responses we have received from people in a variety of professions all over the world. Since then, along with our colleagues, we have taken supervision training into such settings as hospitals, marriage guidance, local government, probation, psychotherapy and counselling. In each new setting, new questions and new issues have emerged. Over time we have come to realize some of the omissions of our first book, and to recognize that both we and the world of supervision have moved on.

In particular we have been struck by how much the importance of supervision has been recognized in the intervening years. This is in part due to the more widespread acceptance of counselling which requires supervision, but also to a recognition of the importance of supervision per se. Supervision courses have increased both in number and length. Ethical guidelines, systems of accreditation and professional standards have been established by a number of the professional associations. Research papers and supervision books have gone from famine to flood.

This combination of factors – our continued learning and development, the dramatic increase in interest, research and literature, and the feedback we have received – have all led us to write a second edition. A further factor is the change in the social and political context. Local government social work departments have had increasing demands made on them with shrinking resources. Their role has changed in emphasis from providing services to commissioning and registering services often provided by others. In the health service there has been constant change. Health trusts emerged with the coming of legislation to split the purchasers and providers of health care. General practitioner (GP) doctors have been able to become fundholders, and many health-related occupations have developed quite large organizations – for example, community psychiatric nurses, practice nurses, health visitors and counsellors. Accountability has become increasingly prominent, as our culture moves towards increased professionalization. This is paralleled in supervision with its emphasis on accountability and professionalization.

In this second edition we have kept the format of the book the same – namely, the individual, group and organizational approaches discussed in turn. We have inserted an extra chapter – Chapter 7, in order to correct a major omission in the first edition, that of looking at how differences, including race, class, gender, etc. inform and affect the supervisory relationship. Much of this chapter has been drafted by Judy Ryde who has been carrying out research in this area through the University of Bath.

In Part 1, which is mainly addressed to the supervisee, there is new material on working with post-traumatic stress, in Chapter 3.

In Part 2, a new section on ethics has been included in Chapter 4. Like trainings everywhere in this field, the training chapter (Chapter 8) in Part 2 has also been expanded in its length and range. There are new sections on training in such areas as ethics and transcultural competence as well as a section on the critical areas of evaluation and accreditation.

In Part 3, on group supervision, we have included two new models that have arisen out of our attempts on training courses to simplify the complexity of levels and development stages in such supervision groups.

We have made changes to Part 4, which includes a new section on the 'addictive organization' as well as an exploration of how supervision can feed back into the learning of a whole organization and profession. The chapter on organizational change (Chapter 13) has been made much more specific, to show the necessary steps in setting out to introduce or develop the practice and policies of supervision in an organization.

We have also provided in this edition some additional aids for the reader. There is a fuller contents list giving all the sub-sections of the chapters, and at the end of the book there is a list of key terms used, along with sections reproducing in full the BAC Code of Ethics and Practice and Criteria for Accreditation.

One of the features of the first edition was our process model. It has been described as a humanistic model, but we think of it as more of a holistic and integrative model which draws upon psychodynamic, humanistic, cognitive, behavioural and systemic approaches to therapeutic work. Indeed the model has been used by workers from all these orientations. The model is also very rooted in an intersubjective approach that focuses on the intersubjective relationship between supervisor and supervisee. Since the first edition the whole field of intersubjective psychotherapy has grown rapidly and this has further informed our thinking (see Atwood and Stolorow 1984; Stolorow *et al.* 1987; Stolorow and Atwood 1992). As well as making this more explicit by devoting space to the relationship, we have also expanded the aspect of the model that focuses on the wider social and organizational context of the work.

In this edition we wanted to retain our original freshness. We have kept many of the early chapters as they were originally written. We want to honour the continuing validity of our writing in the 1980s while expanding it with our later experience and updating it into the current context. What remains constant for both of us is that supervision and supervision teaching is an important part of our lives, and as long as we continue to work with people it will remain so. We hope the love and passion we feel and the pleasure we get from empowering ourselves and others will transmit itself through the theories, models and stories in this new edition of our book.

Peter Hawkins and Robin Shohet

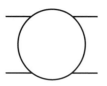

Acknowledgements

We would like first to thank the late Brian Wade of Changes bookshop for the initial idea of writing this book and also Jacinta Evans of Open University Press who has encouraged us to write this second edition and has shown enormous patience over how long it has taken us.

Much of the material on which this book is based has been developed over the last 20 years or more in the training courses in supervision we have been running through the Centre for Staff Team Development. Joan Wilmot made a substantial contribution to both the creation and teaching of these courses and has been a source of inspiration to us both. We would also like to thank others who have taught with us and the many who have attended these courses from whom we have also learned a great deal.

For this second edition we are particularly grateful to Judy Ryde who not only wrote much of the first draft of the new Chapter 7 and the new glossary, but also gave valuable help to other parts of this edition.

For the first edition many colleagues were very generous with their own ideas and experience of supervision, especially Frank Kevlin, Alix Pirani, Brigid Proctor, Helen Davis, Terry Cooper and Hymie Wyse. Mary Parker and Michael Carroll helped us find our way around the North American literature on supervision.

For this second edition we also benefited greatly from those who have written books for our Open University Press series on 'Supervision in Context': Allan Browne and Iain Bourne; Meg Bond and Stevie Holland; and Maria Gilbert and Ken Evans. Also Elizabeth Capewell, who provided specialist advice on supervising those working in traumatic situations.

In preparing the text we have had enormous support from the administrative staff at Bath Consultancy Group, especially Alison Stephenson and Pauline Allsop.

Finally we would once more like to thank our partners Judy Ryde and Joan Wilmot and all our children for their patience and their support in the anti-social activity of writing the book.

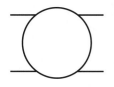

Part One

The supervisee's perspective

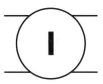

'Good enough' supervision

The late Donald Winnicott, paediatrician and psychoanalyst, introduced the concept of the 'good enough mother' – the mother who, when her child throws the food back at her, does not overreact to this event as a personal attack, or sink under feelings of inadequacy and guilt, but can hear this event as the child's expressing its temporary inability to cope with the external world. Winnicott points out that it is very hard for any mother to be 'good enough' unless she herself is also held and supported, either by the child's father or other supportive adult. This provides the 'nursing triad', which means that the child can be held even when they need to express their negativity or murderous rage.

This concept provides a very useful analogy for supervision, where the 'good enough' counsellor, psychotherapist or other helping professional can survive the negative attacks of the client through the strength of being held within and by the supervisory relationship. We have often seen very competent workers reduced to severe doubts about themselves and their abilities to function in the work through absorbing disturbance from clients. The supervisor's role is not just to reassure the worker, but to allow the emotional disturbance to be felt within the safer setting of the supervisory relationship, where it can be survived, reflected upon and learned from. Supervision thus provides a container that holds the helping relationship within the 'therapeutic triad'.

In choosing to help, where our role is to pay attention to someone else's needs, we are entering into a relationship which is different from the normal and everyday. There are times when it seems barely worthwhile, perhaps because we are battling against the odds, or because the client is ungrateful, or because we feel drained and have seemingly nothing left to give. In times of stress it is sometimes easy to keep one's head down, to 'get on with it' and not take time to reflect. Organizations, teams and individuals can collude with this attitude for a variety of reasons, including external pressures and internal fears of exposing one's own inadequacies.

At times like this, supervision can be very important. It can give us a chance to stand back and reflect; a chance to avoid the easy way out of blaming others – clients, peers, the organization, 'society', or even oneself; and it can give us a chance to engage in the search for new options, to discover the learning that often emerges from the most difficult situations, and to get support. We believe that, if the value and experience of good supervision are realized at the beginning of one's professional career, then the 'habit' of receiving good supervision will become an integral part of the work life and the continuing development of the worker.

In the last 20 years there has been an enormous increase in the use of counselling and therapeutic approaches in many of the helping professions. This has in part been fuelled by the move away from more traditional forms of institutional containment to 'community care' for those needing help and support. This move has led to an ever increasing demand, not just on families and relatives, but also on the whole range of helping professionals who have had to learn new ways of relating to the distress, disturbance and fragmentation of their clients. At the same time there has been an increased acceptance by the general public that most people need some form of counselling at certain stages of their lives.

This enormous upsurge in both counselling and psychotherapy, and in counselling and therapeutic approaches within many of the helping professions, has brought in its wake the recognition that such work needs to be properly supervised. The need for skilled supervisors, good training in supervision, and for theory and research in this area has increased much faster than the provision. When we wrote the first edition of this book there were very few books on supervision in Britain, and those that did exist were mainly limited to one profession. There was also a dearth of theoretical papers and descriptive accounts by those practising supervision. Only in the late 1980s did the British Association of Counselling start to look at the training and accreditation of supervisors, and psychotherapy training institutes start to provide training courses in this crucial area of work. Since the first edition appeared in 1989, there has been an enormous upsurge in both publications and training in this area. This has included important books by Carroll (1996), Page and Wosket (1994), Brown and Bourne (1996), Bond and Holland (1998), Carroll and Holloway (1999), Gilbert and Evans (forthcoming), Holloway and Carroll (1999) and Inskipp and Proctor (1993, 1995), as well as many others.

In the USA they have been concerned with this core area of practice much longer. There has been a great number of American papers and books on supervision. However, much of the work has been within the discipline of 'counselling psychology' and has mostly centred around one particular model – 'the developmental approach' (see, particularly, Stoltenberg and Delworth 1987). Although this is a significant contribution (see Chapter 5), it attends to only one of the many important aspects of the supervisory process. More recently Holloway has done important work synthesizing American approaches to supervision and creating an integrated approach (Holloway 1995; Holloway and Carroll 1999).

The supervisor has to integrate the role of educator with that of being the provider of support to the worker and, in most cases, managerial oversight of the supervisee's clients. These three functions do not always sit comfortably together (see Chapter 5), and many supervisors can retreat from attempting this integration to just one of the roles. Some supervisors become quasi-counsellors to their supervisees; others turn supervision into a two-person case conference, which focuses on client dynamics; others may have a managerial checklist with which they 'check up' on the client management of the supervisees. It is our intention in this book to help the supervisor develop an integrated style of supervision. We are not only advocating integration of the educative, supportive and managerial roles, but also a supervisory approach which is relationship based.

Sometimes, even in the best supervisory relationships, there will be times of being stuck, of wariness and even of avoidance. For one reason or another fear and negativity can creep in and it is useful for both parties to be able to recognize this and have tools for going through and beyond it. This book is addressed to both supervisor and supervisee, for we think that both have some responsibility for the quality of supervision; both form part of the same system geared towards ensuring quality of work. As part of taking joint responsibility for the supervisory relationship which we are advocating, we have therefore given guidelines to check out the process, especially around the initial forming of a contract for the working relationship. This working contract can be very important as it forms the boundaries and baseline to which both parties can refer.

Before entering this relationship, however, we believe that supervision begins with self-supervision; and this begins with appraising our own motives and facing parts of ourselves we would normally keep hidden (even from our own awareness), as honestly as possible. By doing this we can lessen the split that sometimes occurs in the helpers, whereby they believe they are problem free and have no needs, and see only their clients as sick and needy. As Margaret Rioch says: 'If students do not know that they are potentially murderers, crooks and cowards, they cannot deal therapeutically with these potentialities in their clients' (Rioch *et al.* 1976: 3).

Our experience has been that supervision can be a very important part of taking care of oneself and staying open to new learning, as well as an indispensable part of the helper's ongoing self-development, self-awareness and commitment to development. In some professions, however, supervision is virtually ignored after qualifying. We think that lack of supervision can contribute to feelings of staleness, rigidity and defensiveness which can very easily occur in professions that require us to give so much of ourselves. In extremes the staleness and defensiveness contribute to the syndrome which recent writers have termed 'burnout'. Supervision can help to stop this process by breaking the cycle of feeling drained which leads to a drop in work standards, which produces guilt and inadequacy, which lead to a further drop in standards, and so on.

Supervision, like helping, is not a straightforward process and is even more complex than working with clients. There is no tangible product and very little evidence whereby we can rigorously assess its effectiveness. One person brings to another a client, usually never seen by the supervisor, and reports very selectively on aspects of the work. Moreover, there may be all sorts of pressures on either or both of them from the profession, organization or society in which they both work. So, as well as dealing with the client in question, they have to pay attention to their supervisory relationship and the wider systems in which they both operate. There is a danger that both the supervisees and the supervisor can be overwhelmed by the degree of complexity and become like the centipede who, when asked which foot it moved first, lost the ability to move at all.

In order to encompass the complex interconnecting levels of the supervision process and yet write a book that is comprehensible, we have divided the book into four parts.

In Part 1 we have addressed supervisees, with the intention of encouraging them to be proactive in managing to get the support they need to do their work. Helping organizations and managers have an important responsibility to attend to the well-being of their staff, but it is only the workers themselves who can ensure that they get the particular type of support that is most appropriate for them and their work situation. There is a danger for workers to see support as coming only from higher up in their organization and to fail to see that support for their work can arrive from many different directions. Even within the supervisory relationship it is important that supervisees can find a way of being active in ensuring that they make the most of the relationship. In this section we have also included a chapter on the motives for being a helper which is relevant for supervisor and supervisees alike.

In Part 2 we look at making the transition from working with clients to becoming a supervisor, the different roles and functions that are involved, and the maps and models which we have found useful. Some of the same ground as Chapter 3 will be covered, but from the point of view of the supervisor. Chapter 6 is an in-depth exploration of the various aspects and levels of the supervisory relationship. This chapter is particularly addressed to those supervisors who supervise counsellors, psychotherapists or other professionals who are working in intensive therapeutic relationships (such as psychiatrists, psychologists, nurse therapists, etc.).

Chapter 7 is a new chapter which addresses issues of power both from one's role as well as from the cultural differences that can exist between supervisor and supervisee and client. These cultural differences may be rooted in such areas as ethnicity, nationality, gender, class, sexual orientation or professional background.

Part 2 ends with a chapter which explores the training needed for different types of supervisor – beginning supervisors; those who supervise students or trainees; those who supervise teams; and those who supervise departments or whole organizations. This chapter is both for those supervisors who want to think about what training they need for themselves and also for trainers, training officers and others who are responsible for providing training in supervision.

In Part 3 we look at forms of supervision other than the one to one, such as supervision in groups, peer groups and work teams. Part 3 explores the advantages and disadvantages of supervising individuals in a group setting and some of the ways of managing the group dynamics. It also explores how to supervise teams in a way that recognizes that the team is more than the sum of the individuals contained within it.

In Part 4 we focus on how to help an organization develop a learning culture where supervision is an intrinsic part of the work environment.

We have found that the organizational context in which supervision occurs has a major influence on the supervisory relationship.

Focusing on this wider context helps in the understanding of the wider system in which supervision occurs. This understanding can be useful in not over-personalizing a problem which is also a symptom of the organizational dynamics and in realizing that it is not just individual workers nor indeed just work teams that need supervision, but whole helping organizations. In Chapter 12 we also look at the need for supervising situations where a number of professional helpers and organizations are involved and the specialized skills that this requires.

Chapter 13 pulls together the various themes of the book and returns us to the concluding theme: ourselves as wounded helpers.

We see the four parts as increasing in complexity, starting with one person, the helper, then examining a supervisory relationship, then groups, then organizations. However, we recognize that looking at the internal processes of ourselves can be as complex as looking at organizational dynamics – it just involves fewer people. Our choice of topic and order of presentation has been meaningful for us, but our hope is that the actual topics become less important in themselves and become triggers for your own experience and action.

Another notion that we take from Winnicott is that learning is most creative when it emerges in play. In the supervision that we give we try and create a climate which avoids the sense of expert and student both studying the client 'out there' and instead creates a 'play space' in which the dynamics and pressures of the work can be felt, explored and understood; and where new ways of working can be co-created by both supervisor and supervisees working together. Likewise in this book we have shared our experience of the feelings, issues and possibilities of supervision in order to create more choices and options for both supervisees and supervisor.

We also recommend that you choose your own order for reading the chapters, for as we have indicated above, each section (and indeed each chapter) is addressed to a slightly different audience. However, we suggest that all readers start with Chapters 2 and 3, as, no matter how experienced you are as a supervisor, or even as a trainer of supervisors, we all share in common the need constantly to look at why we are in the work and how we get appropriate support for ourselves.

2 Why be a helper?

Introduction

> With great puzzlement and a furrowed brow he said, 'I don't understand why you are so angry with me. I wasn't trying to help you'.
> (Attributed to Wilfred Bion and quoted by Symington 1986: 278)

Helping and being helped is a difficult and often ambivalent process. In this chapter we will look at some of the complex motives for wanting to work in the helping or caring professions. Ram Dass and Paul Gorman (1985: 191) write very beautifully about the motivations and struggle to be a helper. 'How can I help', they write, 'is a timeless enquiry of the heart'. They go on to say: 'Without minimizing the external demands of helping others, it seems fair to say that some of the factors that wear us down, we have brought with us at the outset'.

We believe that it is essential for all those in the helping professions to reflect honestly on the complex mixture of motives that have led them to choose their current profession and role. For as Guggenbühl-Craig (1971: 9) writes: 'No one can act out of exclusively pure motives. The greater the contamination by dark motives, the more the case worker clings to his alleged objectivity'.

Exploring these mixed motives involves facing the shadow side of our helping impulse, including the lust for power and how we meet our needs through helping others.

Facing our shadow

The role of helper carries with it certain expectations. Sometimes clinging to our role makes it difficult to see the strengths in our clients, the vulnerability in ourselves as helpers, and our interdependence. As Ram Dass and Gorman (1985: 28) say: 'The more you think of yourself as a "therapist", the more pressure there is for someone to be "patient"'. In choosing to start here, we are again saying that a willingness to examine our motives, 'good' or 'bad', pure or otherwise, is a prerequisite for being an effective helper. Aware of what Jungians call our 'shadow' side, we will have less need to make others into the parts of ourselves we cannot accept. The crazy psychiatric patient will not have to carry our own craziness, while we pretend to be completely sane; in the cancer patients who cannot face their impending death, we will see our own fear of dying. Focusing on our shadow, we will be less prone to omnipotent fantasies of changing others or the world, when we cannot change ourselves (see also Page 1999).

One aspect of his own shadow – the wish for praise/adulation – happened to Robin while we were writing this book.

> I was running a residential therapy group abroad on my own. After a group member had worked on her feelings involving the death of a child, the group began to share at a very deep level, with one person's work triggering off another's. As the group facilitator I found the work both rewarding and moving as people resolved some of their deep pain. Staying with the process was for me tiring, yet paradoxically effortless in the way people's openness allowed their work to unfold. I could not remember any group which had consistently managed to face such trauma, and work through it successfully. At times like this I remember how privileged I am to be a witness to such work. At times like this ego creeps in. 'Look what *I* have done as facilitator'. After the fourth session we sat around for dinner. I missed not having a co-leader and was wanting the group to give me some validation for (my) wonderful work. Just then a wasp came and joined us. I ran. There was much laughter. 'So you are human after all.' I laughed too, but not before I had caught a feeling of resentment at being lovingly mocked and not revered.

How often we find ourselves caught in the shadow side of helping, letting ourselves and others think we are special, creating that illusion, and then being disillusioned when people want to take us down a peg or two.

The idea that we are helpers as opposed to a channel for help is a dangerous one. We want the praise for the success, but not the blame for the failure. Both of us struggle with the idea of non-attachment, telling students and clients who thank us for good pieces of work that it is not us, but themselves they should thank, yet secretly saying '. . . and me'. It is hard to accept the possibility of being only the vehicle of help. Yet this acceptance is the only way to get off the roundabout of being addicted to praise and fearful of blame, and to stop ourselves lurching wildly between impotence and omnipotence.

Non-attachment does not mean not caring. On the contrary it may be the nearest we can get to real caring as we do not have to live through our clients, dependent on their successes for our self-esteem.

In different ways we were given the opportunity to learn this lesson early on in our helping careers working in a residential therapeutic community. The supervisor of the home came fortnightly to supervise the head of the establishment and then to do a group supervision for all the staff. In one of these sessions the staff were engaged in an intense exchange around how to treat one of the residents. The supervisor stopped the discussion in its tracks by saying:

> You are not here to treat the residents, nor are you here to heal them or make them better. The job of the staff is to maintain the structure and keep open the space in which the residents can learn and grow. You are merely the servants of the process.

We had to learn (and are still learning) to give up the struggle for omnipotence, to let go of the idea that we were the ones that cured people, and learn the humility of being the caretaker of the therapeutic space.

Yet humility too is not without danger. The word 'caretaker' reminds us of a Jewish joke:

> One day a rabbi has an ecstatic vision and rushes up before the ark in his synagogue and prostrates himself, saying: 'Lord, Lord, in Thine eyes I am nothing.' The *cantor* (singer) of the synagogue, not wishing to be outdone, also rushes up to the altar and prostrates himself saying: 'Lord, Lord, in Thine eyes I am nothing.' The *shamash* (caretaker) sees the other two and decides to do the same. He rushes up and prostrates himself with the same words: 'Lord, Lord, in Thine eyes I am nothing.' Whereupon the rabbi turns to the *cantor* and says: 'Look who thinks he's nothing.'

Exploring our motivations

A book that deals very succinctly and challengingly with the shadow side of helping is *Power in the Helping Professions* by Guggenbühl-Craig (1971). He writes (p.79):

> To expand our understanding . . . perhaps it is necessary to go more deeply into what it is that drives the members of these ministering professions to do the kind of work they do. What prompts the psychotherapist to try to help people in emotional difficulty? What urges

the psychiatrist to deal with the mentally ill? Why does the social worker concern himself with social misfits?

Here is Peter's story in response to that question:

> I originally believed that I would work in the creative arts and that I was destined for a career in the theatre or television, but I was drawn away from performance to working in community arts, dramatherapy and from there into mental health work. I worked with people who were actively psychotic, who had murdered, burnt down churches, were violent, suicidal, alcoholic etc. – the whole gamut of human anguish, distress and pain. In this work I found relief, which many of my friends found strange, but which I now know was the relief that my own buried disturbance, hidden and denied within my family, school and culture within which I grew up, now had an outward reality. It was all being played out in the therapeutic community in which I worked.
>
> Looking back I can recognize that I both did some very good work which came from a genuine wanting (and needing) to meet these people in their pain, but also I had, eventually, to move on from this work as I had not got to the stage where I could re-own the full depths of my own shadow disturbance that these clients were living out for me. I had not truly faced my own inner murderer, my paranoid fear, my fragmentation, my despair. So I was unable to meet them fully as equals and was only able to come alongside in an unequal relationship where they carried the dis-ease and I was reinforced in my role of the coping, caring and containing worker.
>
> The journey from facing my own dark inner self through others, back home to facing the shadow deep within myself has been and is a long and painful process. It isn't one simple cycle, but many small waves of discovering depths within others that I then need to go back and find in myself. When I was working as a psychotherapist I had a simple rule that if I found myself saying something more than twice to different clients, trainees or supervisees, I assumed that I was also saying it to myself and I would go away, write it down and explore it.

The lust for power

For most of us the answer to the question of 'why' would include the wish to care, to cure, to heal – an attraction to the 'healer–patient arche-type'. Alongside this, however, may be a hidden need for power, both in surrounding oneself with people worse off, and being able to direct parts of the lives of the people who need help. Guggenbühl-Craig (1971: 8–9) also addresses this issue:

In my years of analytical work with social workers, I have noticed time and time again that whenever something must be imposed by force, the conscious and unconscious motives of those involved are many faceted. An uncanny lust for power lurks in the background . . . Quite frequently, the issue at stake appears to be not the welfare of the protected, but the power of the protector.

This is especially difficult to recognize, because at times of having to make decisions about clients, or their children, the worker very often feels incredibly powerless. This contrasts markedly with the power that he or she has and is seen to have. Here is an example which demonstrates the discrepancy in feelings of power, the value of supervision, and the relevance of understanding motives even when it initially appears irrelevant to do so:

A client with a record of considerable violence threatened to kill his experienced social worker for removing his child from home. The social worker was understandably anxious at this, the anxiety escalated and could not be held within a loose framework of supervision. I was consulted and felt inadequate to contain this life threatening anxiety. I decided that the only way I could help was to concentrate on a thorough understanding of the dynamics of the case, although this hardly seemed to be the crisis response that was being asked for. With this focus, we began to understand the covert rivalry between the worker and the parent to be the better parent, and the murderous, unmanageable rage the client experienced when his inferiority was confirmed and concretized by the making of a Care Order. An appreciation of the rivalry served to contain the anxiety in the worker, the agency and myself by providing pointers to planning the work. This served to release the anxious paralysis. The client, I am thankful to say, responded sufficiently for the situation to become diffused. I quote this example to illustrate my point that agencies concerned with public safety, and indeed the safety of their workers . . . let supervision go at their peril.

(Dearnley 1985)

We have come to believe that this case is not as exceptional as it may at first look. In our experience, once workers have made a shift in acknowledging some aspect of their shadow side – in this case the competition – there is very often a shift in the client right from the start of the very next meeting.

The issue round the potential misuse of power was put very simply by one worker: 'We dabble in people's lives and make enormous assumptions about what we do. We don't sit back and think about what it really means. We can create dependency, undermine the client's worth . . .' (quoted in Fineman 1985). This can be done on a very subtle level. Here is an example from one of our supervisees. It comes from weekly psychotherapy where a male therapist had been seeing a female client in her mid-30s for about 18 months:

The client's presenting problem at the therapy session was her difficulties at work. There was a staff member there who was very offhand with her, treating her almost like some kind of servant, and she could not confront him with his obnoxious behaviour, although she very much wanted to. It transpired that this allowing him to treat her like an object even extended to his going to bed with her whenever he wanted. She did not know how to say no, and at some level they both knew this, which is why he could treat her with such contempt.

During the session the therapist suggested that she made an agreement with him, if she wanted, not to sleep with this man for three months, and see if it made any difference to her relationship with him. The following week she came back and said she had felt a lot stronger in the way she interacted with this man, and was very glad about the agreement. The therapist was pleased, but something did not feel right. He took the case to his fortnightly supervision, and realized that he had become just another man telling her what to do – perhaps with more benign intentions, but nevertheless undermining her. The fact that she had agreed to the suggestion and was happy with the outcome almost completely missed the point – namely her underlying problem in all relationships with men, which obviously included the therapist, was that she could not say no. The therapist knew that his suggestion was not a permanent solution, but had not realized how much he and his helpful suggestion were also part of the client's process of giving power to men. In supervision the therapist faced the fact that it was the 'victim' part of himself which he felt so uneasy about, that had prompted his rush into this premature intervention. He came to realize that rushing into premature solutions was his way of attempting to deal with his own fear of powerlessness. In doing what he had done, he was creating an unnecessary dependence on himself for a behavioural solution instead of doing his job which was to help explore a fuller understanding of how she repeatedly got herself into such situations.

Meeting our own needs

Another aspect of shadow we would like to look at is the helper's attitude to needs – their own needs, both of the job and of their clients. As part of our training we are taught to pay attention to client needs, and it is often difficult to focus on our own needs. It is even considered selfish, self-indulgent. Yet our needs are there nonetheless. They are there, we believe, *in our very motives for the work we do*. As James Hillman (1979: 16) writes:

Analysts, counsellors, social workers are all trouble shooters. We are looking for trouble, even before the person comes in to take the waiting chair: 'What's wrong?' 'What's the matter?' The meeting begins not only with the projections of the person coming for help, but the trained and organized intention of the professional helper. In analysis we would say that the countertransference is there before the transference begins. My expectations are there with me as I wait for the knock on the door.

In fact countertransference is there from the beginning, since some unconscious call in me impels me to do this work. I may bring to my work a need to redeem the wounded child, so that every person who comes to me for help is my own hurt wounded childhood needing its wounds bound up by good parental care. Or the reverse: I may still be the wonderful son who would lead his father or mother out of their mistaken ways. This same parent–child archetype may also affect us, for instance, in the need to correct and punish an entire generation, its ideals and values.

My needs are never absent. I could not do this work did I not need to do this work . . . just as the person who comes to me needs me for help, I need him to express my ability to give help. The helper and the needy, the social worker and the social case, the lost and the found, always go together. However we have been brought up to deny our needs. The ideal man of western protestantism shows his 'strong ego' in independence . . . Needs in themselves are not harmful, but when they are denied they join the shadows of counselling and work from behind as demands . . . Demands ask for fulfilment, needs require only expression.

It is not the needs themselves, but the denial of them that we believe can be so costly. In the next chapter we will look more at the denial of needs, particularly in relation to support. Another need we would like to mention here, however, is the need to be liked, valued, to be seen as doing one's best, to have good intentions even if we sometimes have to make difficult decisions for the 'client's own good': in short, to be seen as the 'good person'. It is not easy for us, even after many years of working with people and attempting to face our shadow side, to accept a picture of ourselves, painted by a client, which does not correspond with how we see ourselves. It seems so unfair to be told that one is cold, rigid or misusing power. The temptations are either to alter one's behaviour to be more 'pleasing', to counter-attack subtly or otherwise, or stop working with the person for 'plausible' reasons. The ingratitude is sometimes hard to accept. We may find ourselves thinking, 'After all I've done for you', words we heard from a parent or teacher, and which we promised never to repeat.

One of the best ways we have found of accepting some of these negative feelings from clients (which usually have at least a grain of truth in them) is for us to remember how *we* feel as clients. We can also remember how in our own supervision, when we feel inadequate, we want to criticize our supervisors in order to make them feel as we do.

The wish to heal

It would seem from the above that it is almost worth packing it in. This chapter has been full of lurking power drives, needy children, unclear motives, hostility to parents. To think this would be to miss the point alluded to above – namely, it is only the *denial* of needs, shadow, image, power that makes them dangerous. Knowing ourselves, our motives and our needs makes us more likely to be of real help. In that way we do not use others unawarely for our own ends, or make them carry bits of ourselves we cannot face. For we believe that the desire to help, in spite of the unclarity surrounding it, is fundamental, and agree with Harold Searles (1975) when he says that:

> innate among man's most powerful strivings towards his fellow men, beginning in the earliest years and even earliest months, is an essentially psychotherapeutic striving. The tiny percentage of human beings who devote their professional careers to the practice of psychoanalysis or psychotherapy are only giving explicit expression to a therapeutic devotion which all human beings share . . . I am hypothesizing that the patient is ill because, and to the degree that his own psychotherapeutic strivings have been subjected to such vicissitudes that they have been rendered inordinately intense, frustrated of fulfilment or even acknowledgement, admixed therefore with unduly intense components of hate, envy and competitiveness: and subjected therefore to repression. In transference terms the patient's illness expresses his unconscious attempt to cure the doctor.

In other words the wish to heal is basic to helpers and non-helpers alike.

Conclusion

We have found that when we have been able to accept our own vulnerability and not defend against it, it has been a valuable experience both for us and our clients. The realization that they could be healing us, as much as the other way round, has been very important both in their relationship with us and their growth. It is another reminder that we are servants of the process.

Finally, we believe that we are only in a position to give when our own needs go some way to being acknowledged and satisfied. To give when we feel that we have something to give, and not just when the client demands, or when we feel we 'ought' to. This puts a lot of responsibility on helpers to be active in trying to satisfy their own needs. It is this we will turn to in the next chapter.

Getting the support and supervision you need

Introduction

A social worker spoke with poignancy about her difficulties in coping with the demands of a particular client when added to her home pressures. I asked her if she had shared her concerns with her colleagues. 'Oh no!' she retorted, 'I wouldn't want to be social worked by them.' She then recoiled with a look of horror on her face, 'God, what am

I saying? I can use my social work skills on clients but I can't accept them for myself?'

(in Fineman 1985)

Many helpers, when they themselves are suffering are incapable of accepting support, or at least receiving it easily. Yet they may be impatient with those they're working with for not accepting aid or counsel readily enough. Chances are, if you can't accept help, you can't really give it.

(Ram Dass and Gorman 1985: 86)

'I cannot get the support and supervision I need to do my job as my manager is either too busy or too inadequate to give me good supervision.' This is regularly said to us by workers in a great variety of helping professions. Teachers, probation officers, social workers and doctors will often complain that they are constantly drained by supporting so many clients and patients, but receive very little support themselves.

In the previous chapter we explored how this in part may be due to the addiction to giving, which is a defence against being a person who needs support oneself. In this chapter we will look at how, even when you acknowledge the need for support, it is still possible to remain stuck blaming others for not providing it. We will explore ways of moving out of this passive position into taking responsibility for ensuring that you get the support and supervision you need. This is a fundamental shift from being reactive and dependent to being proactive concerning your own support system.

It is in the spirit of being proactive that we would like you to read this chapter. As you read through it, we would like to give you the opportunity to take stock of your own support system, your stress and how you manage it. We would also like you to evaluate your own supervision and explore how it can better meet your needs. This chapter is also for supervisors, for to be a good supervisor is also to be a proactive supervisee, ensuring that you continue to arrange and use support for yourself, and can model this to your staff. We also hope that the chapter will provide ways in which supervisors can encourage autonomy and proactivity in their supervisees.

Mapping your support system

We would like you to start by taking a large sheet of paper (A3 or bigger) and on it draw a map of your support system at work. In the middle of the paper draw a symbol or picture of yourself. Then around this picture or symbol draw pictures, symbols, diagrams or words to represent all the things and people that support you in learning and being creative at work. These may be the walk to work, books you read, colleagues, meetings, friends, etc. We would like you to represent the nature of your connection to these supports. Are they near or far away? Is the link strong and regular, or tenuous, or distant? Are they supporting you from below like foundations or are they balloons that lift you up? These are only suggestions; allow yourself to find your own way of mapping your support system.

When you are satisfied with your initial map, we would like you to take a completely different colour and draw on the picture symbols that represent those things that block you from fully using these supports. It may be *fear of* being criticized or interruptions or the relative unavailability of these supports. It may be blocks within you, within the support, or in the organizational setting. Draw whatever you feel stops you getting the support you need.

When you have done this, we would suggest that you choose someone with whom to share your picture. This could be a colleague, partner, supervisor or friend, or even someone who has also done the exercise (you could get your whole staff team to do it!). When you have shared your picture with them, they should first respond to the overall picture. What impression does it create? Then they can ask you the following questions:

- Is this the kind of support you want?
- Is it enough? What sort of support is missing? How could you go about getting such support?
- What support is really positive for you to the extent that you must ensure that you nurture and maintain it?
- Which blocks could you do something about reducing?

Your partner could then encourage you to develop some specific action plans as to how you might improve your support system. An action plan should include *what* you are going to do; *how* you are going to do it; *when and where* you are going to do it; and involving *whom*?

If there is no one that you want to share this process with, it is possible to do the exercise by yourself and ask yourself these questions, but it is much more difficult. Also, involving another is a good first step in proactively asking for support!

Stress

What happens if you do not have enough support is that you absorb more disturbance, distress and dis-ease from your clients and patients than you are able to process and let go of and then you become overburdened by the work. Stress is not only absorbed from the clients but may also come from other aspects of the work and the organization in which you work. These stressors (factors causing stress) will in turn interact with your own personality and the stressors that are currently happening in your own life outside work.

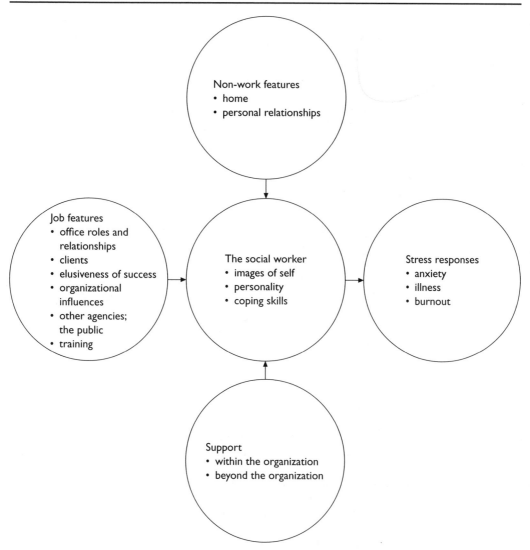

Figure 3.1   Facets of social worker stress
Source: Fineman (1985: 34)

Fineman (1985) provides a useful and simple model illustrating the interconnectedness of stress and support (see Figure 3.1). The diagram underlines the importance of not only attending to, and taking responsibility for, your own support system, but also ensuring that you are taking responsibility for responding actively to the stressors in your own work and home life.

Some stress is inevitable and can be positive in activating the body, mind and energies of the worker. It can awaken our energies ready for action and for dealing with a threat or a crisis. However, so often in the

Table 3.1 Symptoms of stress

Physical
• Migraines or headaches
• Diarrhoea, indigestion, constipation
• Insomnia
• Over-tiredness
• Loss of appetite

Mental
• Inability to concentrate
• Compulsive worry
• Paranoid thoughts – seeing yourself as victim

Behavioural
• Pretending to care, and playing the role of carer, but the actions and feelings are incongruous
• Avoiding clients, colleagues or situations
• Turning to drink, overeating or smoking too much

Emotional
• Sudden swings in feelings
• Not wanting to get up in the mornings
• 'Floating anxiety'
• Hating clients

helping professions the stressors of the work charge our mental and bodily systems ready for action, but there is no possibility for discharging this energy into action. We are left having to sit with the pain of the patient; or having to contain the frustration of not being able to secure the funding to meet client needs that we are in touch with; or having to cope with situations in which we feel undertrained or emotionally inadequate.

Stress that is not discharged stays within the body and can emerge as physical, mental or emotional symptoms. It is important to know your own tendencies for responding to stress, so you can be alert to the build-up of tension within you. In Table 3.1 we offer examples of some of the most common symptoms of being stressed, but suggest that you stop and make a note of the symptoms that inform you that you are overstressed. You might also take the opportunity to ask those who work with you how they notice that you behave under pressure.

It is very important that, as helpers, we take responsibility for noticing the signs that our systems are overloaded; and that we ensure that we get the support, not only to deal with the symptoms of stress that are emerging within us, but also to tackle the cause of the stress. The earlier this is done the better. If we ignore the stress symptoms for too long then we are in danger of being overwhelmed and being left in a situation where the only things we can attend to are the resultant symptoms within us. When this happens we have entered the state that is often referred to as burnout.

Burnout

The term 'burnout' has, in recent years, become much overused. It has become the helping professions' equivalent to what the British army called 'shell shock' or the Americans 'battle fatigue'; what our parents' generation called 'nerves' and the present generation calls 'depression'. They become catch-all phrases that signify 'not coping'. Burnout is not an illness that you catch, neither is it a recognizable event or state, for it is a process that often begins very early in one's career as a helper. Indeed its seeds may be inherent in the belief systems of many of the helping professions and in the personalities of those that are attracted to them (see previous chapter).

Edelwich and Brodsky (1980) explore how unrealistically high expectations of what can be achieved can create the background for the later development of disillusionment and apathy. Many professions also encourage their trainees to develop the image of themselves as heroic helpers who can continually provide for others, solving their problems, feeling their pain, meeting their needs, while remaining themselves strong and happy. This can be coupled with the personality of those attracted to such work who may have been the people who contained the pain and were always helpful in their own families.

Pines *et al.* (1981) define burnout as:

> the result of constant or repeated emotional pressure associated with an intense involvement with people over long periods of time. Such intense involvement is particularly prevalent in health, education and social service occupations, where professionals have a 'calling' to take care of other people's psychological, social and physical problems. Burnout is the painful realization that they no longer can help people in need, that they have nothing left in them to give.

Fineman (1985: 38) follows Maslach (1982) in saying that burnout represents:

> (a) a state of emotional and physical exhaustion with a lack of concern for the job, and a low trust of others, (b) a depersonalization of clients; a loss of caring and cynicism towards them, and (c) self-deprecation and low morale and a deep sense of failure.

We would contend that the best time to attend to burnout is before it happens. This involves: looking at your shadow motivation for being in the helping professions (see the previous chapter); monitoring your own stress symptoms and creating a healthy support system (see above); and ensuring that you have a meaningful, enjoyable and physically active life outside the role of being a helper.

In an earlier work (Hawkins 1986) we explored another aspect of burnout that is ignored in most of the literature, which is the apathy and loss of interest which develop in helpers who stop learning and developing in mid-career. They begin to rely on set patterns of relating to clients and patients and treat new clients as just repeat representatives of clients and patients they met earlier in their career. A preventative approach to burnout needs to include creating a learning environment that continues right through one's career as a helper.

Post-traumatic stress

More recently a cluster of symptoms known to be part of post-traumatic stress has been recognized. It is now accepted that in dealing with traumatic incidents like shootings, fires, crashes or rapes the workers can experience parallel trauma to the trauma of the people they work with. While some of the symptoms are similar to those of stress and burnout, one of the essential differences is that trauma happens suddenly and unexpectedly. This requires very different responses from managers and supervisors and some of these are formulated in Brown and Bourne (1996, Ch. 7). They draw a very useful distinction between internal and external stressors. The former originate from re-experiencing some of the effects of the traumatic incident, and unlike external stress cannot be reduced, say, by simply lightening the workload or changing another aspect of the work environment.

It is also beginning to be recognized that it is not only the front line workers who are traumatized but such people as telephonists and clerical staff who receive distressed calls from relatives, friends and the media; legal secretaries; caretakers; cleaners; leisure centre staff; cooks; registrars of deaths; and people who operate rest centres, body identification centres, drop-in centres and helplines. Managers are in particular need of supervision as they are making key decisions, often without prior training, which affect the whole response and staff care process (Capewell 1997). The burden of responsibility they carry exacerbates the impact on them, yet they rarely feel they need support (doing so is seen as weakness) and believe those on the front line need or deserve it more.

Supervisors, if they are working with supervisees in this area, need to familiarize themselves with the symptoms of post-traumatic stress, and how they differ from symptoms of stress, which build up over time. Often those working on the front line can resort to denial in order to get the work done, and the symptoms can emerge much later.

Arranging appropriate supervision

There are many reasons to be proactive in getting good supervision for ourselves.

First, supervision is a central form of support, where we can focus on our own difficulties as a worker as well as have our supervisor share some of the responsibility for our work with the clients.

Second, supervision forms part of our continual learning and development as workers, including eventually helping us to learn how to be supervisors. A good supervisor can also help us to use our own resources better, manage our workload and challenge our inappropriately patterned ways of coping. We think that, if we are helping clients take more charge of their own lives, it is essential that we are doing the same.

Finally, there is research to show that good supervision correlates with job satisfaction (Cherniss and Egnatios 1978).

Blocks to getting supervision

Part of arranging for good supervision is recognizing blocks and finding effective ways of overcoming them. In this section we will briefly look at the following blocks: previous experiences of supervision; personal inhibition; difficulties with authority; role conflict; practical blocks, such as finance or geography; difficulties in receiving support; and organizational blocks.

Previous experiences of supervision

Previous experiences of supervision, both good and bad, can influence the current supervision. A bad experience can lead a supervisee to be wary, but a good one can lead to comparisons such as 'no one will be as good as my last supervisor'. Taking a more positive stance, you might like to make a résumé of past experiences of supervision and what you learned from them both in terms of managing the relationship, yourself and skills. How do your needs differ now from then?

Personal inhibition and defensive routines

Sometimes just being in a one-to-one relationship can restimulate painful feelings. Here is an account of one supervision relationship from a supervisee on a counselling course:

> When I started supervision I found that I was not going to be
> directed in any way and that all the ideas had to come from me.
> This felt very uncomfortable and I felt very much 'on the spot' –
> in fact it gave an insight as to how a client would feel. Painful
> emotions were just below the surface brought there by the
> insecurity of the position I seemed to be in. I felt very vulnerable
> as if the supervisor's attention was scrutiny. My defensive reaction
> to this was anger and one week I was on the point of walking out.
> I actually started to gather my things together. The supervisor
> stopped me and I realized that I was checking to see if he could

cope with my anger. I had a shock of recognition at this scene as it reminded me of how I test out other relationships.

Although these sessions were painful I realized how important supervision was and how necessary for our particular work especially the 'coping collusion' which permeates our work, our denial of how much we are affected by the client group. Finally the blocks in supervision were self-imposed and therefore having another supervisor would not have solved these blocks but brought out others.

The idea of being on the spot, even though objectively there is no assessment, can relate to internal judging. As the above supervisee said:

> In all the supervision sessions there was a third person present, a part of myself – very critical – who looked at all my thoughts, actions and feelings and commented on them. Somehow it seemed as if my own analysis of my behaviour served to paralyse me. I always had a counter argument for anything I came up with. It seems as if this is the way I keep control.

We can certainly identify with this, and have often found ourselves being needlessly defensive in supervision, protecting ourselves from being judged, when in fact we are usually the worst judges of ourselves. It can certainly feel very exposing to bring cases to supervision to find out that one has missed something which in retrospect seems very obvious.

You might like to ask yourself here how much you hold back in supervision and for what reasons. Can you share any of these reasons with your supervisor even if it feels a bit risky? Recognizing that supervision can produce anxiety in supervisees, Kadushin (1968) has written about the various strategies adopted by supervisees for dealing with such feelings and we would recommend his paper. There is also a later one by Hawthorne (1975) which looks at supervisor strategies for dealing with their anxieties, which we will be referring to later. Ekstein and Wallerstein (1972) also describe some of what Argyris and Schön (1978) term 'professional defensive routines' that we can all adopt to avoid being vulnerable and open to new learning. These are developed by Gilbert and Evans (forthcoming) and they describe the following types of defensive routine:

- The pre-packaging approach: 'I've got it all sewn up in advance and here is my supervision contract for today.'
- The information flooding approach: 'You don't understand unless I give you every detail about my client.'
- Energetic denial of any need in the face of input from supervision: 'This is not really new to me . . . I'm familiar with that already . . . Yes, I've already tried that approach . . .'
- The self-flagellation approach (magnifying one's own shortcomings): 'I know I have made a mess of this session . . . I'll just never get it

right . . . whatever you tell me, I seem to forget as soon as I sit in front of the client.'

- The approach to supervision as a personal assault: 'I know that you will criticize what I have done here . . . I think the problem is really the difference in our orientations to clients . . . I feel terrified coming to supervision because it always ends in an argument . . .'
- The fault-finding or 'nitpicking' approach to supervision: 'You make a good point there but I'm not sure it would apply to this particular client.'
- The displacing of the problem in supervision onto the supervisor: 'I certainly do not have any angry feelings towards this client: are you sure you are not angry here?'

Difficulties with authority

Transference difficulties, usually the projecting of critical or uncontaining parental images, are often present in supervision, just as in therapy, but are less easy to recognize. Page and Wosket (1994: 21) recognize that the supervisory relationship has a more adult–adult component than a counselling relationship, which has more of a nurturing parent–child aspect. However, they point out the paradox that the supervisory relationship is both more equal and more authoritative, as it also contains a critical parent–child aspect. As one worker said in Fineman's study (1985: 52): 'I fear authority and always feel I need to *prove* to my supervisor that I can do my work'. So supervisors are often not seen for who they are; sometimes they are given too much power, at other times they may be defensively seen as useless. Sibling rivalry can also occur in terms of who can manage the client better, and this can come just as much from the supervisor as the supervisees.

Conflict of roles

There can also be problems around the dual roles in supervision of management and support:

> I have regular meetings with my supervisor, but always steer clear of my problems in coping with my report work. Can I trust her? I need her backing for my career progress, but will she use this sort of thing as evidence against me? There are some painful areas that are never discussed but need discussing so much. It's an awful dilemma for me.
> (in Fineman 1985: 52)

There was also an appreciation of the dilemma of the supervisor: 'Currently I get supervised by the team leader – but he's in a conflict situation between being a manager and being my supervisor' (in Fineman 1985: 52).

The conflicting roles of support person and assessor can also create conflict when the supervisee is on a training course, in which their supervisor is providing an evaluation (see Chapter 8).

Although supervisors might try to protect their workers from their own stress, the stress is inevitably picked up. Sometimes the supervisees have the attitude 'They've got enough on their plates without my problems', but often there is resentment at not having the support they feel they have a right to.

A mismatch of expectations that never get tackled can play a part in reducing the worth of supervision: 'My supervisor doesn't really provide what I want. He tends to pick on things which are important to him, not me' (in Fineman 1985: 52).

We will explore later in this chapter the importance of ensuring that you have a clear supervision contract with your supervisor, and that roles and expectations within the supervision are explored and regularly reviewed.

Practical blocks

Besides the many personal and organizational blocks to supervision, some people also face practical difficulties in getting the supervision that they need. These could be financial ('I can't afford supervision'), or geographical (living in a very isolated place), or availability (being head of an establishment and one's manager not having the specialized skills).

All these blocks require the supervisees to have an even higher degree of proactivity and also to think laterally. Isolated therapists who work alone may have to look outside their own training to find a skilled practitioner of another orientation who is sympathetic enough to support the therapist in developing within his or her own style and school of work. Some geographically isolated therapists have arranged infrequent supervision with supervisors to whom they have to travel great distances, but have supplemented these visits with either correspondence, telephone calls or teleconferencing.

In Chapter 9 we look at ways of setting up and conducting peer supervision and support groups. This can either be with a group of other similar practitioners in your area, or be a reciprocal arrangement with one other practitioner who is also in the position of not being able to get appropriate supervision within his or her organizational structure. We also give examples of how one can use professional organizations or training courses to provide a network within which to establish such peer supervision contracts.

Difficulty in receiving support

Another difficulty or block in receiving support or supervision has been referred to in the last chapter and in the quotes at the beginning of this chapter – namely the difficulty in receiving. To receive makes one potentially more vulnerable and exposes need. It is often felt to be safer to work with clients who have to express *their* needs and leave us safe in our roles of providing.

Although this might be a personal difficulty, it is certainly culturally reinforced. To quote Hillman (1979: 17) again: 'We have been brought up to deny our needs . . . To need is to be dependent, weak; needing implies submission to another'. This attitude certainly is there in individuals and is strongly reinforced by work cultures. In Fineman's (1985: 100, 101) study of social workers, when talking about the double standards of giving and not receiving, he quotes one worker as saying:

> It was an odd feeling for those who found themselves facing, and contributing, to a wall of interpersonal evasiveness or even indifference inside the office, while professing just the opposite to clients outside the office . . . They felt helpless victims of a climate which provided little of the emotional support they desired.

and continues:

> This is a particular caring group of people, but they play a charade with each other's problems and stresses. There's a sort of collusive arrangement not to talk to people about their stresses. If it's linked to a home situation there's a shame that they, as social workers, feel stressed . . . No one stops to ask why this should be the case.

Organizational blocks

From the above quotes it can been seen that there is an interplay between an individual's process and the way a work culture might reinforce an individual's own inner feelings about asking for help. The culture of some organizations will discourage individuals to expect and ask for supervision: 'in spite of grumbling about lack of good supervision, there can be an unwillingness to really do something about it' (Fineman 1985). Other organizations will encourage individuals to overcome their inner resistances. This is explored at length in Chapter 12 on organizational cultures.

There is also a very useful exploration of the interface of the personal and organizational blocks in the nursing profession in Chapter 2 of Bond and Holland (1998).

Overcoming blocks: Geraldine's story

Here is part of an article from one of our supervisees who is a speech therapist. We have included it because she writes very clearly and openly about how her chosen profession's blocks around supervision reinforced her own, and because she demonstrates the changes she made to break her personal patterns. She also ends by asking some very relevant questions which do not only apply to speech therapists but all helping professions. You might try to answer these questions for yourself about your own work setting.

> As a disillusioned speech therapist who has considered leaving the profession several times I was interested to read that the majority of

speech therapists in full-time posts were mainly newly qualified, and those who have left the profession were mainly experienced fulltimers. It struck me that these therapists had left without speaking out and saying why. Here is my story:

I started training at the age of 21. I knew that speech therapy was a small profession and that therapists were poorly paid. In fact I was already earning more than a senior speech therapist in my previous job in catering. However I liked working with people and had a genuine interest in communication problems. I wanted job satisfaction and felt that this would be more satisfying than a large salary.

I attacked my first job with a vigour and enthusiasm that I now recognize in many newly qualified therapists. I was keen to put into practice all that I had learnt. I was highly motivated. However, I should have begun listening to the messages behind the questions and comments I was receiving from other professionals, friends and relatives:

'Speech therapy must be a very lonely job.'

'Who do you go to for support?'

'Do you receive supervision?'

I can remember my replies were of the following nature:

'I like being my own boss.'

'I don't need support.'

'I am qualified and no longer need supervision.'

My first Senior 1 post, two years after qualifying, was very challenging. My job was divided between setting up an advisory speech therapy service to a social services department and introducing speech therapy into a language unit which had been open for one year without a speech therapist. I felt I was appointed because I presented as a self-starter who could work without supervision and enjoyed challenges.

Even as I write this, a voice inside me is saying, 'What is wrong with that?' and 'Maybe you just don't have what it takes to be successful.' I have enough faith in myself to know these voices are wrong. If we do not question the assumptions or challenge the rationale behind such management decisions, we become guilty of perpetuating these fantasies. Being a self-starter often means taking up a post which has been poorly set up, then not being given the power to make necessary changes. I feel the personality of those attracted to the caring professions lends itself to exploitation and denial of their own needs. How many times have you heard 'We are here to help our patients'. This is, of course, what may have attracted us to our work, but at what price? The reverse side of the coin often appears to be 'My needs don't matter'.

Despite starting a counselling course, I still believed that I did not need support or require supervision. During the first year I refused to join a support group as it sounded too much like something found in a Californian suburb!

I found my new job very difficult and the team leader for the social work team started questioning me on how much support I received. She was shocked when she realized I saw my line manager very infrequently. She suggested that she and I met fortnightly to discuss the job. These meetings became supervision, even though the team leader was not my line manager, and were very supportive.

Through discussing my work during these supervision sessions and through greater self-awareness, gained as a result of my counselling course, I began to realize that I was going through 'professional burnout'. By this I mean that I had reached a point when I no longer had the enthusiasm to keep injecting into the job because I felt that my efforts were not effective or appreciated. The side effects of burn-out for me were tiredness, lethargy, poor timekeeping and boredom. I had believed that I would always remain as highly motivated as I had been in my first job only four years ago.

The two things that kept me going through this period were supervision and praise (something we tend to give to the patients much more than to other staff). I feel I achieved a lot during this period, by learning how to use the support systems both on the course and at work.

After two years in this post I felt the need for a change. Where did I go from here? I decided to move into an area of work that had always interested me, 'speech therapy within psychiatry'. I found myself with another challenging post. After the initial excitement of the new job, etc. I realized I was back at the beginning of the long uphill struggle of getting a new service going.

There was no formal supervision or support system set up. The voice inside me said: 'Of course, you should be able to do this without support.' When I spoke about the difficulties of the post I heard the responses from others as criticism. I even found myself saying the job was going well. It was difficult to admit, the therapist in me did not want to admit, that I could not cope. Eventually I called out for support. Then my overworked and, probably, unsupported GP also wanted to find a solution to my problem and put me on antidepressants.

The speech therapy profession is concerned about why so many experienced staff are leaving four or five years after being trained. I think my story illustrates one of the main reasons. Therapists who are working in the field need support and supervision. If they are not rewarded and valued by members of their own profession, what hope is there of receiving this from other professions and the government in the future?

I have thought about some questions that each speech therapist should ask before accepting a post:

- Does the district therapist see all new employees shortly after they commence and at regular intervals thereafter?
- Are there regular staff appraisals?
- Is there supervision for all staff members at all levels?
- Are support groups facilitated by an independent person encouraged?
- Are therapists encouraged to meet their colleagues regularly and is there provision made in the timetable for this?

Perhaps by identifying our needs and finding ways of getting them met, we will not have to take such drastic steps as leaving the profession.

(Geraldine Rose, unpublished work, 1987)

In the above the writer was quite open about her own resistance as well as the profession's shortcomings. Good experiences of supervision enabled her to see what she was missing. She was not only lacking supervision, but until she went on the counselling course she was also lacking peer support. Even in social work, where supervision is more acceptable, we think it is important that the worker receive good supervision and be in a supportive peer culture. Too much reliance on one individual supervisor can create unhealthy dependence.

In view of what has been written above about the various personal, interpersonal, practical and organizational blocks to getting supervision, you might like to return to the map of your own support system and review the blocks you experience. Awareness of the blocks is the first step in overcoming them and it is to this that we now turn.

Self-supervision

This is a form of supervision that is always relevant, even if you are receiving good supervision elsewhere. One aim of all supervision is to help practitioners develop a healthy internal supervisor which they can have access to while they are working.

An important aspect of self-supervision is to be able to reflect on one's own working. Borders and Leddick (1987) provide some very useful questions for such a reflection process, and these are listed in Box 3.1.

Box 3.1   Reflecting on your own working

Self-observation (linking counsellor thoughts, feelings and actions with client behaviours):

- What was I hearing my client say and/or seeing my client do?
- What was I thinking and feeling about my observations?
- What were my alternatives to say or do at this point?
- How did I choose from among the alternatives?
- How did I intend to proceed with my selected response(s)?
- What did I actually do?

Self-assessment (evaluating counsellor performance by observing client response):

- What effects did my response have on my client?
- How, then, would I evaluate the effectiveness of my response?

(Borders and Leddick 1987)

This reflection process can also be deepened by the supervisee developing their own system of writing up their casework. This should not only record the facts necessary for professional practice, but should reflect on the process of the work and monitor body sensations, breathing, feelings, thoughts and actions while with the client.

These written processes of reflection can be further deepened by using audio and visual tape-recording of work with clients and patients and developing ways of using these tapes to further one's own self-supervision. Kagan (1980) has done much to develop ways of learning through seeing videotapes of ourselves working and we have written elsewhere about our own systems for self-supervision (CSTD 1999).

What is essential for all forms of self-supervision is giving oneself enough time and also being willing to confront one's own ways of working. Many of our trainees have found their first attempts to learn from listening to themselves on tape to be both challenging and instructive.

Being proactive within supervision

The need to be proactive does not stop at the point where you have set up both a good support system and have found a good supervisor or supervisory situation. It is all too easy at this point to slide back into dependency and just accept the style and level of supervision that the supervisor provides. To ensure you get the supervision you want, you need to take full responsibility for your part in contracting and negotiating how the supervision will operate, what it will focus on and how the process will be monitored and reviewed.

Contracting

Pat Hunt (1986) emphasizes the value of having a clear supervision contract: 'Supervision can become a more effective and satisfying activity for both supervisor and supervisee in any setting if there is a more *explicit* contract on what it is about'. She talks about the need for a 'supervisory alliance' and this includes: 'more openness and clarity on the methods to be used in supervision, and why they are used, the style of supervision, the goals of supervision, the kind of relationship it is hoped to achieve and the responsibilities of each partner in the supervisory relationship'.

When contracting with your supervisor, both parties need to have the opportunity to say how they see the purpose of the sessions, explore how much their expectations match, and look at their hopes and fears concerning the working relationship. Where there is a mismatch in expectations it is important that these differences are further explored and some form of negotiation takes place. As much as possible any conflict of purpose should be talked over, as should any issues of style, assumptions and values. Ground rules need to be established about frequency, duration and place and about how cases are to be brought; also, how the supervision contract and the work will be reviewed and evaluated. Finally, if relevant, what procedures are there for emergencies?

The need for such explicit contracting has been clearly expressed by Brigid Proctor (1988a):

> If supervision is to become and remain a co-operative experience which allows for real, rather than token accountability, a clear – even tough – working agreement needs to be negotiated. The agreement needs to provide sufficient safety and clarity for the student or worker to know where she stands: and it needs sufficient teeth for the supervisor to feel free and responsible for making the challenges of assessments which belong with whatever role – managerial, consultative, or training – the context requires.

Proctor develops this further (see Inskipp and Proctor 1993: 49) with guidelines for the exploratory contracting interview and also a checklist as to what the new supervisee might be looking for (p. 39).

We explore contracting in greater detail in Chapter 5.

Evaluating your supervisor

When exploring blocks to receiving supervision (see p. 23) we mentioned that one of the most common fears of supervisees is how they will be judged and evaluated by their supervisor. What most supervisees forget, or do not even consider, is that supervisors may also be anxious about how they are being judged or evaluated by their supervisees. Evaluation and review should be a two-way process and needs to be regularly scheduled into the supervision arrangements. This ensures that fears on both sides about 'how I am doing' can be brought into the open, and there is a chance to give clear feedback and, where necessary, to renegotiate the supervision contract.

Borders and Leddick (1987) provide a very useful checklist of 41 points for evaluating your supervisor. This list includes:

- helps me feel at ease with the supervision process;
- can facilitate and accept feedback from the supervisees;
- helps me clarify my objectives in working with clients;
- explains the criteria for any evaluation of my work clearly and in behavioural terms;
- encourages me to conceptualize in new ways regarding my clients;
- enables me to become actively involved in the supervision process.

We would invite you to write your own evaluation criteria. Some will be something you might ask of any supervisor and some might be of this particular supervisor at this particular time, related to the current work situation.

Taking appropriate responsibility as a supervisee

Inskipp and Proctor (1993) have drawn up a list of responsibilities for the student/supervisee. By terming them 'responsibilities' they point out that being more active in getting the right sort of supervision also involves more ongoing responsibility. The responsibilities of the supervisees include:

- identify practice issues with which you need help and ask for help;
- become increasingly able to share freely;
- identify what responses you want;
- become more aware of the organizational contracts that affect supervisor, clients and supervisees;
- be open to feedback;
- monitor tendencies to justify, explain or defend;
- develop the ability to discriminate what feedback is useful.

In stressing the essential equality of the relationship we do not want to overlook the fact that in most supervisory relationships there is a managerial responsibility carried by the supervisor. The supervisee needs to be aware of this, and both parties need to work at integrating the managerial aspects of supervision so that they do not invalidate the opportunity for equality.

Self-reflection

At regular intervals it is important to stand back and reflect on the supervision you need and want in relation to what you are currently receiving. You then need to ask yourself what are the blocks to the supervision being more effective, and what can you do to initiate unblocking the process. Here are some questions to help you consider ways of being more proactive about both your support and supervision:

- What are the strengths and weaknesses of your present support system? What do you need to do about improving it?
- How do you recognize that you are under stress? What methods do you use to alleviate this stress? Do these coping mechanisms provide just short-term relief, or do they change the cause of the stress?
- What are your specific needs from supervision and how far do your present supervisory arrangements meet them?
- Do you need to renegotiate the contract with your supervisor, supervision group or work team? Make as many of the transactions and assumptions as explicit as possible. Are all/both parties clear about the purpose of supervision?
- Are there additional forms of supervision (peer supervision, etc.) that you need to arrange for yourself?
- How open do you feel to supervision and feedback? If you are reticent about them, are there personal changes you could make to open up communication?

- Are you frightened of being judged and assessed? Have you tried check-ing out whether your fears are justified or a fantasy?
- Can you confront your supervisor and give him or her feedback? If not, are the constraints internal or external?
- What defensive routines do you fall into using? What do you need in order to move beyond these?
- Are you stuck in blaming others for what you yourself can change? We often find on our courses that supervisees 'depower' themselves, by having an investment in believing that they cannot change what their supervisor or organization does to support them. When confronted by this, they have gone back and found that many more changes are possible than they previously believed.
- Do you carry some of your supervisor's anxieties, so that you have to look after them?
- Is it feasible to have a more equal relationship? How far is it appropri-ate and is it what you want, given that more equality means more responsibility?

When supervision fails

Supervision is a co-created process within a relationship. Often when we bemoan the fact that we do not have 'good enough' supervision, we forget that there are a number of steps we can take to rectify this situ-ation. Sometimes, however, our own efforts will not be enough and we will need to change our supervisor, take out a formal complaint, or join with others in bringing to the attention of the organization the lack of appropriate supervision.

It is important to begin any attempts to improve your supervision *within* the supervision relationship. Even when you decide to take action beyond the supervision boundaries, this is likely to be most effective when it is framed, not as a blaming attack on the individual, but as a clear request for receiving appropriate support and development to carry out your work.

Conclusion

This chapter has shown how getting good supervision for yourself starts with *you*. First you need to be aware of the whole range of your current support system and how to develop it. Then you need to become aware of your own levels of stress and distress and how you can reduce the stressors and increase your coping mechanisms. Finally, we explored how you might proactively overcome the blocks to receiving supervision, both those inside yourself and those in the work environment.

Your organization's efforts to improve your own supervision can become an important part of the organization developing its collective supervision practice. In Chapter 13 we will show how an organization can either introduce supervision or radically improve the policies and practice of the supervision it provides. Such change processes are often initiated by enough staff in an organization or agency responsibly speaking out about the need for better supervision.

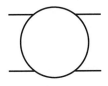

Part Two

Becoming a supervisor and the process of supervision

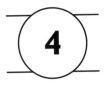

4 Becoming a supervisor

Introduction

Suddenly becoming, or being asked to be, a supervisor can be both exhilarating and daunting. Without training or support the task can be overwhelming: 'Supervising is new to me. It's OK, I suppose, but I'm anxious – I'm never quite sure whether I'm giving the people I'm supervising exactly what they are wanting . . . I'm really afraid about what they will say about me so I don't ask. To be judged by a colleague is just too much' (Fineman 1985: 52).

This chapter and the other four in this section will provide you with some core frameworks for not only carrying out supervision but also for reviewing and evaluating your supervisory work and for receiving quality feedback on your sessions.

If you are reading this book having just become a supervisor, we would encourage you not to start with this chapter, because as we mentioned in the previous chapter, you cannot expect to give good supervision unless you have first learned how to receive supervision and be a proactive supervisee.

Why be a supervisor?

There are many reasons why you might become or might have already become a supervisor. For some it is the natural progression that comes with promotion. They become nursing tutors, senior social workers or area youth officers, and discover that, instead of spending time seeing clients, for which they had been trained, they are now spending all their time seeing junior staff. Some counsellors or therapists find that they have become, over time, one of the most senior practitioners in their area, and supervisees start coming to them. Some staff find that they greatly miss the direct contact with clients and are nostalgic for their earlier days in the work. Such staff can be prone to turning their supervisees into substitute clients, to keep their hand in with therapeutic work.

Others turn to supervision to get away from the pressures of client work, in the false hope that seeing staff provides a quiet life! After several years as a helping professional they opt, not for a specialist post, but to go into student supervision or to become a tutor in their chosen profession. For some the role of supervisor fits more easily than for others. They find themselves at home in a role that requires both personal development and educational skills.

Others get promoted into management because they are better administrators than they are at working with people, but unfortunately for such people and their organizations management positions in the helping professions nearly always include some supervision responsibilities. These staff then become the reluctant supervisors, who are always too busy with 'important meetings' and finishing 'essential reports' to see their supervisees.

Some staff are so able to arrange their work that they can mix some direct work with clients with being a supervisor of others. We would recommend that wherever possible staff who supervise or teach should still be practising whatever they teach or supervise. It is all too easy to get out of touch with the realities of being at the 'coal face' and to wonder why your supervisees are making such heavy weather of what seems perfectly straightforward from your perspective as a supervisor. The mix of work can have advantages in both directions. Many new supervisors in several professions have remarked to us how having to supervise other staff helped them revitalize their own work with clients and start to think afresh about what they did themselves.

Many staff become and stay supervisors through being attracted to the challenge and scope of the role. Here is an account from a colleague:

> I feel most challenged and excited in supervision by the tension between the loving relationship and holding my own authority. Supervision is the place in my work where I can be at my most free ranging – playful, free to think aloud, able to comment on the process, challenge, take a journey into the unknown. Then there is the opposite side when I really have to hold the boundaries, own my own authority and risk the good relationship for the sake of the truth. Each time this has happened, I have found it risky, self-challenging, lonely for a while, but also very mind-clearing and transformational and ultimately very strengthening to both ourselves and the relationship.

Being a supervisor provides an opportunity to develop one's educative skills in helping other staff to learn and develop within their work. As a new supervisor you are impelled to stop, reflect upon and articulate the ways you have worked as a practitioner, many of which you may have begun to take for granted. The challenge is then to use your own experience to help supervisees develop their own style of working and their own solutions to difficult work situations.

Another reason, which is often denied, for becoming a supervisor can be that of becoming one up on the other staff. Many of us will remember the joy when we entered our second year at a school – we were no longer the youngest or most gullible, there were now others we could tell 'what is what' to. New supervisors can be eager to mask their own anxieties by using their supervisees to bolster up their own pseudo-role of expert – the one who has all the answers.

Finally, another hidden motive in giving supervision can be when staff who do not know how to get decent supervision for themselves compensate by giving to other staff the sort of supervision they need and want, in the vain hope that this will magically lead to someone offering it to them. This is equivalent to those who find it difficult to ask for counselling help going into training as a counsellor, a pattern that Relate termed 'training as the preferred mode of treatment'.

Getting started

The first prerequisite for being a good supervisor is being able actively to arrange good supervision for yourself (see Chapter 3). A useful question to ask yourself is: 'Am I currently receiving adequate supervision, both for the other work I am doing and for being a supervisor?'

Before you give your first supervision sessions, we think it is useful for you to sit down and reflect on your own overt and covert motives that you bring to supervision. This is not in order to suppress the more shameful motives but to find some appropriate way to meet the needs those motives represent.

It would also be worthwhile to sit down and write out examples of positive and negative supervision experiences you yourself have received. What are your positive role models and what sort of supervisory experiences would you want to avoid repeating for your own supervisees?

Your expectations may well set the tone of what happens in the supervision sessions you give. If you go into supervision expecting the sessions to be full of conflict or to be problematic they may well end up that way. If you go in expecting them to be interesting, engaging and cooperative, you may well produce the necessary climate for that to happen.

Brigid Proctor (1988a) suggests that it is most useful to start with the assumptions

that workers in the human service professions can be relied on
- to want to monitor their own practice;
- to learn to develop competence; and
- to respond to support and encouragement.

Starting with these basic assumptions, even though at times they may not appear totally true, is helpful in setting a positive tone.

It is, however, possible that you are part of an organization where a negative culture about supervision has already developed, or where supervision is totally absent. You may find it supportive to recognize that some of the difficulties are not all yours and to read Chapters 12 and 13.

Qualities needed to be a good supervisor

Carifio and Hess (1987: 244) quote a variety of sources in looking at the qualities of the 'ideal supervisor' which they see as similar to the qualities of the ideal psychotherapist, but employed differently. These qualities include empathy, understanding, unconditional positive regard, congruence, genuineness (Rogers 1957); warmth and self-disclosure (Coche 1977); flexibility, concern, attention, investment, curiosity and openness (Gittermann and Miller 1977; Hess 1980; Aldridge 1982; Albott 1984).

Gilbert and Evans (forthcoming) provide a much fuller list of supervisor qualities based partly on the work of Leddick and Dye (1987), and we have developed this in Box 4.1. You will notice that most of these qualities and

---

Box 4.1 Supervisor qualities (developed from Gilbert and Evans, forthcoming)

- **Flexibility:** in moving between theoretical concepts and use of a wide variety of interventions and methods.
- **A multi-perspectival view:** being able to see the same situation from a variety of angles.
- **A working map of the discipline in which they supervise.**
- **The ability to work transculturally:** (see Chapter 7).
- **The capacity to manage and contain anxiety:** their own and that of the supervisee.
- **Openness to learning:** from supervisees and from new situations that emerge.
- **Sensitivity to the wider contextual issues:** that impact on both the therapeutic and supervisory process.
- **Schooled in anti-oppressive practice:** can handle power appropriately (see Chapter 7).
- **Humour, humility and patience.**

skills are ones you will already have or have developed in order to be a competent practitioner within the helping professions. Good counselling skills are a prerequisite for being a competent supervisor. Brigid Proctor (1988a) makes this point well when she says:

> The task of the supervisor is to help him (the supervisee) feel received, valued, understood on the assumption that only then will he feel safe enough and open enough to review and challenge himself, as well as to value himself and his own abilities. Without this atmosphere, too, he is unlikely to be open to critical feed-back or to pay good attention to managerial instructions.
>
> It will also be the case that a worker often comes to supervision stressed, anxious, angry, afraid. It is our assumption that only if he feels safe enough to talk about these uncomfortable feelings, and fully acknowledge them for himself will he be 'cleared' to re-evaluate his practice.

As a supervisor you may recognize how relevant to this new task are the wealth and experience you have had as a practitioner. Some new supervisors need to be helped to adapt their useful counselling skills to this new context; others hold onto their counselling skills too tenaciously and, as mentioned earlier, turn their supervisees into quasi-clients.

To start supervising you will first find it important to understand the boundaries of supervision and to be able to make clear and mutually negotiated contracts. In Chapter 3, we discussed the importance of contracting clear supervision for the supervisees, and in Chapter 5 we will explore how the supervisor can manage this process. Many new supervisors are concerned about where supervision ends and therapy or counselling begins. Some new supervisors are anxious they will be flooded by their supervisees' personal problems. Others are only too eager to play therapist with their supervisees. Sometimes supervisees want to turn their supervisor into a 'quasi-therapist'.

When training therapists, one of us became aware that several of his own supervisees were half secretly wishing to have therapy with him rather than supervision. In exploring this further he became aware of another factor in this dynamic; that their wish for replacing the supervision of their work with the client with quasi-therapy for themselves was partly due to envy of their clients, to whom they were not only giving the attention in their therapy that they wished for themselves, but were also giving yet more attention in the supervision. He began to realize that this envy needed to be made conscious and that the supervisees should be helped to look at what other forms of support they needed or wanted for themselves.

Kadushin (1968) describes a similar pattern in social work, when supervisees play the game of 'Treat me, don't beat me'. This game can be extremely alluring to the supervisor in several ways:

1 Because the game appeals to the . . . worker in him . . . who is still interested in those who have personal problems.

2 Because it appeals to the voyeur in him (many supervisors are fascinated by the opportunity to share in the intimate life of others).
3 Because it is flattering to be selected as therapist.
4 Because the supervisor is not clearly certain as to whether such a redefinition of the situation is not permissible.

Good supervision inevitably focuses some of its attention on the dynamics of the supervisees, but this must always arise out of work-related issues and be done in the service of understanding and being able to manage the work better.

You need to develop your framework for supervising, which is appropriate to the setting in which you work. This framework needs to be clear enough to be explainable to your supervisees, but also flexible enough to be adapted to meet the changing needs of different supervisees, at different levels and with a variety of situations.

The most difficult new skill that supervision requires is what we call the 'helicopter ability'. This is the ability to switch focus between the following areas:

- the client that the supervisees are describing;
- the supervisees and their process;
- your own process and the here and now relationship with the supervisees;
- the client within their wider context (and to help the supervisees do likewise);
- the wider context of the organization and inter-organizational issues.

This skill cannot be learned before you start and indeed takes many years to develop. What is important is to know of the existence of all the possible levels and perspectives and then gradually expand your focus within the sessions (see Chapter 6). However, do not try to get all the possible perspectives into every session, or your supervisees will get indigestion.

Finally, before we go on to present the different maps and models of supervision, we would like to spend some time looking at the complex roles that a supervisor has to combine. Clarifying your role(s) as supervisor is half the battle to achieving a clear framework.

Supervisor roles

As supervisor you have to encompass many functions in your role:

- a counsellor giving support;
- an educator helping your supervisee learn and develop;
- a manager with responsibilities both for what the supervisee is doing with and to the client;
- a manager or consultant with responsibilities to the organization which is paying for the supervision.

Table 4.1 Helping roles

Helping role	What you take to them	What you expect to receive
Doctor	Symptoms	Diagnosis, cure
Priest	Sins, confessions	Penitence, forgiveness
Teacher	Ignorance, questions	Knowledge, answers
Solicitor	Injustice	Advocacy
Judge	Crimes	Retribution
Friend	Yourself	Acceptance, listening ear
Mother	Hurts	Comfort
Car mechanic	Mechanical failure	Technical correction and servicing

Several writers have looked at the complexity of roles for the supervisor (Bernard 1979; Hess 1980; Hawkins 1982; Holloway 1984, 1995; Ellis and Dell 1986; Carroll 1996). Among the 'sub-roles' most often noted are:

- Teacher
- Monitor evaluator
- Counsellor
- Colleague
- Boss
- Expert technician
- Manager of administrative relationships

In our training course on the fundamentals of supervision we involve all the trainee supervisors in looking at the variety of helping relationships that they have experienced in their lives and the expectations and transactions that these roles involve. We ask them to brainstorm the type of people they have gone to for help in their lives, what needs they take to these people and what they expect to receive. We end up with a list that typically looks like Table 4.1.

When the roles are not clearly contracted for and defined in supervision, and to a lesser extent even when they are, supervisors and supervisees will fall back on other patterns of relating which may be one of the typical transactions mentioned above. It is possible to have *collusive*, *crossed* or *named* transactions.

A *collusive transaction* happens when you go to your supervisor expecting a reassuring mum and your supervisor obligingly plays out that role by constantly telling you that everything is fine. Such a collusive transaction may feel good to both parties at the time, but is unproductive as it feeds the neurotic needs of both parties rather than the needs of the supervision.

If on the other hand you went expecting a reassuring mum and your supervisor played the judge, you would have a *crossed transaction*. In this case you would probably feel misunderstood and put down and that your supervisor was very unsupportive.

A *named transaction* is when one or other of the parties names the patterns and the games that are being played, so that they become a choice rather than a compulsive process.

The supervisor has to be able to combine the roles of educator, supporter and, at times, manager, in an appropriate blend. As Hawthorne (1975: 179) notes: 'It requires effort and experience to integrate these into a comfortable and effective identity'.

Taking appropriate authority and power

Much of the conflict around the role of the supervisor emerges from the difficulty that many supervisors have in finding an appropriate way of taking authority and handling the power inherent in the role. Lillian Hawthorne (1975: 179) has written about this difficult and yet crucial task:

> Many supervisors, especially new ones, have difficulty adjusting to their new authority . . . The balance which they have worked out for their personal lives between dominance and submission is upset by the new responsibility. The supervisory relationship is complex, intense and intimate . . . Sometimes the effort [to take on authority] is hampered by the supervisor's unfamiliarity with the requirements of his role, by difficulties stemming from personal experiences with authority, or by discomfort in the one-to-one relationship.

Hawthorne goes on to describe the sort of games supervisors play either to abdicate power or to manipulate power. These draw on the work of Eric Berne and other writers in transactional analysis approaches to counselling and psychotherapy. Abdication games include:

- *'They won't let me'*: I would like to agree to what you are asking, but senior management won't let me.
- *'Poor me'*: I'm sorry about having to cancel our weekly conferences, but you have no idea how busy I am with these monthly lists for the director.
- *'I'm really a nice guy'*: look at how helpful and pleasant I am being to you.
- *'One good question deserves another'*: how would *you* answer that question?

Manipulation power games include:

- *'Remember who is boss'*: artificially asserting the power of one's role.
- *'I'll tell on you'*: threatening to pass on information about the supervisees to more senior management.
- *'Father or mother knows best'*: acting in a parental or patronizing manner.
- *'I am only trying to help you'*: defending against criticism from the supervisees by pleading altruism.
- *'If you knew Dostoevsky like I know Dostoevsky'*: showing off your knowledge to make the supervisees feel inferior.

In Chapter 7 on transcultural supervision, we explore the interplay between personal power, cultural power and role power. With the role of supervisor comes the responsibility to be aware of your own power in each of these three areas and to learn ways of utilizing this power in ways that are appropriate, well intentioned, anti-oppressive and sensitive to the particular background of the supervisee.

In the next chapter we will go on to look at positive ways of combining the roles of educator, supporter and manager, and at taking the appropriate authority, depending on the experience of the supervisees and the supervision contract you have with them.

Ethics

It is important before starting supervising to revisit the ethical standards that underpin your professional client work and to consider how each of these standards applies to working as a supervisor. Alternatively you can start afresh and list the principles you would wish your supervisor and yourself as supervisor to espouse and enact. Page and Wosket (1994) provide a whole chapter where they build their ethical principles for supervision from studying writings in moral philosophy. Following on from their work we would propose six basic principles:

1 balancing appropriate responsibility for the work of the supervisee with respect for their autonomy;
2 due concern for the well-being and protection of the client with respect for their autonomy;
3 acting within the limits of one's own competence and knowing when to seek further help;
4 fidelity – being faithful to explicit and implicit promises made;
5 anti-oppressive practice (see Chapter 7);
6 openness to challenge and feedback combined with an active commitment to ongoing learning.

We should also be guided by Hippocrates' injunction to first and foremost 'do no harm'!

Bramley (1996) also has two very readable and useful chapters on ethics, which make useful links with the ethical importance of respecting cultural difference (see Chapter 7). Bramley ends his list of injunctions with 'Do for heaven's sake laugh!'.

Michael Carroll (1996) acknowledges that acting ethically is full of complexity and ambiguity. He provides a four stage process for ethical decision making:

1 *Creating ethical sensitivity*: involves becoming aware of the implications of behaviour for others and insight into the possibility of ethical demands within interpersonal situations.
2 *Formulating a moral course of action*: an interplay between the facts of the situation, professional ethical rules and our own ethical principles.

3 *Implementing an ethical decision*: the need to follow through and implement the ethical decisions made while coping with the resistances both inside and outside, such as politics, self-interest, protection of a colleague or fear of making a mistake.

4 *Living with the ambiguities of an ethical decision*: coping with doubt and uncertainty.

We discuss this issue further at the end of Chapter 8. We also include in Appendix 1 a copy of the British Association for Counselling's *Code of Ethics and Practice for Supervisors of Counsellors* (1996) as an example of one profession's ethical framework for supervision. We recommend that you familiarize yourself with your own profession's latest code of practice and ethics for supervision.

Conclusion

To be a supervisor is both a complex and enriching task. It is deceptively similar to, and uses the same sort of skills as, one's work with clients, but the supervisor must be clear about how supervision is different in content, focus and boundaries and entails a more complex ethical sensitivity. It is also important to explore your feelings, motives and expectations in relation to the role of supervisor, as they will have a large effect on the supervision climate that you set in the sessions.

Above all, supervision is a place where both parties are constantly learning, and to stay a good supervisor is to return regularly to question not only the work of the supervisees, but also what you yourself do as a supervisor and how you do it.

5 Maps and models of supervision

Introduction

In this chapter we want to pause and provide a theoretical background and framework for supervision. The chapter is written particularly for new supervisors to help them take a broad survey of what supervision is – the various types, aspects and styles that are possible – so that they can identify their own style of supervision and then find the particular sort that is most appropriate for the supervisee and the setting within which they work. The chapter also covers the issues that a new or experienced supervisor needs to consider and provides the basis for thinking about what training you might need in supervision.

What is supervision?

Hess (1980: 25) defines supervision as: 'a quintessential interpersonal interaction with the general goal that one person, the supervisor, meets with another, the supervisee, in an effort to make the latter more effective in helping people'. This is similar to the other most commonly used definition of supervision by Loganbill *et al.* (1982): 'an intensive, interpersonally focused, one-to-one relationship in which one person is designated to facilitate the development of therapeutic competence in the other person'.

The British Association for Counselling have created some ground rules for supervision. In their first document on supervision (1987) they also include an awareness of supervision being not only for the supervisee, but also for the benefit of the client. They state that: 'The primary purpose of supervision is to protect the best interests of the client' (p. 2).

But this is only the beginning of the story, because the task of supervision is not only to develop the skills, understanding and ability of the supervisee, but, depending on the setting, may have other functions. Combining the multiple functions of supervision is at the heart of good practice.

Supervision functions

Kadushin (1976), writing about social work supervision, describes three main functions or roles, which he terms as *educative, supportive* and *managerial*. Proctor (1988a) makes a similar distinction in describing the main processes in the supervision of counselling, for which she uses the terms *formative, restorative* and *normative*.

The educative or *formative* function, which is the one stressed in the definitions quoted in the previous section, is about developing the skills, understanding and abilities of the supervisees. This is done through reflection on and exploration of the supervisees' work with their clients. In this exploration they may be helped by the supervisor to:

- understand the client better;
- become more aware of their own reactions and responses to the client;
- understand the dynamics of how they and their client were interacting;
- look at how they intervened and the consequences of their interventions;
- explore other ways of working with this and other similar client situations.

The *supportive* or *restorative* function is a way of responding to how any workers who are engaged in intimate therapeutic work with clients are

necessarily allowing themselves to be affected by the distress, pain and fragmentation of the client and how they need time to become aware of how
this has affected them and to deal with any reactions. This is essential if
workers are not to become over-full of emotions. These emotions may have
been produced through empathy with the client or restimulated by the
client, or be a reaction to the client. Not attending to these emotions soon
leads to less than effective workers, who become either over-identified with
their clients or defended against being further affected by them. This in time
leads to stress and what is now commonly called burnout (see Chapter 3).
The British miners in the 1920s fought for what was termed 'pit-head
time' – the right to wash off the grime of the work in the boss's time,
rather than take it home with them. Supervision is the equivalent for those
that work at the coalface of personal distress, disease and fragmentation
(see also Chapter 3).

The *managerial* or *normative* aspect of supervision provides the quality
control function in work with people. It is not only lack of training or
experience that necessitates the need in us, as workers, to have someone
look with us at our work, but our inevitable human failings, blind spots,
areas of vulnerability from our own wounds and our own prejudices. In
many settings the supervisor may carry some responsibility for the welfare
of the clients and how the supervisee is working with them. Supervisors
may carry the responsibility to ensure that the standards of the agency in
which the work is being done are upheld. Nearly all supervisors, even when
they are not line managers, have some responsibility to ensure that the work
of their supervisees is appropriate and falls within defined ethical standards.

Brigid Proctor (1988a) gives some interesting vignettes to illustrate the
different functions of supervision and to show how one can move from
one to another:

> A teacher in a young person's treatment centre is leaving after five
> demanding years. She asks for time to review the skills she has
> developed. It soon becomes clear that, before she can do that, she
> needs to talk about her feelings of loss and disorientation as she
> leaves the close, battering, intimate, structured environment. (*An
> apparently formative task becomes restorative.*)

> A pregnancy adviser talks about her ethical and legal dilemmas in
> respect of a 15-year-old client. After giving her the 20 minutes
> she asked for, the group decides to spend all the following week's
> supervision on issues of confidentiality that arise in their work.
> (*A normative task.*)

> A teacher in a disruptive unit starts to discuss a boy he is counselling.
> Through a socio-drama initiated by the supervisor the group helps
> him notice the complex system he and the boy are in and the differ-
> ent expectations placed on them . . . by parents, headmaster, social
> worker and others. At the end, he says he is clearer about his chosen
> task and role. (*Formative, normative and restorative.*)

Table 5.1 Primary foci of supervision

Main categories of focus	Kadushin category
To provide a regular space for the supervisees to reflect upon the *content* and *process* of their work	Educational
To develop understanding and skills within the work	Educational
To receive information and another perspective concerning one's work	Educational/supportive
To receive both content and process feedback	Educational/supportive
To be validated and supported both as a person and as a worker	Supportive
To ensure that as a person and as a worker one is not left to carry, unnecessarily, difficulties, problems and projections alone	Supportive
To have space to explore and express personal distress, restimulation, transference or countertransference that may be brought up by the work	Managerial/supportive
To plan and utilize *personal* and *professional* resources better	Managerial/supportive
To be proactive rather than reactive	Managerial/supportive
To ensure quality of work	Managerial

In our work training supervisors we have elaborated the Kadushin (1976) supervisory functions by listing what we see as the primary foci of supervision, and relating these to the Kadushin categories (see Table 5.1). The Table shows that supervision has educative, supportive and managerial components, although in different settings some aspects will be more prominent than others and also the differing aspects are not totally separate but are combined in much of the supervisory focus. We have described elsewhere (Hawkins 1982) our own model that illustrates how these three areas are both distinct but also greatly overlap. A good deal of supervision takes place in the areas where managerial, supportive and educative considerations all intermingle.

Types of supervision

It is important to form a clear contract for every supervisory relationship, and in this contract to decide what managerial, educative and supportive responsibilities the supervisor is carrying. The first step in contracting is to be clear which of the main categories of supervision is being requested by the supervisees and being offered by the supervisor and what sort of match or mismatch exists. The main categories are as follows.

Tutorial supervision

In some settings the supervisor may have more of a tutor role, concentrating almost entirely on the educative function, helping a trainee on a course explore his or her work with clients, where someone in the trainee's workplace is providing the managerial and supportive supervisory functions.

Training supervision

Here the supervision also emphasizes the educative function and the supervisees will be in some form of training or apprenticeship role. They may be student social workers on placement or trainee psychotherapists working with training clients. The difference from tutorial supervision is that here the supervisor will have some responsibility for the work being done with the clients and therefore carry a clear managerial or normative role.

Managerial supervision

We use this term where the supervisor is also the line manager of the supervisees. As in training supervision the supervisor has some clear responsibility for the work being done with the clients, but supervisor and supervisee will be in a manager–subordinate relationship, rather than a trainer–trainee relationship.

Consultancy supervision

Here the supervisees keep the responsibility for the work they do with their clients, but consult with their supervisor, who is neither their trainer nor their manager, on those issues they wish to explore. This form of supervision is for experienced and qualified practitioners.

So far we have described only supervision which is *vertical*, by which we mean a more experienced supervisor working with a less experienced supervisee. It is also possible to have *horizontal* supervision contracts between supervisees of the same level. This will be addressed further in Chapter 9 on group supervision when we consider peer-group supervision. It is also possible to have a one-to-one peer supervision contract. This would normally be a form of consultancy supervision, but it may also have a peer learning element.

Forming the contract

All forms of supervisory relationship need to begin with a clear contract which is created and formed by both parties, and also reflects the expectations of the organizations and professions involved. Page and Wosket (1994: 44) propose that a contract should attend to the following:

- Ground rules
- Boundaries
- Accountability
- Expectations
- Relationship

Carroll (1996: 98) elaborates four principle areas that need to be explored:

- Practicalities
- Working alliance
- Presenting in supervision
- Evaluation

We propose that in contracting there are five key areas that should be covered:

- Practicalities
- Boundaries
- Working alliance
- The session format
- The organizational and professional context

Practicalities

In forming the contract it is necessary to be clear about the practical arrangements such as time, frequency, place, what might be allowed to interrupt or postpone the session, and clarification of any payment that is involved, etc.

Boundaries

A boundary that often worries both supervisees and new supervisors is that between supervision and counselling or therapy. Clearly, working in depth in any of the helping professions can restimulate personal feelings, distress, anger or unhappiness. These feelings need to be shared and explored if the worker is going to be able to function well and learn from the restimulative event. To give an example from a youth club:

A youth club leader had spent a lot of time with a 14-year-old boy whose father had just died. He came to the supervision very angry about how the boy was receiving very little help at school. It gradually emerged that his own father left home when he was quite young and he had to support his mother emotionally, with very little outside help.

The basic boundary in this area is that supervision sessions should always start by exploring issues from work and should end with looking at what the supervisee does next with the work that has been explored. Personal material should only come into the session if it is directly affecting, or being affected by, the work discussed; or if it is affecting the supervision relationship. Thus, in the above case, it would be important to explore how the youth club leader's own personal material was being restimulated by the death of the young boy's father and how this was colouring his perspective on the boy's needs. If such an exploration uncovered more material than could be appropriately dealt with in the supervision, the supervisor might suggest that the worker get counselling or other forms of support in exploring these personal feelings. Page and Wosket (1994: 20) provide a very useful summary of the differences between counselling and supervision.

A supervision contract should also include clear boundaries concerning *confidentiality*. Confidentiality is an old chestnut which brings concern to many new supervisors. So many supervisors fall into the trap of saying or implying to the supervisees that everything that is shared in the supervision is confidential, only to find that some unexpected situation arises where they find it is necessary to share material from the supervision beyond the boundaries of the session.

Clearly this is more likely to be the case in training or managerial supervision, where the supervisor has an agency function and responsibility, of which the supervision is part. But even in consultancy supervision there are circumstances in which material from the session may be appropriately taken over the boundary. The consultant supervisor may feel a personal need for supervision on how he or she is supervising this worker. Another, although less likely, possibility is that within the supervision, gross professional misconduct may be revealed which the supervisee refuses to take active responsibility to redress. The supervisor may feel ethically or legally incumbent to take action, informing appropriate authorities.

Thus, in contracting the appropriate confidentiality boundary for any form of supervision, it is inappropriate either to say everything is confidential that is shared here, or, as in the case of one supervisor we knew, to say nothing here is confidential. The supervisor should rather be clear what sort of information participants would need to take over the boundary of the relationship; in what circumstances; how they would do this; and to whom they would take the information. Clearly every possible situation cannot be anticipated, but by such a general exploration the possibility of sudden betrayal is diminished.

We also give our supervisees the undertaking that we will treat everything they share with us in a professional manner and not gossip about their situation.

Working alliance

Forming the working alliance starts by sharing mutual expectations. What sort of style of supervison do the supervisees most want and which of the possible foci do they wish the supervisor to concentrate on? The supervisors also need to state clearly what their preferred mode of supervising is, and any expectations they have of the supervisees. We find it useful at the contracting phase to not only share conscious expectations but also hopes and fears. It can be useful to complete sentences such as: 'My image of successful supervision is . . .'; and 'What I fear happening in supervision is . . .'

A good working alliance is not built on a list of agreements or rules, but on growing trust, respect and goodwill between both parties. The contract provides a holding frame in which the relationship can develop, and any lapses in fulfilling the contract need to be seen as opportunities for reflection, learning and relationship building, not judgement and defence (see Shohet and Wilmot 1991: 95).

Session format

As well as sharing hopes, fears and expectations, it is useful to ground the discussions in an exploration of what a typical session format might be like. Will all the time be spent on one case? Are supervisees expected to bring written-up case notes or verbatim accounts of sessions? Is there an expectation that all clients will be discussed within a certain time frame? Are supervisees required to check with or inform their supervisor whenever they take on a new client?

Organizational and professional context

In most supervisory situations there are other critical stakeholders in the supervisory contract besides the direct parties. There are the expectations of the organization or organizations in which the work is being carried out. The organization may have its own explicit supervision policy where the organizational expectations of supervision are clarified (see Chapter 13). Where a clear policy does not exist, it is still essential that the implicit expectations of the organization are discussed. This could include what responsibility the organization might expect the supervisor to take in ensuring quality work and what report they require on the supervision. Likewise it is important to clarify the professional and ethical codes of conduct that both parties may be party to. In many cases the supervisor and the supervisee may be part of the same profession, but on some occasions the supervision may be happening across professions or across orientations with different codes.

Most professional associations have codes of conduct and statements of ethics which stipulate the boundaries of appropriate behaviour between a worker and a client or patient, and also provide the right of appeal for the client against any possible inappropriate behaviour by the worker. Many professions are not as clear about their code of practice for supervision. We do not want to prescribe what we think are appropriate ethical standards for supervisors, because this must invariably vary from one setting to another. However, we do consider it imperative that all new supervisors check whether there are ethics statements covering supervision within their profession and/or organization. If no such statements exist, we suggest that you review the ethical standards for work with clients and become clear within yourself which of them you feel apply to the supervision context. It is important that all supervisors are clear about the ethical boundaries of their supervisory practice and are able to articulate these to their supervisees (see the sections on ethics in Chapters 4 and 8).

A number of works including Page and Woskett (1994), Brown and Bourne (1996), Carroll (1996) and Holloway and Carroll (1999) have detailed sections on the process of contracting.

Negotiating the contract

Inskipp and Proctor (1995) have provided a very helpful checklist of areas to be covered in an initial exploratory contracting meeting by a counselling supervisor. We have slightly amended this in Box 5.1 to be appropriate for all the helping professions.

Supervision arrangements

So far we have concentrated on contracts for formal one-to-one supervision. However, it is also possible to have supervision arrangements that are more informal or ad hoc. In some residential or day care agencies much of the supervision will be outside formal individual sessions. Payne and Scott (1982) have produced a format for recognizing the choices between formal and informal, planned and ad hoc supervision. This is very useful in helping teams to recognize that a great deal of supervision happens in times and places other than those officially designated for supervision. Once this is recognized, the quality of the informal or ad hoc supervision can also be negotiated and improved.

However, there are dangers in informal supervision arrangements. Although there is a lot of creative scope for more informal types of supervision, it is easy to use these less structured types of supervision to avoid the rigours and concentrated focus of regular, formal individual sessions. We have talked extensively in this book about the natural resistances and defences to both giving and receiving supervision, and without a formal

Box 5.1   The exploratory contracting meeting

Negotiate	The working alliance	Information to supervisee about me
Time, length, when, frequency, where? Cost: how much? Method of payment: who pays, when, invoice/cheque/cash? Missed sessions: payment holidays, notice	Beginning to set up a trusting relationship to produce a working alliance by communicating empathy, respect, genuineness	Theoretical background and training experience as a professional, supervisor etc. Present work Support for supervision Membership of professional associations
Discuss and negotiate	**Basic relationship skills**	**Information wanted from the supervisee**
Recording • client • supervision • agreement Boundaries Reviews Evaluation/ assessment Code of ethics	For relationship building, exploring and negotiating Paraphrasing, reflecting, summarizing, focusing, questioning, self-disclosure, immediacy and purpose; stating and preference stating	Experience, qualifications Theoretical model(s) Professional organization Code of ethics Freelance/ organization/agency Where working? Number of clients, and other counselling work Any agency requirements? Professional needs and development In counselling or therapy?
Final decision	**Can and will we work together?**	

Source: Inskipp and Proctor (1995)

structure these resistances can produce a lot of avoidance behaviour from both the supervisor and the supervisee. It is easy to create a climate where supervision is only requested when you have a recognizable problem and at other times you have to be seen to 'soldier on'. The dangers of this type of culture are explored more fully in Chapter 12.

Supervisory styles

Having looked at the various functions and modes of supervision, we will now look at how the style of supervision can vary within each of these different types. In this chapter we provide you with a broad-brush distinction between different supervisory styles and then in Chapter 6 we present our own model for more finely delineating and developing your own supervisory style.

One's style as a supervisor is affected by the style of one's practitioner work. If you are a Rogerian counsellor it is most likely that your style of supervision will be non-directive and supervisee-centred (see Hess 1980, Ch. 12). If your training has been psychoanalytic, as a supervisor you may tend to concentrate on understanding the unconscious processes of the client or the supervisee (see Hess 1980, Ch. 11). If you are trained as a behaviourist, then as a supervisor you will tend to concentrate on client behaviour and the methodology of the worker (see Hess 1980, Ch. 13). It is also possible to integrate several different therapeutic approaches into your own supervision style and this is explored by Boyd (1978).

Sometimes we are asked whether the supervisor should always have the same type of training as the supervisee. There is no easy answer to this question, but both supervisor and supervisee need to share enough of a common language and belief system to be able to learn and work together. Sometimes having a supervisor with a different training means that he or she is more able to see what your own belief system is editing out.

Supervisory style is also greatly affected by your own gender, age and cultural background, as well as your personality. It is important to be aware of how all these affect the way you will view both the supervisees and the clients they will present to you. This is especially relevant when there is a match between the age, gender and background of the worker and the supervisor, but the client has a different age, background or gender (e.g. if the client is an old, working-class, West Indian man, and the worker and supervisor are both young, middle-class, white women). In such cases the supervisor has to work doubly hard to help the supervisee explore how his or her own background and attitudes are affecting how she or he sees and works with the client. (This whole area is explored at length in Chapter 7.)

Eckstein (1969) offers a simple way of thinking about such issues, through considering our *dumb spots*, *blind spots* and *deaf spots*. Dumb spots are those where supervisees or supervisors are ignorant about what it is like to be in the position of the client. They lack the experience to understand what it means to be a homosexual, frightened of parental disapproval, or a member of an oppressed ethnic group. Blind spots are where the supervisee's own personal patterns and processes get in the way of seeing the client clearly (see the discussion of countertransference in Chapter 6, Mode 4). Deaf spots 'are those where the therapist not only cannot hear the client, but cannot hear the supervisor either. These are likely to involve particularly defensive reactions based on guilt, anxiety or otherwise unpleasant and disruptive feelings, or hostility to authority figures' (Rowan 1983).

A developmental approach to supervision

In the upsurge of literature on supervision in the field of counselling psychology in the USA, the main model that has emerged is the developmental approach. This approach suggests that supervisors need to have a range of styles and approaches which are modified as the counsellor gains in experience and enters different definable developmental stages.

One of the first seminal works in this field was by Hogan (1964) working in the area of training psychologists as psychotherapists. Many writers have followed since then, most notably Worthington (1987) and Stoltenberg and Delworth (1987). Rather than describe each of these models (they are well described in Stoltenberg and Delworth 1987: 18– 30) we will integrate them into a combined developmental model of four major levels of supervisee development.

Level 1: self-centred

The first level is characterized by trainee dependence on the supervisor. The supervisees can be anxious, insecure about their role and their own ability to fulfil it, lacking insight, but also highly motivated. A recent study by Hale and Stoltenberg (1988) suggests that the two main causes of anxiety in new trainees are evaluation apprehension and objective self-awareness. 'Objective self-awareness' is a term borrowed from social psychology and is used to suggest that 'the process of being videotaped, audiotaped, or otherwise made to focus on oneself . . . can elicit negative evaluations of one's performance and concomitant feelings of anxiety' (Stoltenberg and Delworth 1987: 61).

New trainees have not had the experience to develop grounded criteria on which to assess their performance and consequently can feel very dependent on how their supervisor is assessing their work. This apprehension may be linked to the supervisor having some formal assessment role in their training or in their work evaluation. It will also be present on a more day-to-day basis as concern about how the supervisor is viewing their work, and how they compare to other supervisees that their supervisor sees.

We have found this concern to be particularly present when the taping of sessions is employed, or where trainees are asked to bring 'verbatims' or accounts of sessions. However, supervision generally must help the supervisee to reflect back on themselves, and for the new trainee this is inevitably anxiety provoking.

Level 1 workers tend 'to focus on specific aspects of the client's history, current situation, or personality assessment data to the exclusion of other relevant information. Grand conclusions may be based on rather discreet pieces of information' (Stoltenberg and Delworth 1987: 56). It is difficult for workers at this level to have an overview of the whole therapeutic process as they have usually only worked with clients in the early stages of therapeutic work. This may make them impatient or fearful that the process will ever move on from a current sticking place.

In order to cope with the normal anxiety of Level 1 trainees, the supervisor needs to provide a clearly structured environment which includes positive feedback and encouragement to the supervisees to return from premature judgement of both the client and themselves to attending to what actually took place. 'Balancing support and uncertainty is the major challenge facing supervisors of beginning therapists' (Stoltenberg and Delworth 1987: 64).

Level 2: client centred

Here the supervisees have overcome their initial anxieties and begin to fluctuate between dependence and autonomy, and between over-confidence and being overwhelmed.

We have written elsewhere (Hawkins 1979, 1980) about how this stage manifests itself in residential workers in therapeutic communities. This paper, entitled 'Between Scylla and Charybdis', describes how the staff trainee has to be supported by tutors and supervisors to steer a course between submergence and over-identification (representing Charybdis on the one side) and flight into over-professionalism (being Scylla on the other side). This is how a staff member disappearing into the whirlpool of Charybdis was described:

> the staff member stops reading books or writing letters; he becomes unable to objectify his experience in case conferences or supervision; he finds it difficult to set limits, say no to residents (clients) or to protect his off-duty hours . . . unable to separate other people's difficulties from one's own intra-psychic dynamics, or investing one's own success or failure and validation in the success or failure of the residents.
>
> (Hawkins 1980: 195)

The staff member who is dashed on the rocks of Scylla becomes: 'defensively over-clinical to avoid any personal involvement . . . staff trainees become unable to meet clients on a person-to-person basis, desperately hold on to a false persona of adequacy and retreat into administration' (Hawkins 1979: 222–3).

In their work with clients the Level 2 trainee begins to be less simplistic and single focused both about the development process of the client and their own training: 'the trainee begins to realize, on an emotional level, that becoming a psychotherapist (or other helping professional) is a long and arduous process. The trainee discovers that skills and interventions effective in some situations are less than effective at other times' (Stoltenberg and Delworth 1987: 71).

Loss of the early confidence and simplicity of approach may lead some trainees to be angry with their supervisor whom they see as responsible for their disillusionment. The supervisor is then seen as 'an incompetent or inadequate figure who has failed to come through when he or she was so badly needed' (Loganbill *et al.* 1982: 19). Some writers have likened this level of development to that of adolescence in normal human development, with Level 1 being similar to childhood, Level 3 to early adulthood and Level 4 being full maturity.

Certainly Level 2 can feel to the supervisor like parenting an adolescent. There is a testing out of one's authority, a fluctuation in moods and a need to provide both space for the trainees to learn from mistakes and a degree of holding and containment. In this stage the trainees can also become more reactive to their clients, who, like the supervisor, may also be felt to be the cause of their own turbulence.

The supervisor of Level 2 trainees needs to be less structured and didactic than with Level 1 trainees, but a good deal of emotional holding is necessary as the trainees may oscillate between excitement and depressive feelings of not being able to cope, or perhaps even of being in the wrong job.

Level 3: process centred

The Level III trainee shows increased professional self-confidence, with only conditional dependency on the supervisor. He or she has greater insight and shows more stable motivation. Supervision becomes more collegial, with sharing and exemplification augmented by professional and personal confrontation.

(Stoltenberg and Delworth 1987: 20)

Level 3 trainees are more able to adjust their approach to clients to meet the individual and particular needs of those clients at that particular time. They are also more able to see the client in a wider context and have developed what we call 'helicopter skills'. These are the skills of being fully present with the client in the session, but being able simultaneously to have an overview that can see the present content and process in the context of:

• the total process of the therapeutic relationship;
• the client's personal history and life patterns;
• the client's external life circumstances;
• the client's life stage, social context and ethnic background.

At Level 3 it is less possible to recognize what orientation the trainee has been schooled in, as they have by this stage incorporated the training into their own personality, rather than using it as a piece of learnt technology.

Level 4: process in context centred

This level is referred to as 'Level 3 integrated' by Stoltenberg and Delworth (1987). By this time the practitioner has reached 'master' level 'characterized by personal autonomy, insightful awareness, personal security, stable motivation and an awareness of the need to confront his or her own personal and professional problems' (Stoltenberg and Delworth 1987: 20). Often by this stage supervisees have also become supervisors themselves and this can greatly consolidate and deepen their own learning. Stoltenberg and Delworth (1987: 102) quote a colleague: 'When I'm supervising, I'm forced to be articulate and clear about connections across domains and that makes it easier for me to integrate'.

We often find that we say things to our supervisees that we need to learn. It is as if our mouth is more closely linked to our subconscious knowing than is our mental apparatus! Mulla Nasrudin, when he was asked how he had learned so much, replied: 'I simply talk a lot and when I see people agreeing, I write down what I have said'.

Certainly Level 4 is not about acquiring more knowledge, but allowing this to be deepened and integrated until it becomes wisdom; for as another Sufi teacher put it: 'Knowledge without wisdom is like an unlit candle'.

It is possible to compare the developmental stages of supervisees development to other developmental approaches. We have already mentioned the analogy to the stages of human growth and development. We can also posit the analogy to the stages of development within the medieval craft guilds. Here the trainee started as a *novice*, then became a *journeyman*, then an *independent craftsman* and finally a *master craftsman*.

The model also has parallels in the stages of group development. Schutz (1973) describes how groups begin with the predominant concerns being *inclusion/exclusion*: can I fit in and belong here? Once this has been resolved the group will normally move on to issues of *authority*: challenging the leader, dealing with competitiveness, etc. Only then will the group move on to look at issues of *affection* and *intimacy*: how to get close to the others and what is the appropriate closeness. This progression of themes seems to be paralleled in the supervision–developmental approach, particularly where supervision is part of training which is being carried out with other trainees (see also Chapter 9).

Finally, the four stages of supervisee development can be seen as characterized by where the centre of supervisees' focus and concern is located (see Table 5.2).

We will return to this 'map' in Chapter 6 when we explore the developmental aspects of our own model of supervision.

Table 5.2 Developmental stages of the supervisee

Level 1	Self-centred	'Can I make it in this work?'
Level 2	Client centred	'Can I help this client make it?'
Level 3	Process centred	'How are we relating together?'
Level 4	Process in context centred	'How do processes interpenetrate?'

Reviewing the developmental approach

The developmental model is a useful tool in helping supervisors more accurately to assess the needs of their supervisees and to realize that part of the task of supervision is to help in the development of the supervisee, both within stages and between stages of development. The model also stresses that as the supervisee develops so must the nature of the supervision.

However, there are limits to its usefulness that must be borne in mind. First, there is a danger of using the model too rigidly as a blueprint for prescribing how every supervisee at each stage should be treated, without enough reference to the particular needs of the individual, the style of the supervisor and the uniqueness of the supervisor–supervisee relationship.

Second, Hess (1987) points out that supervisors are also passing through stages in their own development and we must therefore look at the interaction of both parties' developmental stages. This challenge is taken up in part by Stoltenberg and Delworth (1987: 152–67). They suggest a parallel model for supervisors development as follows:

- *Level 1* Tendency of supervisors to be anxious to do the 'right' thing and to be effective in the role. This can lead to being overly mechanistic or attempting to play an expert role.
- *Level 2* 'The supervisor now sees that the process of supervision is more complex and multi-dimensional than he or she had imagined. It is no longer the "great adventure" it once was'. There is sometimes a tendency to go out on one's own as a supervisor, rather than get support for one's supervision practice.
- *Level 3* Most supervisors reach this level if they avoid stagnating at Level 1 or dropping out at Level 2. At this level the supervisor displays a consistent motivation to the supervisory role and is interested in constantly improving his or her performance. Supervisors are able to make an honest self-appraisal (see Chapter 8).
- *Level 4* (Stoltenberg and Delworth call this 'Level 3 integrated'). At this level the supervisor can modify their style to work appropriately with supervisees from any level of development, from different disciplines, different orientations and across cultural differences (see Chapter 7). Such supervisors are able to supervise supervision practice and may also teach or tutor supervision training.

An individual should not embark on giving supervision until they have reached Level 3 or Level 4 of development in their own practice. They then have to cope with being an advanced practitioner and an early-stage supervisor. Stoltenberg and Delworth (1987) suggest that it is very hard for a Level 1 or Level 2 supervisor to supervise practitioners other than those who are at Level 1 in their development. They also need good supervision on *their* supervision practice. It is important not to apply the developmental model too rigidly, but it can be a useful map for matching the right supervisee to the right supervisor, or to explore difficulties in the supervision relationship.

Carroll (1987) warns those working outside the USA of another of the limitations of the developmental model, which is that it has been developed entirely within an American context and: 'We need to be careful that we do not transport theories that work well in other climates to Britain without serious investigation that they will adapt well to the changing environment. Counselling supervision may not be a good traveller'. Carroll quotes the research by O'Toole (1987) which shows significant differences between the counselling climates in the USA and the UK. In the fields of psychotherapy and social work there are also major differences between the cultures on each side of the Atlantic.

Finally, we would do well to remember that we can become egotistic and over-inflated in thinking that we are responsible for another person's development. Here is a story that beautifully makes this point: 'A man once saw a butterfly struggling to emerge from its cocoon, too slowly for his taste, so he began to blow on it gently. The warmth of his breath speeded up the process all right. But what emerged was not a butterfly but a creature with mangled wings'.

Despite our reservations, we would particularly recommend some acquaintance with the developmental approach to all supervisors who work in the context of a training course, be it for nurses, social workers, counsellors or psychotherapists, in order that they may plan what supervision is most appropriate for trainees in different stages of the course.

Conclusion: choosing your framework

Our hope is that this chapter has provided readers with the tools to choose and/or clarify:

- the supervision framework they wish to use;
- how they will amend their basic framework depending on the work, needs and developmental stage of the supervisees;
- how they will balance the competing demands of the educative, supportive and managerial functions of supervision;
- what sort of supervision contract they will negotiate, and what issues it will include.

However, the map is not the territory. Before setting off on an expedition into new terrain, you need to ensure that the map is as good as you can get, but once you have embarked on the journey you do not want to spend the whole time buried in your map. You only need the map to send you in the right direction, or to redirect you when you get lost and also to make periodic checks that you are all going in the right direction.

Finally, it is important that the map you develop is accessible to and understandable by your supervisees. Supervision is a joint journey and works best where there is a shared model and framework.

6 A process model of supervision

Introduction

This chapter is written particularly for those who supervise counsellors or psychotherapists, but we hope it will also be of interest to those in other helping professions who supervise in-depth casework. Because of this focus we have used the term 'therapist' for the supervisee throughout this chapter. When reading this, it is possible to substitute the terms 'worker', 'counsellor', 'social worker', 'psychiatrist', etc.

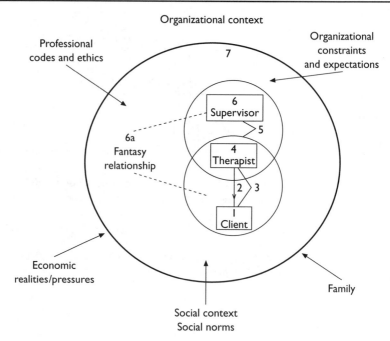

Figure 6.1   The seven-eyed model of supervision

Having presented, in the previous chapter, the main maps and models of supervision that are currently available, we now turn to our own model of the supervision process. Our 'double matrix' model, which we first presented in 1985 (Hawkins 1985), differs significantly from the other ways of looking at supervision. In this model we turn the focus away from the context and the wider organizational issues (discussed in the models in the previous chapter) to look more closely at the process of the supervisory relationship. This model has since been referred to as the 'seven-eyed model of supervision' (Inskipp and Proctor 1995), a name we have now adopted (see Figure 6.1).

The double matrix or seven-eyed supervisor model

Our interest in this dimension began when we were trying to understand the significant differences in the way each member of our own peer group supervised and the different styles of supervision that we had encountered elsewhere. These differences could not be explained by developmental stages, our primary tasks or our intervention styles. From further exploration came the realization that the differences were connected to the constant choices we were making, as supervisors, as to what we focused on.

At any time in supervision there are many levels operating. At a minimum all supervision situations involve at least four elements:

- A supervisor
- A therapist
- A client
- A work context

Of these four, normally only the supervisor and the therapist are directly present in the supervision session, except in live supervision. However, the client and the work context are carried into the session in both the conscious awareness and the unconscious sensing of the therapist. They may also, at times, be brought indirectly into the session in the form of audio/video tapes or written verbatims of sessions, or through role-play.

Thus the supervision process involves two interlocking systems or matrices:

- the therapy system which connects the client and the therapist through some agreed contract, regular time spent together and a shared task;
- the supervision system or matrix which involves the therapist and the supervisor through their agreed contract, time spent together and shared task.

The task of the supervisory matrix is to pay attention to the therapy matrix, and it is in how this attention is given that supervisory styles differ.

Our model divides supervision styles into two main categories:

- supervision that pays attention directly to the therapy matrix, through the therapist and the supervisor reflecting together on the reports, written notes or tape recordings of the therapy sessions;
- supervision that pays attention to the therapy matrix, through how that system is reflected in the here-and-now experiences of the supervision process.

Each of these two major styles of managing the supervision process can be further subdivided into three categories, depending on the emphasis of the focus of attention. This gives us six modes of supervision, plus a seventh mode that focuses on the context in which supervision happens.

The therapy session is reported and reflected upon in the supervision

Reflection on the content of the therapy session

Attention is concentrated on the actual phenomena of the therapy session: how the client presented themselves, what they chose to share, which area of their life they wanted to explore, and how this session's content might relate to content from previous sessions. The aim and goal of this form of supervision are to help the therapist pay attention to the client, the choices the client is making and the relatedness of the various aspects of the client's life.

Exploration of the strategies and interventions used by the therapist

The focus here is on the choices of intervention made by the therapist – not only what interventions were used but also when and why they were used. Alternative strategies and interventions might then be developed and their consequences anticipated. The main goal of this form of supervision would be to increase the therapist's choices and skills in intervention.

Exploration of the therapy process and relationship

Here the supervisor will pay particular attention to what was happening consciously and unconsciously in the therapy process: how the session started and finished; what happened around the edges; metaphors and images that emerged; and changes in voice and posture. The main goal of this form of supervision will be the therapist having greater insight and understanding of the dynamics of the therapy relationship.

Focus on the therapy process as it is reflected in the supervision process

Focus on the therapist's countertransference

Here the supervisor concentrates on whatever is still being carried by the therapist, both consciously and unconsciously, from the therapy session and the client. The countertransference may be of several different kinds which will be explored later in this chapter (see Mode 4).

Focus on the here-and-now process as a mirror or parallel of the there-and-then process

Here the supervisor focuses on the relationship in the supervision session in order to explore how it might be unconsciously playing out or paralleling the hidden dynamics of the therapy session (Searles 1955; Mattinson 1975). Thus, if the client was covertly acting in a passive-aggressive way to the therapist, this might emerge in the supervision by the therapist's becoming unconsciously passive-aggressive to the supervisor as they discuss that particular client.

Focus on the supervisor's countertransference

Here the supervisor primarily pays attention to their own here-and-now experience in the supervision – what feelings, thoughts and images the shared therapy material stirs up in them. The supervisor uses these responses to provide reflective illumination for the therapist. The unconscious material of the therapy session which has been unheard at the conscious level by the therapist may emerge in the thoughts, feelings and images of the supervisor.

Focus on the wider context

Although the six modes of focus are inclusive in so far as they include all the processes within both the therapy and supervisory matrices, the supervisory relationships also exist within a wider context which impinges upon and colours the processes within it. The supervisor cannot afford to act as if the client–therapist–supervisor threesome exists on an island. There are professional codes and ethics, organizational requirements and constrictions, as well as relationships with other involved agencies. All of these need to be taken into consideration.

In Chapter 8 we will explore how the organizational roles and power dynamics may affect the supervisory process, and in the final section of the book (Chapters 12 and 13) we will explore the wider organizational context in which supervision takes place and how to work within it.

It would be very unusual to find a supervisor who remained entirely in one of these seven modes of supervision and we would hold that good supervision must inevitably involve movement between modes. However, distinguishing between the modes in their pure form has many advantages. It allows supervisors to be clearer about their own style, its strengths and weaknesses and which possible modes of supervision they might be avoiding out of habit or lack of familiarity and practice.

Not only does the model provide a way of increasing the options for the supervisor, but it can also be used by the therapist as a language within which to negotiate changes in supervision style, and can be used as a tool in a regular review and appraisal of the supervision.

The model can also be used to train supervisors in the various elements of the supervision process, learning the refinements of each focus separately, so that they can then develop their own style and method of putting the different processes together (see Chapter 8).

It is this approach that we use on our training course for those who supervise counsellors and therapists. We now present each mode of supervision in detail along with a specific training exercise designed to train the course members in that particular mode (CSTD 1999). We liken this to musicians learning to play scales before performing concert pieces.

Mode 1: the content of the supervision session

'It is the task of the Supervisor to enable the supervisees to become more aware of what actually takes place in the session' (Shainberg 1983).

To a supervisor, focusing on what actually happened during the supervision session may sound deceptively easy. But as Shainberg points out in her excellent paper, 'Teaching therapists how to be with their clients', the difficulty for therapists in staying with their not knowing what is happening, and what to do in the therapy session, causes them to fear this relative impotence and rush to make premature sense. This can lead on to premature theorizing and over-early interpretation of what has happened.

Supervisors can both collude and intensify this process with their own anxiety and need to be potent and have answers for their therapists.

Shainberg is not the first to point out this phenomenon. Freud relates how 'a store of ideas is created, born from a man's need to make his helplessness tolerable' (Freud 1927: 18) and Bion (1974) in his writings on therapy constantly entreats us to stay empty with our unknowing, uncluttered by premature judgement, theory and interpretation: 'In every consulting room there ought to be two rather frightened people'. 'True knowing', Shainberg writes, comes from 'being able to observe and describe what is going on in the present in accurate, concrete, and complete detail. This is different from wanting to change or get rid of or compare or assume a fixed meaning about what is happening' (Shainberg 1983: 164).

The first task in every supervisory exploration of clients is to have the therapists accurately describe the clients: how they came to be having therapy; their physical appearance; how they move and hold themselves; how they breathe, speak, look, gesture, etc.; their language, metaphors and images; and the story of their life as they told it.

This task requires the clear focus of a portrait painter or Zen archer and the supervisor's job is to help the therapist to stay with this difficult task. This involves challenging the assumptions that the therapist makes and asking them to return to what they saw or what the client said. It also entails watching for the therapist's 'ideological editor' or belief system that edits what information the therapist is relating to and forms the frame in which they present the clients.

Shainberg shows, in her paper, how often new therapists have a fixed notion of how the therapy should go. They are anxious to apply the theory that they have learned about personality types and pathology to the patients they see before them. This leads them to stop seeing the actuality of the unique human being that they are with and can lead to 'objectification': the seeing of the patient as a challenge to their ther-apeutic prowess. In the second of her two illustrations, Shainberg (1983: 168) describes the 'objectification process' in one of her therapists:

> She then said she did not experience the patient in the same way as she would 'a fellow human being'. She could not feel other than that the patient was 'so far a test of my being a therapist'. I said she had turned the patient into an object 'to be worked on' at this point. She said she felt the gist of it was that 'if *it* is a person you can feel free, but if *it* is a patient you have to do something to change things. Other-wise what are you doing there?' I did not comment on the use of her word *it* but heard it as how remote she experienced the patient at this point from herself, as though the patient were not her fellow being sharing the human condition of suffering, daily conflict, having a mother and a father, being in fear, facing the inevitability of death.

Shainberg (1983: 169) gradually helps therapists to become aware of the internal dialogue inside their own heads – the judgements, expectations, self-doubt, etc. – so that they can return to the actuality of the experience of *being* with the patient prior to *doing*: 'Focus all your attention on seeing as clearly as you can the way this person behaves and what you think and feel being with her. Do not try to find meanings, make connections, or understand. Observe what takes place and your responses'.

There is a place for theorizing and using theory to understand what is happening in work with clients, but it must always come after direct encounter with the client in the fullness of their unique being. Between the stages of concentrating on the direct observation and the content of what the client said, and turning to theoretical consideration, there are several further steps that need to be taken. As Shainberg has already said, the next stage is to attend to the feelings of the therapist while with the patient and this we will talk about more when we look at Mode 3.

After that there are further stages of content focus. There is the exploration of the connections of the content of one part of the session with material from elsewhere in the session, listening for the whole that is contained within each of the parts. Then there is the tentative linking of material from one session to material and sequences from previous sessions. Beginning therapists so often treat each session as if it was a closed system, rather than part of an ongoing process.

Working further out, we can then explore the links of the content to the life of the patient outside therapy and also prior to therapy. In this we can look at the content in the therapy session as a microcosm of the macrocosm of the client's life as a whole.

In focusing on content there are two useful additional processes. One is to concentrate on attending to the first five minutes of the session; to see how the clients first presented and revealed themselves before the dyadic process got fully under way. The other useful approach is to use video or audio recordings of sessions. Here one can move between the actuality of the material and the feelings of the therapist (see Kagan 1980; CSTD 1999).

Mode 2: focusing on strategies and interventions

In this mode the supervisor focuses on what interventions the therapists made in their work with the clients, how and why they made them and what they would rather have done. One psychotherapy trainer that we interviewed uses this approach as the main focus of her supervision: 'I ask them what interventions they have made? What reasons they had for making them? Where their interventions were leading them? How they made their interventions and when? Then I ask what do you want to do with this client now?' (Davies 1987).

It is useful to bear in mind Abraham Maslow's aphorism: 'If the only tool you have is a hammer, you will tend to treat everything as if it is a nail', and it is important to make sure that your therapists not only have a wide range of interventions in their tool box, but also that they use the tools appropriately and are not blunting their chisels by using them to turn screws!

We have often found that in considering how to work with a client, therapists can get stuck in dualistic thinking. They will make statements which we term 'either-or-isms' such as:

- I either have to confront their controlling behaviour or put up with it.
- I didn't know whether to wait a bit longer, or interpret their silence as their aggression towards me.
- I don't know whether to continue working with them.

As you can see, such statements do not always contain the words 'either or', but they are always based on the therapist seeing two opposing options. The job of the supervisor is to avoid the trap of helping the therapist to evaluate between these two choices, but rather to point out how they have reduced numerous possibilities to only two. Once the therapist has realized that they are operating under a restrictive assumption, the supervisor can help them generate new options for intervening.

Generating new options can be done by using a simple brainstorming approach. The basic rules of brainstorming are:

- Say whatever comes into your head.
- Get the ideas out. Don't evaluate or judge the ideas.
- Use the other person's ideas as springboards.
- Include the wildest options you can invent.

Brainstorming is helped by setting a high target for options, for it is only when we have exhausted all the obvious rational choices that the creative unconscious starts to get going. Often it is the craziest idea that contains the kernel of a creative way forward. In a group supervision you could try brainstorming 20 ways of dealing with a therapeutic impasse. In individual supervision you could ask the therapist to invent six or seven different ways of handling the situation with which they are supposedly stuck.

Group supervision offers this mode many creative possibilities. The group contains a greater variety of styles and can avoid the dualism in the dyadic system where there is either the supervisor's or the therapist's approach.

In group supervision there is also a greater range of active role-playing possibilities. Different group members can choose one possible approach they would like to try out from the list of brainstormed possibilities. Then with the therapists playing the client, several different interventions and strategies can be tried and evaluated (see Chapter 9). Even in individual supervision the therapist can try out different interventions. It is possible to use an empty chair or the supervisor to represent the client. If necessary, after trying the intervention, supervisor and therapist can role-reverse and respond to the intervention from within the role of the client.

Many supervisors, when focusing on therapeutic interventions, would offer their own intervention. There are dangers in doing this. It is easy as supervisor to want to show off your therapeutic skill without fully acknowledging how much easier it is to be skilful in the relative ease of the supervisory setting than when face to face with the client. The other danger is that the interventions of the supervisor will be introjected (swallowed whole) by the therapist rather than helping them to develop their own improved interventions.

In Chapter 8 on training supervisors we will describe John Heron's classification of interventions which divides all forms of possible intervention into six categories. We point out how there is no value judgement that one intervention is better than another, but that all interventions can be used *appropriately*, *degenerately* or *perversely*. We do this in order that supervisors may look at which forms of intervention they compulsively use and which they mostly avoid using. From this they can discover some aspects of the strength and weakness of their style, and how they might want to change the balance in the sort of interventions they are using. We find that monitoring our own interventions in such a way sharpens our awareness of the interventions of our therapists.

There is a whole school of strategic therapy which is mainly used for working with families and utilizes a whole range of specific live supervision techniques, with the supervisor delivering strategic interventions to the therapist, often from behind a one-way mirror, through an earpiece or via a telephone. Focusing on strategy should not be confused with 'strategic' approaches to therapy, for all therapists use some form of strategy, be it interpretation, reflection, silence or the active facilitation of bodywork.

Mode 3: focusing on the therapy relationship

In this mode the focus is neither on the client, nor the therapist, nor their interventions, but on the system that the two parties create together. In this mode the supervisor focuses on the conscious and unconscious interaction between therapist and client. To start with the supervisor might ask one or more of the following questions:

- How did you meet?
- How and why did this client choose you?
- What did you first notice about the nature of your contact with this client?
- Tell me the story of the history of your relationship.

These questions must clearly be requesting something different from a case history and must help the therapist to stand outside the therapy relationship in which they might be enmeshed or submerged, and see the pattern and dynamic of the relationship.

Other techniques and questions that encourage this distancing and detachment are:

- Find an image or metaphor to represent the relationship.
- Imagine what sort of relationship you would have if you and the client met in other circumstances, or if you were both cast away on a desert island.

- Become a fly on the wall in your last therapy session; what do you notice about the relationship?

These are all techniques to help the therapist to see the relationship as a whole rather than just stay with their own perspective from within the relationship. But it is the supervisor's job also to listen to the relationship when the therapist is talking from within their own perspective. In this way the supervisor acts like a marital counsellor, in so far as he or she must have the interests of both parties in balance, taking neither the side of therapist nor of the client against the other.

The supervisor listens to the relationship in a variety of different ways. All approaches involve listening with the 'third ear' to the images, metaphors and Freudian slips that collect around the therapist's description of this particular client. Through this form of listening the supervisor is trying to discover the picture that the therapist's unconscious is painting of the relationship. Frank Kevlin (1987) talks about listening to the reported therapy as if it were a dream: 'I look at therapy as a dream. The therapist is telling me a dream and I am doing a dream analysis. The client is the subject being dreamt'.

Attending to the client's transference

The supervisor is also interested in the transference of the client. In Mode 4 we will move on to looking at the countertransference of the therapist, and in many ways it is necessary to move between these two modes and consider the transference and countertransference together. However, for the time being, we will separate the focus and look only at the client's transference.

Many of the questions used above, along with paying attention to the images and metaphors, will give important clues to the transference that is happening. If, for instance, the therapist said that the relationship was like that of two sparring partners in a boxing ring, the transference would be very different from that of a therapist who answered that their relationship was like a frightened rabbit wanting to cuddle up to its mother.

Learning from the patient

When attending to the process between the client and therapist it is important to recognize that somewhere both parties probably know what is really going on and what is getting in the way of their healthy open meeting. This knowing is most likely unconscious, otherwise the case would not have been brought to supervision. The job then of the supervisor is listening to how the unconscious of the client is informing the therapist about what the client needs and how the therapist is helping or getting in the way. Robert Langs (1978, 1985) has developed a complex and very detailed system for attending to and then decoding the latent and unconscious communication of the client and then relating this to the interactions of the therapist and how they were unconsciously received by the client.

A simple way to use this approach is to listen to all the reported content of the client (e.g. stories they told, feelings they have about other people, asides and throwaway comments) as all relating to how the client experiences the therapy and the therapist, especially recent interventions. Langs (1985: 17, 20) gives a good example of this process:

> The final session with a 45-year-old woman who was seen in onceweekly psychotherapy for episodes of depression. She begins this last hour as follows.
>
> *Patient:* One of the boys in the class that I teach at religious school is leaving town. I don't know if I will ever see him again. I wanted to hug him goodbye. My son is leaving for an out-of-town college. I thought of the time my father left us when I was a child. Yesterday, at religious school, I thought of having an affair with the principal.
>
> The patient has largely made use of displacement and symbolization in her allusion to the external danger situation. Rather than alluding directly to the therapist's abandonment . . . the patient mentions the loss of a boy in her class, of her son, and of her father in childhood . . . Each involves an aspect of loss and termination and . . . each expresses in some disguised form a meaning of the ending of the patient's psychotherapy.

Patrick Casement has written about a very similar approach to Langs in a more easily readable book called *On Learning From the Patient* (1985). Here he writes about 'the patient's unconscious search for the therapeutic experience that is most needed'. He gives ample examples of how the client or patient's unconscious is constantly informing the therapist about its need for structure, responsiveness and the appropriate space. However, he cautions us to distinguish between patients' growth needs and their wants: 'I am here making a distinction between needs that need to be met and wants . . . The therapist should . . . try and distinguish between libidinal demands, which need to be frustrated, and growth needs that need to be met' (Casement 1985: 171–2).

Here is an example illustrating the difference between these wants and growth needs drawn from a psychotherapist one of us supervises:

> The therapist was a female worker who looked and acted in a motherly fashion. The client was also a female whose own mother had been very depressed, often not leaving the house for weeks at a time. The client went through periods of wanting the therapist to hug and cuddle her and of trying every way possible for the sessions to overrun the ending time. The libidinal demand was for unbounderied symbiotic mothering, whereas the unconscious

growth need was for a therapist who would provide the clear boundaries that her own mother was unable to give her. Once this had been realized in the supervision, the therapist's anxiety with this client lessened considerably and she was able to set clear boundaries for the client, in a way that the client was able to accept.

Mode 4: focusing on the therapist's process

In this mode the focus of the supervision is on the internal processes of the therapist and how these are affecting the therapy that is being explored. This includes the countertransference of the therapist. It is important to distinguish between four different types of countertransference:

1 Transference feelings of the therapist stirred up by this particular client. This can be either the transferring of feelings about past relationships or situations onto the relationship with this client, or the projection of part of the therapist onto the client.
2 The feelings and thoughts of the therapist that arise out of playing the role transferred on to them by the client (e.g. if the client responds to you as if you were her mother, you may find yourself feeling alternatively protective and angry, in the way her mother did).
3 The therapist's feelings, thoughts and actions used to *counter* the transference of the client. The client treats you as a mother figure and you find yourself becoming very masculine and businesslike to avoid the mother transference.
4 Projected material of the client that the therapist has taken in somatically, psychically or mentally.

What all forms of countertransference have in common is that they involve some form of predominantly unaware reaction to the client by the therapist. It is essential for the therapist to explore all forms of countertransference in order to have greater space to *respond to* rather than *react to* the client. Countertransference used to be thought of as something that had to be made conscious and removed as it formed a negative barrier. More recently psychotherapists have begun to realize that in the countertransference can be the clues to understanding the therapy and client better, and that working with the countertransference is a useful therapeutic tool.

It is clear from what we have said above that it would be hard to work with the countertransference without reference to the client's transference, and so Modes 3 and 4 most often work together. However, there is a difference in focus in whether you are predominantly still trying to understand the client 'out there', or concentrating more on the therapist's own process.

The simplest way to focus on the countertransference is for the supervisor just to pose the question 'What is your countertransference to this client?'. However, as we suggested above, most countertransference is outside awareness and predominantly unconscious, so this question has only very limited effectiveness.

Another slightly more sophisticated technique is 'checks for identity' which we have adapted from 'co-counselling' (see Heron 1974). In this technique the supervisor takes the therapist through four stages in order to elicit any transference from a previous person.

- *Stage 1*: the therapist is encouraged to share their first spontaneous responses to the question: 'Who does this person remind you of?' The supervisor keeps repeating the question until the therapist discovers an answer, which could be a person from their past, a well-known personality, historical or mythic figure or part of themselves.
- *Stage 2*: the therapist is asked to describe all the ways their client is like this person.
- *Stage 3*: the therapist is then asked what they want to say to the person that they discovered in the first question, particularly what is unfinished in their relationship with that person. This can be done in role-play by putting the person on an empty chair or cushion and expressing their feelings to them.
- *Stage 4*: the therapist is then asked in what ways their client is different from this person.

This exercise can lead to surprising discoveries about the most unlikely connections and transferences.

The more unconscious material is often found at the edges of the therapist's communication. It can be in their images, metaphors or Freudian slips of the tongue; or it may be in their non-verbal communication. The supervisor can elicit this material by getting them to free-associate to images or 'slip' words; or by getting them to repeat and exaggerate a movement or gesture that carries a charge. From these interventions can emerge strong feelings that then need to be related back to the work with the client.

Also when looking at the therapist's countertransference it is important to include an exploration of what Frank Kevlin (1987) calls 'the ideological editor'. This is the way the therapist views the client through their own belief-and-value system. This includes conscious prejudice, racism, sexism and other assumptions that colour the way we miss-see, miss-hear or miss-relate to the client. This is explored more fully in Chapter 7.

One way of eliciting this ideological editor is through awareness of the therapist's use of comparatives or associations. If a therapist says about a client: 'She is a very obliging client' the supervisor can ask: 'How is she obliging?'; 'She is very obliging compared to whom?'; or 'Tell me how you think clients should oblige you?' Thus the supervisor is seeking to discover the assumptions about how clients should be that are hidden in this comparative term 'very obliging'. In the terms of construct theory (Kelly 1955) this therapist would be seen as having a bipolar construct obliging/non-obliging.

Here is another example which shows the eliciting of countertransference through spontaneous association. It is taken from a supervision session where Robin is supervising a senior manager in a social services department, whom we will call John:

Robin: Why are you allowing this staff member to drift and not confronting him?
John: Well I do not want to be a punitive boss.
Robin: What would that be like?
John: As you asked that, I got the image of a little boy outside a headmaster's office.
Robin: So your unconscious links confronting to being a punitive head teacher. If you were this staff member's head teacher, how would you want to punish him and what would you be punishing him for?

Having explored this together Robin then encouraged John to try out other ways of confronting the staff member which were less polluted by the punitive countertransference. Thus having started with Mode 4, Robin then moved back into Mode 2.

Mode 5: focusing on the supervisory relationship

In the previous modes the supervisor focused outside themself. In Mode 1 they focused on the client and then increasingly in Modes 2 to 4 they focused on the therapist. Increasingly the supervisor encouraged the therapist to look less for the answers 'out in the client' and to pay more attention to what is happening inside themselves. But the supervisor has so far not started to look inside themself for what is happening. In the final two modes the supervisor practises what they preach and attends to the client's therapy by focusing on how the client's psychodynamics enter and change the supervisory relationship (Mode 5), and then on how these dynamics affect the supervisor (Mode 6). Without the use of Modes 5 and 6 the supervisor would lack congruence between what they were asking the therapist to do and what they were modelling (i.e. the supervisor would be failing to look inside themself).

Harold Searles, an American neo-Freudian, has contributed a great deal to the understanding of this supervision mode in his discovery and exploration of what he terms the paralleling phenomenon:

My experience in hearing numerous therapists present cases before groups has caused me to become slow in forming an unfavourable opinion of any therapist on the basis of his presentation of a case. With convincing frequency, I have seen that a therapist who during occasional presentations appears to be lamentably anxious, compulsive, confused in his thinking, actually is a basically capable colleague who, as it were, is trying unconsciously by his demeanour during the presentation, to show us a major problem area in the therapy with his patient. The problem area is one which he cannot perceive objectively and describe to us effectively in words; rather, he is unconsciously identifying with it and is in effect trying to describe it by the way of his behaviour during the presentation.

(Searles 1955:)

In the paralleling phemonenon the processes at work currently in the relationship between client and therapist are uncovered through how they are reflected in the relationship between therapist and supervisor. For example, if I have a client who is very withholding (who had a mother who was very withholding, who had a mother or father who was very withholding, etc.), when I present them to my supervisor I may well do this in a very withholding way. In effect I become my client and attempt to turn my supervisor into me as therapist. This function, which is rarely done consciously, serves two purposes for the therapist. One is that it is a form of discharge – 'I will do to you what has been done to me and you see how you like it'. The second is that it is an attempt to solve the problem through re-enacting it within the here-and-now relationship. The job of the supervisor is tentatively to name the process and thereby make it available to conscious exploration and learning. If it remains unconscious the supervisor is likely to be submerged in the enactment of the process, by becoming angry with the withholding therapist, in the same way that the therapist was angry with the withholding client.

The important skill involved in working with paralleling is to be able to notice one's reactions and feed them back to the therapist in a non-judgmental way (e.g. 'I experience the way you are telling me about this client as quite withholding and I am beginning to feel angry. I wonder if that is how you felt with your client?'). The process is quite difficult as we are working with the paradox of the therapist both wanting to de-skill the supervisor and at the same time work through and understand the difficult process in which they are ensnared.

Here is a clear example of paralleling written by our colleague Joan Wilmot.

I was supervising a social work student on placement to our thera-peutic community who was counselling a resident with whom she was having difficulty. He was a man in his forties who had been in the rehabilitation programme in the house for about seven months and was now to move on to the next stage which was finding him-self some voluntary work. He was well able to do this but despite the student making many helpful and supportive suggestions, he 'yes but' everything she said. In her supervision with me, despite her being a very able student, her response to all my interventions was 'yes but'. I took this issue to my supervisor, in order as I thought, to obtain some useful suggestions with which to help the student. How-ever, despite the fact that I was usually very receptive to supervision,

> I responded to every suggestion my supervisor made with a 'yes but'. He then commented on how resistant I was sounding and how like the resident in question I was being. This insight immediately rang so true that we were both able to enjoy the unconscious paralleling I had been engaged in and I no longer needed to engage in a resistance game with my supervisor. I shared this with my student who no longer needed to resist me but was able to go back to her client and explore his need to resist. His issues around needing to feel his power by resisting could then be worked on separately from his finding voluntary work and he was able to arrange some voluntary work within the week.
>
> (Wilmot and Shohet 1985)

Margery Doehrman (1976) has done one of the very few pieces of research on paralleling that exist, in which she studied both the therapy sessions and the supervision on the therapy of 12 different people. In the introduction to Doehrman's study, Mayman writes: 'What is strongly suggested by Dr Doehrman's study, a result that she herself admits took her by surprise, was the fact that powerful parallel processes were present in every patient–therapist–supervisor relationship she studied' (Doehrman 1976: 4).

Doehrman discovered that paralleling also went in both directions; not only did the unconscious processes from the therapy relationship get mirrored in the supervision process, but also the unconscious processes in the supervisory relationship could get played out within the therapy process. Mayman concludes by saying: 'I believe parallel processing . . . is a universal phenomenon in treatment, and that the failure to observe its presence in supervision may signal only a natural resistance on the part of the supervisor and/or therapist against facing the full impact of those forces which they are asking the patient to face in himself' (Doerhrman 1976).

The supervisory relationship can also be a forum for modelling new ways of relating. To illustrate this, let us return to the case of Robin's supervision with John, that we used in Mode 4.

> During the session Robin noticed he was irritated with John. He was aware of paralleling, and wondered if this was how John felt about his client. Robin was able to share his irritation in a way that helped John understand his relationship to the client. Also this provided a role model for John of how to share his irritation with the client.

Mode 6: focusing on supervisors' own process

In Mode 5 we explored how the therapeutic relationship invades and is mirrored by the supervisory relationship. In this mode we focus on how the therapeutic relationship enters into the internal experience of the supervisor.

Often as supervisors we find that sudden changes 'come over us'. We might suddenly feel very tired, but become very alert again when the therapist moves on to discuss another client. Images, rationally unrelated to the material, may spontaneously erupt in our consciousness. We may find ourselves sexually excited by our image of the client or shuddering incomprehensibly with fear.

Over the years we have begun to trust these interruptions as being important messages from our unconscious receptors about what is happening both here and now in the room, and also out there in the therapy. In order to trust these eruptions supervisors must know their own process fairly well. I must know when I am normally tired, bored, fidgety, fearful, sexually aroused, tensing my stomach, etc., in order to ascertain that this eruption is not entirely my own inner process bubbling away, but is a received import.

In this process the unconscious material of the therapist is being received by the unconscious receptor of the supervisor, but the supervisor is tentatively bringing this material into consciousness for the therapist to explore.

The supervisor needs to be clear about the countertransference to the therapist: 'What are my basic feelings towards this therapist?'; 'Do I generally feel threatened, challenged, critical, bored, etc.?' All that has been said above about transference and countertransference is relevant to the supervisor relating to their therapists. The main difference is that in supervision you are staying in an adult-to-adult relationship (as far as possible) rather than working *through* the transference. Unless supervisors are relatively clear about their basic feelings towards their therapists they cannot notice how these feelings are changed by the import of unconscious material from the therapists and their clients.

In order to use this mode supervisors not only have to be aware of their own processes, but must also be able to attend to their own shifts in sensation, and peripheral half-thoughts and fantasies, while still attending to the content and process of the session. This may sound a difficult task, but it is also a key skill in being a therapist and it is therefore important that supervisors can model its use to the therapists that they supervise.

Supervisors might use their awareness of their own countertransference by making statements like:

- While you have been describing your work with X, I have been getting more and more impatient. Having examined this impatience it does not seem to be to do with you, or something from outside our work together, so I wonder if I am picking up your impatience with your client?
- I notice that I keep getting images of wolves with their teeth bared, as you describe your relationship with this client. Does that image resonate with your feelings about the relationship?
- I am getting very sleepy as you go on about this client. Often when that happens to me it seems to indicate that some feeling is being shut

off, either to do with the therapy or right here in the supervision. Perhaps you can check what you might be holding back from saying?

Mode 6a: the supervisor–client relationship

So far this model explores the interplay between two relationships: that of the client–therapist and that of the therapist–supervisor; but it ignores the third side of the triangle – namely, the fantasy relationship between the client and the supervisor. Supervisors may have all sorts of fantasies about their therapists' clients, even though they have never met them. The client may also have fantasies about the therapist's supervisor, and we have known some therapy clients to direct a lot of their attention towards the unknown supervisor and their fantasies about what their therapist gets up to in their supervision!

These fantasy relationships complete the triangle and like all triangular processes are laden with conflict and complexity: 'Any pairing ousts the third party, and may at an unconscious level, even revive the first rivalrous oedipal threesome' (Mattinson quoted in Dearnley 1985).

The thoughts and feelings that the supervisor has about the client can clearly be useful, especially in Modes 1 and 6, as described above. Where the feelings of the supervisor are at odds with the experience of the therapist, it can be that some aspect of the client–therapist relationship is being denied and experienced by the supervisor.

Mode 7: focusing on the wider context

Here the supervisor moves the focus from the specific client relationships that are figural in the session to the contextual field in which both the therapy work and the supervision work are taking place. In Chapter 5 we talked about Kadushin's (1976) model and its emphasis on balancing the educative and supportive elements of supervision with the managerial. The supervisor may well have a responsibility to an organization which is responsible for employing them and the therapist. The needs of this organization must also be held in focus in the supervision, including its policies and parameters for carrying out the work. Even when the therapist is an independent practitioner, they will still be part of a professional community with its standards, ethics and professional mores. This is what Proctor (1988a) calls the 'normative' aspect of supervision.

In this mode the supervisor may well ask 'How does your handling of this situation fit with the expectations of your professional body?' Although the supervisor has some responsibility for ensuring ethical and professional work, the focus should not be just on compliance, but also on helping the therapist question how they may be over-constraining their practice because of their assumptions about 'expected practice standards', or because of fear of judgement.

If the supervisor gets trapped in just seeing themselves as the channel of the current wisdom of the profession to the therapist, then the danger is that the profession stops learning. Where supervision is an active enquiry process between supervisor and therapist, it can become an important seedbed for the profession, where new learning and practice are germinated (see Chapter 12).

The situation is further complicated when the therapist is in professional training and the supervisor may well have to write some form of assessment of the therapist's work. When this is the case, then frequently dynamics that emerge in Mode 5 between the therapist and the supervisor will be influenced not just by the case presented but by the training and assessment context. This issue is discussed further in Chapter 8.

Integrating the modes

It is our view that good supervision of in-depth work with clients must involve all seven Modes, although not necessarily in every session. Therefore, part of the training with this model is to help supervisors discover the processes they more commonly use and those with which they are less familiar. We have also found that some supervisors become habituated to using just one process. Always asking 'What is your countertransference?' in response to whatever the therapist shares about their client soon becomes very oppressive.

A parallel model to ours is suggested by Pat Hunt (1986) in her article on supervising marriage guidance counsellors. She suggests that supervision styles can be divided into three types:

- *Case centred approach*: where the therapist and the supervisor have a discussion on the case 'out there'. This is similar to our Mode 1.
- *Therapist centred approach*: which focuses on the behaviour, feelings and processes of the therapist. This is similar to our Modes 2 and 4.
- *Interactive approach*: this focuses both on the interaction in the therapy relationship and the interaction in the supervision. This is similar to our Modes 3 and 5.

Hunt illustrates the dangers of using one of these approaches exclusively. If all the attention is on the client 'out there', there is a tendency to get into an intellectual discussion 'about' the client. There is also a danger of a large 'fudge factor' – the therapists hiding material from the supervisor for fear of judgement. If the approach is exclusively therapist centred it can be experienced by the therapists as intrusive and bordering on therapy. Hunt writes: 'I am not sure how supportive this kind of supervision would feel. I guess quite a lot of learning would occur, but I suspect assessments might be made in terms of the trainee therapist's willingness to open up and talk about himself' (Hunt 1986: 17). If the approach is exclusively interactive centred, there are fewer dangers than in the other two approaches, but a great deal of important information could be ignored in the immersion of attention in the complexities of the two interlocking relationships.

Thus the trainee supervisor, having learned skilfully to use each of the main modes, needs help in moving effectively and appropriately from one mode to another. To do this, it is important to develop the supervisory skills of appropriateness and timing. The supervisor also needs to be aware of how different modes need to be dominant for different therapists, and for the same therapists at different times. The most common pattern of the use of different modes in a supervision session is to begin with Mode 1 (discovering what happened in the session); for this to naturally lead on to Modes 3 and 4 (what happened in the relationship and how this affected the therapist); and if and when this triggers unconscious communication to switch the focus to Modes 5 and 6. At the end of the exploration of a particular client the supervisor might then focus back on what new interventions the therapist might utilize at their next session with this client (Mode 2).

Linking the model to the developmental process

It is also important for the supervisor to be aware of the developmental stage and the readiness of individual therapists to receive different levels of supervision (see Chapter 5).

As a general rule new therapists need to start with most of the supervision focusing on the content of the work with the client and the detail of what happened in the session (Mode 1). As Stoltenberg and Delworth (1987) stress, beginning therapists are often over-anxious about their own performance and need to be supported in attending to what actually took place. New therapists also need help in seeing the detail of individual sessions within a larger context: how material from one session links to the development over time; how it relates to the client's outside life and to their personal history. In helping therapists develop this overview, it is very important not to lose the uniqueness of the therapist's relationship with their client, and for the supervisor not to give the impression that what is new, personal and often exciting for the therapist can easily be put into a recognizable type.

As therapists develop their ability to attend to what *is*, rather than to premature theorizing and over-concern with their own performance, it is then possible to spend more time profitably on Mode 2, looking at their interventions. As stated above, here the danger is that the supervisor habitually tells the therapists how they could have intervened better. We have found ourselves saying to therapists things like 'What I would have said to this client would have been . . .', or 'I would have just kept quiet at that point in the session'. Having said such a line we could kick ourselves for not having practised what we preach and wish we had kept quiet in the supervision session!

As the therapists become more sophisticated, then Modes 3, 4, 5 and 6 become more central to the supervision. With a competent and experienced practitioner, it is possible to rely on their having attended to the conscious material and having carried out their own balanced and critical evaluation of what they did. In such a case the supervisor needs to listen more to the unconscious levels of both the therapist and the reported clients. This necessitates focusing on the paralleling, transference and countertransference processes being played out within the supervision relationship.

There are some contexts in which the new therapists will not require this progression of starting in the more content centred modes, with a later progression into the here-and-now, process centred modes. A psychoanalytic trainee will need their supervisor to use process supervision from the very beginning and more behavioural counsellors may remain predominantly in need of supervision in the content centred modes.

The developmental stage of the therapist is only one factor which will cause the experienced supervisor to shift the dominant mode of focus. Other factors that should influence the choice of focus are:

- the nature of the work of the therapist;
- the style of the therapist's work;
- the personality and learning style of the therapist;
- the degree of openness and trust that has been established in the supervision relationship;
- the amount of personal exploration the therapist has done for themselves (e.g. have they been in therapy?);
- the cultural background of the therapist (see Chapter 7).

Conclusion

In this chapter we have explored in detail the 'double matrix' or 'seven-eyed supervisor model' that we first presented in 1985. We have continued to teach and develop this model ever since and have found that it continues to provide a framework for new levels of depth and new ways of creatively intervening in a supervision session.

We have become increasingly convinced that to carry out effective supervision of any deep therapeutic work it is necessary for the supervisor to be able to use all seven modes of supervision.

The model also provides a framework for the therapist and the supervisor to review the supervision sessions and to negotiate a change in the balance of the focus. Different therapists will require different styles of supervision, and in the next chapter we will explore how the supervisor can increase their ability to work with a greater range of difference. In Chapter 7 we will also revisit each of the seven modes and provide case examples of working with each mode transculturally.

Working with difference: transcultural supervision

Introduction

In this chapter we will focus on the sensitivity and awareness needed to work with different minority groups. We will show how this sensitivity and awareness applies as much, if not more, to our own culture and cultural assumptions as it does to that of others. Minority groups are often discriminated against because of some aspect of their difference to the majority. We will in particular concentrate on the area of culture as it has implications not only for 'race' and ethnicity, but also for class and other groupings which develop their own 'sub'-culture.

Although it is important to take steps to understand other cultures, we have found our usual stance of openness to inquiry also to be useful. This is partly because we generally believe that an open attitude to learning means that we ourselves keep alive and creative rather than formulaic in the work, but also because, if we are to really honour rather than deny cultural diversity, we need to find a way of dialoguing across difference. If we see our task as merely to understand the other's perspective then no real meeting has happened. We are ourselves absent. In a supervisory relationship this means not only a willingness to encourage and explore difference in the supervisee–client relationship, but also an openness to ourselves and our relationship with our supervisees.

Tyler *et al.* (1991) identify three ways of responding to culture:

- *The universalist* denies the importance of culture and puts difference down to individual characteristics. In counselling a universalist will understand all difference in terms of individual pathology.
- *The particularist* takes the polar opposite view, putting all difference down to culture.
- *The transcendentalist* takes a view more similar to our own. Coleman (1999) discusses this perspective as follows: 'both the client and the counsellor have vast cultural experiences that deeply influence their worldviews and behaviour'. He says that 'it is the individual who has to make sense of and interpret those experiences. The transcendent or multicultural perspective suggests there are normative assumptions that can be made about individuals based on cultural factors such as race, gender and class, but that it is just as important to understand how these normative assumptions become reality through the idiosyncratic choices made by individual members of a group'.

Eleftheriadou (1994) makes a helpful distinction between cross-cultural work and work that is transcultural. In the former we 'use our own reference system to understand another person rather than going beyond our own world views' whereas transcultural work 'denotes that counsellors need to work beyond their cultural differences' and need to be able to operate within the frame of reference of other individuals and groupings.

An open attitude to inquiry enhances the ability to work transculturally from a transcendentalist perspective. This inquiry optimally takes place within a dialogue in which both parties participate in the learning.

One particularly complex area is the way issues of power and authority are present for all those concerned. The supervisory relationship is already complicated in this way because of the authority vested in the role of supervisor. In working with difference, power dynamics are compounded because of the inequality of power between majority and minority groups. We will look at how power invested in different roles, cultures and individual personalities comes together to make a complex situation which is nevertheless better explored than ignored or denied.

In this chapter we will see how supervision can play its part in ensuring that differences are understood and responded to appropriately. We explore the importance of taking culture and other areas of difference into account when supervising; cultural factors that need to be worked with; power dynamics and difference; and how difference affects the seven modes of supervision (see Chapter 6). Finally there will be a discussion of best practice in supervision which is sensitive to difference. But first we will explore what we mean by 'culture'.

Understanding culture

> My new client will never be able to use counselling. She kept saying 'I'll do whatever you suggest, doctor'. Actually, I wanted to laugh. Of course, I told her I wasn't a doctor and I wouldn't tell her what to do. She looked really confused when I said that.

This supervisee was a recently qualified English counsellor. Her client was from South East Asia and had recently come to England with her husband. She was working as a nurse and was lonely and frightened much of the time. Her husband's work took him away from home a good deal so she did not even have him as a familiar reference point. A nursing officer had suggested counselling as she was struggling to cope at work. However, the counselling never got beyond the second session as she was told that counselling was not appropriate for her.

This event happened several years ago. We wonder whether the counsellor and the supervisor would now be more aware of the cultural implications in how the client understood the counselling relationship. Would they now be more likely to consider that, by trying to understand the cultural context, some useful work could have been done, even if it was just a place where the client could have articulated the loneliness and confusion she felt in this very alien culture?

We recognize here that the difference in culture had led to an inappropriate response. But what precisely do we mean by 'culture'?

We understand 'cultural differences' as referring to the different explicit and implicit assumptions and values that influence the behaviour and social artefacts of different groups (Herskowitz 1948). An understanding of culture in relation to our clients must also include an understanding of our own cultural assumptions and beliefs. Culture is not just something within us, which we *have*, but rather resides in the milieu in which we live. Culture affects primarily not *what* but *how* we think, although what we think may alter as a result of our cultural assumptions. It exists in the spaces between us, just as an organism is grown in a 'culture' in a laboratory. Hawkins (1994c, 1997) has developed a model of five levels of culture, each level being fundamentally influenced by the levels beneath it:

1 *Artefacts*: the rituals, symbols, art, buildings, policies, etc.
2 *Behaviour*: the patterns of relating and behaving; the cultural norms.
3 *Mind sets*: the ways of seeing the world and framing experience.
4 *Emotional ground*: the patterns of feeling that shape the making of meaning.
5 *Motivational roots*: the fundamental aspirations that drive choices.

This model is further explored in Chapter 13.

Both ethnic groups and different subgroups, based on gender, class, sexual orientation, etc., have different cultural norms. Judy Ryde (1997)

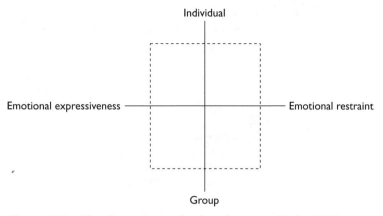

Figure 7.1   The dimensions of cultural norms (Ryde 1997)

has written about two dimensions along which these cultural norms can be distinguished. These are:

- a continuum between the valuing of the experience of individuals and the valuing of the group;
- a continuum between emotional expressiveness and emotional restraint.

To explore the ways in which these dimensions interact they may be arranged as shown in Figure 7.1. We may place a particular culture on the diagram at a position which demonstrates the culture's position in regard to these polarities. For example the dominant British and most north European cultures can be plotted in the individual/emotional restraint box. While the diagram does not cover all possible cultural differences, it does help us to orientate ourselves more easily to two important variables and therefore to think in a more culturally sensitive way.

Other variables which have been identified by a variety of writers (Hofstede 1980; Sue and Sue 1990; Trompenaars 1994) include:

- equality versus hierarchy;
- self-disclosure;
- outer-directed versus inner-directed;
- cause and effect orientation;
- achievement orientation;
- universalist to particularist;
- adaptive versus protectionist;
- time as sequence versus time as synchronization.

The more we can understand the ways in which the world looks different through different cultural lenses, the more able we are to work well across cultures. Weerdenburg and Brinkmann (Weerdenburg 1996; Brinkmann and Weerdenburg 1999) have created and researched a developmental model of 'intercultural sensitivity' based on the work of Dr Milton Bennett (1993) which maps the stages individuals go through as they become more transculturally effective. These are:

- *Denial*: where one sees one's own culture as the only real one.
- *Defence*: against cultural difference, where one sees one's own culture as the only good one.
- *Minimization*: in which elements of one's own cultural world view are experienced as universal.
- *Acceptance*: in which there is a recognition that one's own culture is just one of a number of equally complex world views.
- *Cognitive adaptation*: where one can look at the world 'through different eyes'.
- *Behavioural adaptation*: where the individual can adapt their behaviour to different cultural situations and relationships.

The first three stages of this development are termed 'ethnocentric' and the later three 'ethnorelative'. We would contend that the first two stages represent culturally insensitive work and the second two the beginnings of cross-cultural practice. Only the last two stages equate with transcultural supervision.

The six stages provide a parallel developmental path to the general stages of supervisor development outlined in Chapter 5.

Awareness of cultural and other differences in supervision

Several writers on supervision (Inskipp and Proctor 1995; Brown and Bourne 1996; Carroll and Holloway 1999; Gilbert and Evans forthcoming) have pointed out that the supervision situation creates a more complicated set of relationships than relating one to one. In supervision there are at least three relationships: client–supervisee; supervisee–supervisor; client–supervisor. (There are more than three in group supervision and also if there is a supervisor of a supervisor.) This is complicated further in a situation of cultural difference. Any one of the three may be culturally different and, indeed, all three may be culturally different to each other. In the situation where the client comes from a different cultural background it is particularly important that the supervisee and supervisor do not collude to misunderstand factors which are based in culture rather than personal psychology, as we will see below.

Where there are smaller ethnic groups within a dominant culture, it is not uncommon for the second generation of these groups to experience problems in trying to exist in two cultures at once:

An Asian came from a culture which emphasised the group and emotional restraint. The father of this client lived for some time in America and, while there, trained as a Rogerian therapist. Here he learned to value the individual and emotional expression. Then, when he returned to his own country, he married and had a family. This family became an island of Rogerian values within the predominant culture. The effect on the son was to create a situation which was very similar to that confronting a second generation immigrant with an alien culture. One set of values pertained at home and another in the world beyond it. In going to a psychotherapist in the UK, the son chose someone with a similar but not identical theoretical basis to his father. This possibly showed some 'unconscious hope' (Casement 1985) that the differences in the two cultures could be reconciled. He needed someone who would be somewhat similar to his father but not identical. The impulse of his psychotherapist was to stress the importance of finding his own direction, meeting his own needs and getting in touch with feelings he needed to express. While this may indeed have had value, his supervisor pointed out that this approach did not recognize or help to resolve the cultural differences and tensions that had become almost unbearable for this client.

We can see here how necessary it is for both supervisor and supervisee to be aware of, and sensitive to, cultural difference. It may also be important to notice and honour differences even when they are being denied.

Perceived cultural differences are often focused on physical characteristics: the colour of the skin, the shape of the nose, etc. The dominant group can often be ruthless in denigrating and marginalizing those with real or perceived differences. Rather than face this vicious prejudice people will go to much trouble to disguise difference or deny its effects:

One client of mixed race denied that the colour of her skin led to any difficulties for her. She was a good looking and popular woman and the question of her being black did not seem to arise in her circle of friends or in the counselling. The supervisor remarked on this but found it difficult to engage the supervisee with the issue or keep a focus on it himself. The issue drew itself to the attention of all three rather forcefully when the client related an incident in which a motorist had called her a 'black bastard'. Upon hearing this she had chased him and pulled him out of his car. Subsequently memories and feelings arose about being black which had been previously unexplored.

Other marginalizing differences may not be immediately obvious to the eye but can cause as much alienation through the cultural rejection of people with these differences. Differences in sexual orientation is one of the less visible examples. While moves are being made to ban discrimination on this and other grounds, prejudice remains and is likely to be found, consciously or unconsciously, in the supervisor and supervisee.

Power and difference

Society may be greatly enriched by the multitude of differences brought about by populations of different cultures living side by side. However, the majority culture tends to be more powerful in the community and such imbalances of power are inevitably played out in professional relationships, including the relationship between supervisee and supervisor and between supervisee and client. As we saw above, Brown and Bourne (1996) have pointed to the different combinations of relationships present in supervision and they also explore in some depth the different power relationships. They point out (p. 39) all the different possible combinations that can arise when someone from a minority group is in each of the possible roles, and the complex power dynamics that result. They particularly emphasize race and gender, although other factors such as sexual orientation, disability and class also have inbuilt power imbalance.

Inskipp and Proctor (1995) have also pointed to the dynamics in relationships between black and white in a series of eight triangles showing all the possible combinations of supervisor, client and therapist, with each being black or white. Each triangle has its own dynamic which is influenced by the different power dynamics inherent in the roles and the ethnic grouping.

To draw this out further, we consider there to be another triangle: one which demonstrates the complex power dynamics inevitably present in transcultural supervision. At each corner we can have three different types of power: role power, cultural power and personal power (see Figure 7.2).

- *Role power* points to the power inherent in the role of supervisor which will vary depending on the organizational setting in which supervision is taking place. This includes what has been termed *legitimate* power (invested in the role); *coercive* and *reward* power (meaning, respectively, power to require the supervisee to do something and power to offer or withhold rewards); and *resources* power (the power a supervisor may have to offer or withhold resources) (French and Raven 1967; see also Kadushin 1992, Ch. 3).
- *Cultural power* derives from the dominant social and ethnic group. In northern Europe a person with cultural power would be someone who

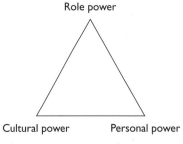

Figure 7.2 Power dynamics in transcultural supervision

was born within the white, western majority group. This power is emphasized if that person is male, middle class, heterosexual and able-bodied.

- *Personal power* points to the particular power of the individual which may be over and above that given to the person through role or culture. It derives from the authority of their expertise as well as from the presence and impact of their personality. It also comprises what French and Raven (1967) term *referent* power, which derives from the supervisee wishing to identify with or be like their supervisor.

When all three different sources of power are brought together in the same person the effect may be quite overwhelming. The dominant cultural and/or personal power does not necessarily lie with the supervisor. When it does, the power dynamics may be simpler but could well be insensitively misused or even overlooked as they are taken for granted. When cultural and/or personal power is not with the supervisor there may be conflict in establishing authority or a need to compensate by overemphasizing it. Whatever the case, power relationships in the supervision are better explored than ignored as we have shown in the paper 'Anti-discrimination and oppression in supervision' (CSTD 1999).

While it is spurious for power, and therefore authority, to be automatically invested in those from a cultural majority, it may be appropriate for a supervisor to carry greater authority through their role:

> One well-intentioned white supervisor felt nervous but excited about having her first black supervisee. The supervisee was a counselling student who had been taken onto a counselling course in spite of the fact that she did not have the initial experience of counselling normally expected of students starting the course. This 'positive discrimination' had been one clear factor that had led the supervisee to struggle to be able to understand and use basic counselling techniques and theories.
>
> The supervisor, not wanting to appear racist, was very tentative in confronting the supervisee on her tendency to advise clients rather than listen to them. In fact the supervisor's worst fears were realized when the supervisee complained to her tutor that her supervisor was racist. This led to a further backing off from confrontation.

In order to understand this complex situation it is helpful to bear in mind Karpman's (1968) drama triangle which illustrates the interconnecting dynamics of the persecutor, victim and rescuer, and was further explored in our paper 'Anti-discrimination and oppression in supervision' (CSTD 1999). This dynamic is characterized by the way in which these roles, having been established, tend to revolve between the players (see also Chapter 11). Here the supervisor appears to be the persecutor, the supervisee the victim and possibly the tutor the rescuer. In this example, the roles changed with the accusation of racism so that the supervisor apparently became the victim.

In fact the role power was with the supervisor. Had she been more experienced and confident she may have been able to work with the supervisee more effectively in the first place to explore the situation in all its complexity: the way the power dynamics of the supervisee–supervisor relationship is compounded by the cultural context of a difference in 'race'; the cultural context in which a student is taken onto a course without the usual preparatory experience; an exploration of the difference experienced by clients in being listened to rather than given advice; and any cultural meanings given to 'being listened to' and 'being given advice' in the different cultures of supervisee and supervisor.

By appropriately keeping her authority and not being afraid to open up the complexity of the issues knotted up in this situation, the supervisee (and supervisor) would have received a rich learning experience which any student might rightly expect where appropriate authority is taken.

If the supervisor had hounded this supervisee out of the course it would have been a clear abuse of power. As it was, the misuse of power was much more subtle: appropriate authority was not taken and the supervisee's difficulties with her course were compounded. One might go so far as to say that the supervisor exhibited, if not racism, then clear cultural prejudice in her assumption that these issues could not be tackled openly and honestly.

Learning to take appropriate authority, while being sensitive to the various aspects of power operating in the therapy and supervision relationships, is an important and challenging task. As Kadushin (1992) writes: 'the supervisor must accept, without defensiveness or apology the authority and related power inherent in his position. Use of authority may sometimes be unavoidable. The supervisor can increase its effectiveness if he feels, and can communicate, a conviction in his behaviour'.

Anti-oppressive practice

To effectively work transculturally it is essential to operate in a framework of anti-oppressive practice, which goes beyond merely avoiding discriminatory behaviour. Brown and Bourne (1996) discuss this issue at length, building on the work of Julia Philipson (1992):

Oppression is a complex term which relates to structural differences in power as well as the personal experiences of oppressing and being oppressed. It relates to race, gender, sexual orientation, age, and disability as separate domains and as overlapping experiences.

(Philipson 1992: 13)

Philipson suggests that whereas anti-discriminatory practice relies on a model of challenging unfairness, and is essentially 'reformist in orientation', 'anti-oppressive practice' works to a model of empower-

ment and liberation and requires a fundamental rethinking of
values, institutions and relationships.

(Brown and Bourne 1996: 37)

To be anti-oppressive entails attending to the experiences of oppression
in both the supervisees and the clients, and also attending to becoming
aware of our own cultural biases and become more adaptive to difference.

Difference and the seven modes

The seven modes of supervision (presented in Chapter 6) can be used to
increase the ability of the supervisor to attend to the cultural differences
between client, therapist and supervisor, as well as the cultural and power
dynamics at play in both sets of relationship:

- *Mode 1*: a focus on the culture of the client and their context. This
  includes attending to possible culture-specific behaviours (e.g. avoidance
  of eye contact).
- *Mode 2*: finding ways of responding to the cultural differences and the
  hidden cultural assumptions implicit in the supervisee's interventions.
- *Mode 3*: the culture inherent in the relationship between the client and
  the supervisee. How the cultural material manifests in the process of
  the work including any 'unconscious supervision' (Casement 1985)
  which might correct the approach to the work.
- *Mode 4*: a focus on the cultural assumptions of the supervisee. Also the
  countertransference of the supervisee which seems to be responding to
  the cultural material (e.g. racist fantasies).
- *Mode 5*: cultural difficulties experienced in the cultural dynamics between
  client and supervisee and how they are mirrored in the supervision
  relationship. Also attending to cultural differences in the supervisee–
  supervisor relationship.
- *Mode 6*: the supervisor attending to their own cultural assumptions and
  their own countertransference which seem to arise as a result of the
  cultural material.
- *Mode 7*: the cultural norms and biases in the wider context in which the
  work is done, particularly organizational, social and political. This will
  include institutional racism and oppressive practice.

Mode 1

In Mode 1 the client's world is explored through the content of the actual
material brought to the sessions both in terms of their behaviour and
through the narrative of the client's life. Here cultural material may be
brought explicitly or implicitly. Explicit problems within the client's world
may be experienced through clashes or difficulties with people from the

majority culture. Implicitly, difficulties may turn out to relate to cultural differences even though the client is unaware that this is the case when the matter is first approached. In Mode 1 the supervisee and supervisor will engage with trying to understand the client's world from the material brought, both verbally and non-verbally. The therapist may try, for instance, to understand to what extent the client's experience is rooted in their culture and how much is special to their individual character:

> A Japanese client was married to a successful Japanese businessman living in England. Since coming to England she had been very depressed. She felt displaced and missed her home and family. This led to her feeling unable to act as the sparkling hostess that both she and her husband expected of her. This inability intensified her depression and feelings of inadequacy. In supervision the supervisee brought her feelings of outrage at what she understood to be the client's acquiescence to her husband. The supervisor, however, quickly returned to the phenomenal world of the client to better understand her cultural position.

Mode 1 will often involve paying close attention to the non-verbal behaviour of the client in order to become aware of their phenomenal world. It is important in supervision not to jump to conclusions about the meaning of non-verbal behaviour so that the 'interpretation' of what is seen becomes mistaken for the real thing. When working transculturally this is particularly true. Within our society we tend to have culturally determined ways of interpreting non-verbal signs. For instance, a client who likes to shake hands with the therapist may be considered inappropriately formal or trying to please. This view would be mistaken if the client came from a culture in which it would be considered unthinkably rude not to shake hands. The avoidance of eye contact also has different meanings in different cultures. In western cultures it is often thought of as shifty and defensive but in some cultures it is considered to be very impolite to look directly at someone with whom you are not on familiar terms or who has a higher status than yourself.

Mode 2

In Mode 2 the supervisee and supervisor explore the interventions made in the session:

> In the example of the Japanese client mentioned above, the supervisor was able to challenge the cultural assumption of the supervisee that it was dependency in the client that led to this attitude to wifely duties rather than it being a normal response within her culture. The therapist's intervention had been to say 'Are you angry with your husband for putting you into such an inferior role?' The supervisor was able to challenge the supervisee's

cultural assumption that the client may be 'angry' and that the 'role' was 'inferior'. The two then explored different interventions that could have been made and decided that it might be useful to ask what it was like for the client to be a hostess in England and in Japan. This would have opened up the area of differences between the two cultures and how it felt for the client to be in both. A better understanding of the cultural differences led the supervisee to be able to intervene in a more genuinely empathetic way and to a useful and undefensive exploration within the context of cultural difference.

Mode 3

Here the supervisory exploration involves the way unconscious material is shown in the process of the work and in particular in the process between the supervisee and the client. It may, for example, be shown in dreams or the kinds of anecdote that the client tells. In the example of the mixed race client who related the story of how she chased a motorist and pulled him from his car, the telling of the anecdote could be understood as being brought as an unconscious prompt to explore the issues. Maybe at some level she wanted to metaphorically pull the supervisee, and, indeed, herself, from her chair and shake them both into realizing the importance of this issue.

> A West African client told of being sent to an aunt in England at the age of 6. She was given an apple to eat on her arrival, a fruit she had never tasted before. It was so delicious that the client thought life in England would be as wonderful as the apple tasted! She soon discovered that this would be far from the case and in fact never returned to her parents in Africa. This was, of course, a very formative experience in the client's life, but it became clear that she had also told the story unconsciously because of a fear that the apparently benign nature of the first few sessions of the psychotherapy may be illusory in the same way.
>
> Following an exploration in supervision her fear was picked up by the supervisee and the work was able to deepen.

Mode 4

In Mode 4 the supervisee explores how their own issues may affect the process of the work. In order to work with these modes it is necessary for the supervisee to be aware of their own prejudiced attitudes and feelings. Again, with the example of the Japanese client, we saw how the supervisee's own concerns about being disparaged by men led to an inappropriate intervention. Understanding our own issues more clearly and how they relate to our own culture can bring about a vital and very fruitful way of working with cultural difference. It brings the whole question right into the room rather than being seen as something that only happens out in the big bad world:

> One supervisee had a paraplegic client who was in a wheelchair. When first discussing this client in supervision he stressed on several occasions how 'intelligent' the client seemed. The supervisor remarked on this and it led to an exploration of the supervisee's expectations of people in wheelchairs. The supervisee discovered in himself an expectation that they were not very bright.

It is often useful in uncovering unconscious prejudice to discover what 'scale' is being used when a description is given. In this example the client was described as 'intelligent' so the supervisor asked what measure was being used in making this observation. In this way the unconscious prejudice was uncovered and not allowed to affect the progress of the work.

Mode 5

In this mode the supervisor and supervisee explore ways in which the relationship with the client is mirrored within the supervisory relationship. This is particularly interesting where there is a cultural difference as it may provide a taste of the way in which a client from a non-dominant culture feels:

> One supervisee started to feel stupid and ridiculed during supervision sessions and the supervisor noticed that he was beginning to feel unusually critical. Things became so difficult that the supervisee had started to look elsewhere for supervision. He announced his intention to leave the supervision rather abruptly while he was presenting a client. This client had felt ashamed in adult life of having failed the eleven plus and being sent to a secondary modern school. Now, in the session being presented, the supervisee related that the client had started to act as if he was being examined. The supervisor also noticed that he was in danger of being seen as critical and so had become patronizingly protective to the supervisee. The parallels between what was happening in the supervision and the therapy struck the supervisor. This led to an exploration in which the supervisee discovered his identification with his working-class client and the hostility he felt to his middle-class supervisor. This enabled the whole area of feeling ridiculed to be opened up between them and led to the supervisee staying with the supervisor. It subsequently led to a greater ability to work with his client's lack of self-esteem and his emerging judgmentalness in the relationship with the client.

Mode 6

Mode 6 involves the reactions and responses that the supervisor notices in themself during a session:

One supervisor often found herself feeling uneasy when a certain client was being presented. When she focused on this feeling she thought it was fear. As this feeling grew she mentioned it to her supervisee saying she wondered how her feeling might be related to what was being shared. The supervisee was at first very surprised. He felt rather in awe of this very bright client who was a foreign student newly in this country but who was having difficulties concentrating on his work. The supervisor's feelings of fear became the first clue to the terror that the student felt at being away from home. In his own culture it was rare to leave the village, let alone the country. The supervisor was experienced enough to value rather than fear her own responses and had faith that they may provide valuable countertransference clues. She also knew that this was often true when the supervisee and supervisor had different responses. In this case it provided much needed insight for helping the work to move on.

We have also described a slightly different form of Mode 6 called Mode 6a. Here the emphasis is on the supervisor's specific responses to the client which may be quite different to those of the supervisee. In the example above the feeling was pervasive rather than attached to the particular client. The following is an example of Mode 6a:

A supervisee tended to find a client interesting while the supervisor found that she dreaded having to listen to accounts of the client's life. In this case both the supervisor and the client came from the same African country. The supervisor's unease eventually became a clue to unexpressed feelings that were disguised by the client often telling an apparently interesting story. The supervisor and supervisee had different responses to these stories: the supervisor was irritated and the supervisee was beguiled by hearing unfamiliar stories about life in Africa. By paying attention to her countertransference, the supervisor was able to draw attention to important material.

Mode 7

In Mode 7 the focus is on the organizational, social and political context in which the work takes place.

Where the social and political context for working with culture in supervision is hostile then it is harder for supervisors to focus clearly on these issues. The necessity to work towards a more conducive environment in the social and political world may become pressing. It may become part of the supervisor's task within Mode 7 to ensure that the context for doing the work is supportive. Some of this work may be by raising awareness within the session but may also entail work outside it on the political stage, such as within national and local professional bodies or by having more personal contact with key people within organizations, such as those running the training programmes.

Developing transcultural supervision

Transcultural supervision as well as transcultural therapeutic practice are both still in the very early stages of development. Leong and Wagner (1994), in their review of the literature, conclude that little has been written about cultural issues in supervision and most of what has been is very recent. As we increasingly operate in a transcultural society, it is essential that both individuals and organizations put a strong emphasis on developing their ability to work transculturally.

Coleman (1999) stresses the need for training to ensure that students are well versed in cultural awareness and that supervisors bear this in mind in the same way as they would ethical practice. Gilbert and Evans (forthcoming) provide a very useful case example of one training institution's attempt to address its own oppressive practice and develop its ability to work more transculturally. They also provide a very useful and simple audit for therapeutic organizations to examine their own 'make-up in terms of ethnicity, gender, sexual orientation, religion, political affiliation, class, status, age and disability'. This includes examining:

- Recruitment from different groupings
- The make-up of the staff
- Patterns of interaction between the staff
- The make-up of the client groups
- The training curriculum

As well as looking at how much time is given to addressing the issues of culture and difference, and developing the skills of transcultural work, it is also important to reflect on cultural biases inherent in all aspects of the theories taught, the learning processes adopted and how trainees are evaluated. Supervision training needs to include specific focus on both transcultural supervision and awareness of power imbalances in supervision practice.

At the personal level, all of us as supervisors continually need to develop our ability to work with a greater range of difference and with more awareness of our own culturally defined behaviour, mind sets, emotional ground and motivational roots. Working in a culturally sensitive way is never easy. We cannot be culturally neutral and so we will inevitably view the world from our own cultural perspective.

In order to increase our transcultural ability it is useful to hold in mind the following:

- It is important to become conscious of our own culture.
- Habitual ways of thinking may arise out of cultural assumptions and not out of personal pathology.
- We as professionals also exist in a culture which is no more or less valid than the client's, but may lead to us holding different values and assumptions.
- The dialogue between us will throw up cultural clashes and may be a fruitful way of understanding and negotiating cultural differences.
- We will work more sensitively if we familiarize ourselves with the types and range of differences that may exist in order that we can recognize them when they arise.
- It is good to be sensitive to the differences that might emerge both in the supervisory and the therapy relationship. To best facilitate this sensitivity we need not only to take an active interest in other cultures and areas of difference but also must never assume that we understand the client's cultural world. We can then start with an interest in finding out from the other while also accepting our own not knowing.

If we are to be non-dogmatic we cannot hold onto our own theories tenaciously. We may need instead to be more interested in phenomena as we experience them. This may be a more useful guide to our practice than rigid theories. This phenomenological approach to the work means that the focus of interest, both for the supervisor and the supervisee, is their own experience and their interest in that of the client. The work thus becomes like a research project (Reason 1994) in which the experienced world of all three is made known more richly.

It is important to understand in working transculturally that we ourselves are not culturally neutral. Every individual is embedded in their culture and, if we are to work effectively with people from cultures different from our own, we need to have an understanding of our own culture and the assumptions we take as read because of this cultural context. If the supervisor espouses this attitude it will help the supervisee to be less defensive in presenting work in the supervision. Certain attitudes and feelings cease to be either wrong or right but *interesting*. This approach helps to open up a space in which real experience can 'come in' and be valued.

It is not enough just to rely on an openness to other's experience. Unless the professionals also have or acquire some knowledge of the sorts of differences that may be found transculturally, they are likely to miss vital pieces of information. Pat Grant cogently points out the arrogance of assuming that it is not necessary to know the cultural background of a client (Grant 1999). The factors mentioned at the beginning of this chapter begin to alert us to the kinds of difference we may find. Nevertheless we need to guard against assuming that we know everything about a person's culture by having read about it, for we are unlikely to know the subtleties and we could be in danger of reducing all to culture (Coleman 1999).

Conclusion

Working with cultural difference is demanding. It is often fraught with difficult and even violent feelings, particularly when cultural difference has been ignored and denied over a period of years. It is nevertheless of utmost importance to work with this dimension, particularly in our multicultural society.

Possibly because of power imbalances which are often denied or unrecognized, the whole area of difference, often subsumed under the heading of 'equal opportunities', has been very painful and fraught with conflicts. These range from the extremes of race hatred leading to many deaths in minority groups, including ethnic and gay groups, to less extreme but very damaging injustices such as those in the workplace, higher education and the professions. In the face of these painful clashes simple prescriptions have been sought for 'getting it right'. Many of these prescriptions, such as an insistence on using 'correct' words, have helped to draw attention to areas of inequality. However, there is a danger that merely prescribing correct behaviour may do nothing but drive real feelings underground so that lip-service only is paid to greater tolerance and full explorations are curtailed for fear of vilification. An open-hearted and undefensive attitude can lead to a deeper understanding of the issues and real exploration of difference.

Supervisory sessions that accept that prejudiced feelings are inevitable given our cultural heritage may open up genuine explorations in which such feelings can be challenged and changed. This open supervision does not put into question the basic worth of the supervisee who reveals prejudiced or culturally insensitive attitudes. They could indeed be praised for their courage in being prepared to own to difficult thoughts, feelings and beliefs. Having been voiced and explored, a genuine change of attitude is the most likely outcome, particularly if there is a real meeting across difference.

We will end with a salutary story from the Sufi Middle Eastern fool, Mulla Nasrudin, who, as the story goes, became a psychotherapist. He decided to have a well-earned rest by taking a cruise:

> The first night of the voyage he was given a table with a
> Frenchman. At the beginning of the meal the Frenchman greeted
> him with 'Bon appetit'. Nasrudin thought that the Frenchman was
> politely introducing himself, so he responded by saying 'Mulla
> Nasrudin'. They had a pleasant meal.
>
> However, the next morning breakfast started with the same
> ritual, the Frenchman saying 'Bon appetit' and Nasrudin who now

thought the Frenchman must be a little deaf said more loudly, 'Mulla Nasrudin'.

At lunch the same thing happened and by now Nasrudin was getting a little irritated with what he thought must be a very dim-witted Frenchman. Luckily that day he got talking to a fellow passenger who spoke French and was, by extraordinary coincidence, a transcultural supervisor. He was able to enlighten Nasrudin and tell him that 'Bon appetit' was a polite French greeting that meant 'have a nice meal'.

'Ah! Thank you,' said the enlightened and relieved Nasrudin. All afternoon he practised his next intervention, walking up and down the deck of the boat. That evening he very proudly sat down at dinner, smiled and said to his new French friend, 'Bon appetit.'

'Mulla Nasrudin,' the Frenchman replied.

Introduction

This chapter is addressed both to those new or experienced supervisors who want to assess their own learning and development and plan what future training they want for themselves, and to those who are responsible for providing training in supervision. In addition to providing the background to training needs, the chapter outlines a variety of possible training courses to meet different supervisory training needs.

Assessing your learning needs

There are two attitudes that are often held by new supervisors:

- Now I have been made a supervisor I should know how to do it and should just get on and do the job.

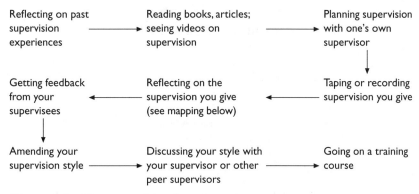

Figure 8.1 The supervision learning process

- I do not know anything about supervision and the only way I am going to learn to be a proper supervisor is from a full supervision training course.

Both ways of thinking are unhelpful and prevent new supervisors from carefully assessing their own knowledge and abilities and what they need to learn beyond these. Also, such thinking prevents them from realizing that learning to be a competent supervisor can come from a great variety of sources. We believe that a good training course is an essential component of any supervisor's development, but it should be only one of several components. For most supervisors there are a great variety of learning possibilities that can be used in different combinations to feed into each other. A possible learning programme or cycle is presented in Figure 8.1.

This learning cycle can flow in any of the directions shown and can be reordered in any way so as to most suit the learning needs and opportunities of the supervisor. However, if you are to learn systematically you need to start the process by carrying out a self-appraisal and a learning needs assessment. Box 8.1 provides a possible format for such an assessment, but this is only a blueprint which you can amend and rewrite to fit your circumstances and needs.

This form of assessment can be done collaboratively, either by using it as a format for requesting feedback from your supervisees, or by sharing your self-appraisal with your supervisor or your work team, and receiving their feedback and appraisal of your work.

Setting up training courses

In Chapter 4 we argued that it is important that all new supervisors not only obtain supervision on their supervision, but also receive some training for the new role of being a supervisor. For some staff it might seem preferable that they receive training before they embark on giving any

Box 8.1 Self-assessment questionnaire for supervisors

	Learning need		*Competent*		*Expert*
	1	2	3	4	5

1 Knowledge
1.1 Understand the purpose of supervision
1.2 Clear about the boundaries of supervision
1.3 Understand the following elements:
　　managerial
　　educative
　　supportive
1.4 Know the various types of supervision
　　contract

2 Supervision management skills
2.1 Can explain to supervisees the purpose of
　　supervision
2.2 Can negotiate a mutually agreed and clear
　　contract
2.3 Can maintain appropriate boundaries
2.4 Can set a supervision climate that is:
　　empathic
　　genuine
　　congruent
　　trustworthy
　　immediate
2.5 Can maintain a balance between the
　　managerial, educative and supportive functions
2.6 Can end a session on time and appropriately

3 Supervision intervention skills
3.1 Can use the following types of intervention
　　(see p. 115):
　　prescriptive
　　informative
　　confrontative
　　catalytic
　　cathartic
　　supportive
3.2 Can give feedback (see p. 113) in a way that is:
　　clear
　　owned
　　balanced
　　specific
3.3 Can usefully focus on (see Chapter 6):
　　reported content

	Learning need		*Competent*	*Expert*
	1	2	3	4	5

supervisee's interventions
supervisee–client relationship
supervisee's countertransference
supervision relationship
own countertransference
the wider context

3.4 Can describe own way of working
3.5 Can offer own experience appropriately
3.6 Can develop self-supervision skills in
supervisees

4 Traits or qualities
4.1 Commitment to the role of supervisor
4.2 Comfortable with the authority inherent in
the role of supervisor
4.3 Can encourage, motivate and carry appropriate
optimism
4.4 Sensitive to supervisee's needs
4.5 Aware of, and able to adapt to, individual
differences due to:
gender
age
cultural and ethnic background
class
sexual orientation
personality
professional training
4.6 Sense of humour

**5 Commitment to own ongoing
development**
5.1 Have ensured own appropriate supervision
5.2 Committed to updating own practitioner and
supervisory skills and knowledge
5.3 Recognize own limits and identify own
strengths and weaknesses as supervisor
5.4 Get regular feedback from:
supervisees
peers
own supervisor/senior

6 For group supervisors
6.1 Have knowledge of group dynamics
6.2 Can use the process of the group to aid the
supervision process
6.3 Can handle competitiveness in groups

	Learning need		Competent		Expert
	1	2	3	4	5
7 For senior organizational supervisors					
7.1 Can supervise interprofessional issues					
7.2 Can supervise organizational issues					
7.3 Have knowledge of stages in team and organizational development					
7.4 Can 'surface' the underlying team or organizational culture					
7.5 Can facilitate organizational change					
7.6 Can create a learning culture in which supervision flourishes					

supervision, so that they have clarity about what they are providing and how they are going to function, before they even start. However, the limitation of this approach is that, like all pre-training, trainees have no direct experience to reflect on and work with during their training course, other than their experience of being supervised.

We would recommend that all new supervisors receive a training course at some time during the first year of their functioning as a supervisor. If the new supervisor is in a situation where they do not currently receive good supervision, which can act both as a model and a support for their new role, then the training should precede their embarking on the new role. However, in such cases it is grossly inadequate just to send them on a short supervisor training course and then expect them to function well as a supervisor. The most important part of the development of good supervisors comes not from their attending a training course, but from their being well supported in planning and reflecting on the supervision that they give. If there is no possibility of new supervisors receiving this form of support from the person responsible for supervising them, then the training course should set up an ongoing peer or led support group for new supervisors to meet and reflect on their supervisory practice.

Another important feature is that all supervisory training should be action based, and not just teaching theory. This means that the course should ideally be a short sandwich course, where the trainees have time in the middle of the course to return to work and carry out some action learning on the supervision that they either give or receive. Then they will have the opportunity to return to the course and explore their actual experience and how they can handle certain situations differently.

Another way of ensuring that courses are practical is to make them substantially experiential, with much of the time given over to the trainees working together giving, receiving and observing supervision, and then giving structured feedback to each other. On the courses that we run ourselves, much of the time is spent in different triads, with each member having the opportunity to be supervisor, supervisee and observer. Course members report that this is often the most valuable part of the course, with a great deal of learning being experienced in all three roles.

A different way of using triads in training is described by Spice and Spice (1976):

> Working in groups of three, beginning supervisors take turns functioning in three different roles: beginning supervisor, commentator, and facilitator. The beginning supervisor presents samples (e.g., audiotape, videotape, case report) of an actual supervision, the commentator reviews the sample and then shares observations and encourages dialogue about the session, and then the facilitator comments on the present, here-and-now dialogue between the beginning supervisor and the commentator. Four processes are taught in the triadic model: a) presentation of supervision work, b) art of critical commentary, c) engagement of meaningful self-dialogue, and d) deepening of the here-and-now process.

Harold Marchant, who has done much to develop supervision training in the areas of youth and community work, writes: 'Supervision involves knowledge, skills and techniques. Above all it involves attitudes and feelings of a supervisor in a relationship with another person' (Marchant, in Marken and Payne 1988). It is thus important that supervision training includes not only the relevant knowledge, skills and training to equip a competent technical supervisor, but also concentrates on exploring the attitudes and assumptions of the trainees. It must also focus on 'exploring the concept of empathy and . . . working out its expression in the supervisory relationship' (Marchant, in Marken and Payne 1988: 40). All supervisor training must therefore focus on how to build a relationship, with a wide range of supervisees, that is built on trust, openness, awareness of difference and a sense of mutual exploration. In doing this the trainers need to be very aware of how the course itself is providing a role model and should endeavour to provide a setting which is warm, open and trusting, where trainees feel able to explore both their experiences and inadequacies, despite their inevitable fears and vulnerabilities. This is a difficult task, for as Barbara Dearnley (1985) says: 'I have come to learn that looking in detail at supervisory practice is widely experienced as a very exposing affair, much more so than discussing one's own difficult cases. It is as if the public confirmation that one is sufficiently experienced to supervise leads to persecutory personal expectations that supervisors should say and do no wrong'.

Being made a supervisor can decrease the space we give ourselves to be open to learning, for now we can believe that we should have the answers, be the experts and should certainly not let on that we do not know what we are doing! Guy Claxton (1984) described the four beliefs that get in the way of adults' learning as being:

- I must be *competent*
- I must be in *control*

- I must be *consistent*
- I must be *comfortable*

All these four beliefs can easily be reinforced when a practitioner becomes a supervisor, and doubly reinforced when a supervisor starts training other supervisors!

A training course needs to set a climate that challenges these attitudes and creates a climate where making mistakes, trying out very different approaches and being vulnerable are valued. To set this climate trainers have to model not being 'super-competent in-control experts', but, rather, experienced supervisors who are still open to knowledge and needing to learn and who are also open about their vulnerabilities.

Much of the material that needs to be included in courses is common to all types of trainee supervisors, but there are also different training needs depending on the context in which the trainee supervisor will be functioning. We propose five distinct types of course. These are:

- A core supervision course for new supervisors.
- A core supervision course for student and practice supervisors.
- Courses in team and group supervision.
- Therapeutic supervision courses for those who supervise in-depth counselling, or psychotherapy, or other therapeutic work.
- Advanced supervision courses for those who have to supervise across teams and organizations, or teach supervision, or want to become advanced practitioners.

We will now look at what each of these courses might include, and we will illustrate this by describing some of the content of our own courses.

Core supervision course (for new supervisors)

It is useful to begin this type of course by ascertaining what experience the course members have of both supervising and being supervised. Both kinds of experience will provide useful material to learn from and will also colour the attitudes and assumptions with which the course members begin their training.

In our early days of teaching supervision we naively used to expect course members to be coming on the course already believing that supervision was a good thing and eager to learn how to give it. We were soon disillusioned. Many staff, who had spent years as social workers, doctors, occupational therapists or probation officers, had never received any formal supervision. There were others whose experience of supervision was very negative. Supervision was a place where they had been made to feel very inadequate by over-critical supervisors. Others had been led to trust their supervisors and share their difficulties and sense of inadequacy, only to find that this had later been used against them by more senior management.

We discovered that it helped course members to be more open if we drew out all the bad experiences and negative attitudes to supervision at a very early stage of the course, as this not only stopped them from covertly sabotaging the course, but was also useful learning material. As new supervisors they could explore how not to repeat the negative scenarios that they and their fellow course members had experienced.

We also learned from experience to avoid the process whereby we would be very evangelical about supervision and its benefits, and the course members would have to carry the negative attitudes. On some courses we introduced a debate where some of the course members would argue for the effectiveness and the benefits of supervision and the others would argue its costs and negative side-effects. Halfway through the debate we would ask them all to switch sides and carry on the heated exchange, but now arguing the opposite case. This ensured that the course was not divided into pro- and anti-supervision factions, and both the costs and benefits of supervision were clearly recognized.

The next stage is to explore what supervision is. There are many maps and models in Chapter 5 that can be used for this purpose. At this stage trainees should not be overloaded with too many different theories and maps, but given a clear and simple framework which can help them identify the boundaries and roles involved in supervision.

This naturally leads on to the issue of contracting for supervision, and the attendant issues of confidentiality, responsibility and appropriate focus. We also find it necessary to explore the setting in which supervision is carried out. Where, when and how does supervision take place? Is it done in a cluttered office with the phone always ringing? Is it done across a desk? What is allowed to interrupt the supervision, or cause its postponement?

We also look at who takes responsibility for arranging the time for the supervision and ensuring that it happens – the supervisor or the supervisee? Also, how does the supervision start? We often find that the first two or three minutes of a supervision session set the stage and the atmosphere for the rest of the session. Early on in the course it is also important to introduce basic ethical guidelines for supervision as well as an awareness of the power relationship and the importance of an anti-discriminatory practice base (see Chapter 7).

The rest of the time on the first part of our courses is divided between providing new supervisors with maps and models with which to reflect on their supervision, and teaching and practising supervisory skills.

The first skill that we teach is the skill of giving good feedback, as this is not only essential to being a competent supervisor, but is also a skill that the course members will be using throughout the training course as they work with each other.

Supervisory feedback skills

The process of telling another individual how they are experienced is known as feedback. Giving and receiving feedback is fraught with difficulty and anxiety because negative feedback restimulates memories of being rebuked as a child, and positive feedback goes against injunctions 'not to have a big head'. Certainly most people give or experience feedback only when something is amiss. The feelings surrounding feedback often lead to its being badly given, so fears of it are often reinforced. There are a few simple rules for giving and receiving feedback that help it to be a useful transaction which can lead to change.

Giving feedback

A mnemonic to help remember how to give good feedback is CORBS: clear, owned, regular, balanced and specific:

- *Clear*: try to be clear about what the feedback is that you want to give. Being vague and faltering will increase the anxiety in the receiver and not be understood.
- *Owned*: the feedback you give is your own perception and not an ultimate truth. It therefore says as much about you as it does about the person who receives it. It helps the receiver if this is stated or implied in the feedback (e.g. 'I find you . . .' rather than 'You are . . .').
- *Regular*: if the feedback is given regularly it is more likely to be useful. If this does not happen there is a danger that grievances will be saved up until they are delivered in one large package. Try to give the feedback as close to the event as possible and early enough for the person to do something about it (i.e. do not wait until someone is leaving to tell them how they could have done the job better).
- *Balanced*: it is good to balance negative and positive feedback and, if you find that the feedback you give to any individual is always either positive or negative, this probably means that your view is distorted in some way. This does not mean that each piece of critical feedback must always be accompanied by something positive, but rather that a balance should be created over time.
- *Specific*: generalized feedback is hard to learn from. Phrases like 'You are irritating' can only lead to hurt and anger. 'It irritates me when you forget to record the telephone messages' gives the receiver some information which he or she can choose to use or ignore.

Receiving feedback

It is not necessary to be completely passive in the process of receiving feedback. It is possible to share the responsibility for the feedback you receive being well given. What is done with the feedback is almost entirely the responsibility of the receiver. The following may be helpful when receiving feedback:

- If the feedback is not given in the way suggested above you can ask for it to be more clear, owned, regular, balanced and/or specific.
- Listen to the feedback all the way through without judging it. Jumping to a defensive response can result in the feedback being misunderstood.

- Try not to explain compulsively why you did something, or even explain away positive feedback. Try and hear others' feedback as *their* experiences of you. Often it is enough just to hear the feedback and say 'Thank you'.
- Ask for feedback you are not given but would like to hear.

Our own emphasis on feedback has been paralleled by that of Freeman (1985). His conclusions are summarized by Hess (1987):

Freeman (1985) comprehensively outlined a number of important considerations for the supervisor delivering feedback. It should be a) systematic (objective, accurate, consistent and reliable feedback that is less influenced by subjective variables); b) timely (feedback is delivered soon after an important event); c) clearly understood (both positive and negative feedback are based on explicit and specific performance criteria); and d) reciprocal (feedback is provided in two way inter-actions in which suggestions are made, not as the only way to approach a problem, but as only one of a number of potentially useful alternatives).

Supervisory intervention skills

The other major area of skill learning that needs to be included in any basic supervision training is to review the practitioner facilitation skills of the course members and help them adapt and develop them in an appropriate way for supervision. One useful tool in doing this is the Heron model of six categories of intervention. Heron (1975) developed a way of dividing all possible interventions in any facilitating or enabling process into six categories. They apply equally to one-to-one and group situations. Their use is in helping us to become aware of the different interventions we use, those we are comfortable with and those we avoid. Following on from that we can, with practice, begin to widen our choices. The emphasis is on the intended effect of the intervention on the client. There is no implication that any one category is more or less significant and important than any other. Heron's six categories of intervention are:

- *Prescriptive*: give advice, be directive (e.g. 'You need to write a report on that'; 'You need to stand up to your father').
- *Informative*: be didactic, instruct, inform (e.g. 'You will find similar reports in the filing cabinet in the office'; 'This is how our card index works').
- *Confrontative*: be challenging, give direct feedback (e.g. 'I notice when you talk about the home's supervisor you always smile').
- *Cathartic*: release tension, abreaction (e.g. 'What is it you really want to say to your client?').
- *Catalytic*: be reflective, encourage self-directed problem-solving (e.g. 'Can you say some more about that?' 'How can you do that?').

• *Supportive*: be approving, confirming, validating (e.g. 'I can understand how you feel').

These six types of intervention are only of any real value if they are rooted in care and concern for the client or supervisee. They are valueless when used degenerately or perversely. *Degenerate interventions* happen when the practitioner is using them in an unskilled, compulsive or unsolicited way. They are usually rooted in lack of awareness, whereas a *perverted intervention* is one which is deliberately malicious.

We have widely used this model in helping supervisors look at their own style of intervention. We ask them to appraise themselves in terms of which category they most dominantly use and which category they feel least comfortable using. We then have all trainee supervisors carrying out individual supervisions with a fellow trainee, while a third trainee records the pattern of interventions they use.

This opens up the possibility of the trainees deciding to develop one of their less-used intervention skills. Also for many new supervisors it provides an opportunity to consider how their intervention style needs to be different as a supervisor compared with what it was as a practitioner. A non-directive counsellor may find that their previous training and experience have led them dominantly to use catalytic interventions and that as a supervisor they have to incorporate more informative and confrontative interventions.

We have also found that some workers completely switch styles and abandon many of their very useful counselling skills when they move into a managerial or supervisory role. These workers need help in revaluing their own practitioner skills, albeit within a new context and role.

This model can also be used by trainee supervisors in mapping their own supervision style. Some trainees have recorded their supervision sessions and then scored each of the interventions that they have used. Others have used the model for both the supervisees and themselves to reflect back on the session and in particular the supervisors' interventions. They then explore how each party would like the emphasis in intervention style to change.

Bond and Holland (1998, Chs 4, 5 and 6) give detailed guidelines on how to develop each of the Heron intervention styles.

Mapping supervision

The other main system for mapping supervision that we provide for trainee supervisors is a model that helps them chart the content focus of a session – i.e. how it shifts from management issues to client issues to areas of supporting the supervisee. The model also looks at who is responsible for the shift in focus. This is published elsewhere (Hawkins 1982; CSTD 1999).

As mentioned above, the main emphasis of any good supervision course should not be on teaching these skills and models or any others, but on the course members using these skills and models as a language with which to reflect on the practice supervisions they give on the course and also the supervision that they then give back at work. This is why a central part of the course is the trainees' returning to work with an action learning project, using one of the skills, models or maps as a research tool in order to find out more about their own supervision.

The course needs to reconvene in order to harvest the learning from these action learning projects, so that course members are learning not only from their own experience but also from that of their colleagues. To harvest this learning both discursive case presentations and more action-based methods like group sculpting (see Chapter 10), role-play and enacted stakeholder role-plays can be used (see Chapters 9 and 10). This part of the course can be thought of as an extended group supervision of the course members' supervisory work.

Core supervision course (for practice and student supervisors)

There are two types of student supervisor: those who are college based and those who are responsible for supervising students on practice. A training course for both types of student supervisor has to include most, if not all, of the material recommended for new supervisors, but the context and the emphasis of the course need to be slightly different.

First, the college based student supervisor is working within a different supervision contract, where the emphasis is on the educative and supportive aspects of supervision and where the managerial aspects are being carried by the practice supervisor or manager. Even the practice supervisor will have a greater emphasis on the educative side of supervision.

One of the difficulties for many college based supervisors is that they are often more at home in a teaching role than a supervisory role. The danger of this is that their supervision may turn into a series of didactic tutorials and the supervisees, instead of being enabled to reflect on their own experience, have theoretical references thrown at their 'inadequacies': 'If only you had read X, then you would not have been so foolish' is the attitude that the student experiences. This is similar to the 'game' that Kadushin (1968) calls: 'If you knew Dostoevsky like I know Dostoevsky'. He points out it can be played by either the supervisor or the supervisee (see Chapter 4).

The college based supervisor needs to provide a climate that goes against the common educational culture of dependency and instead provide a setting in which supervisees are encouraged to be responsible for their own learning and can rely on the support, trust and openness of their supervisor.

At the former South West London College counselling course, where one of us taught and supervised counselling, the students were encouraged to work out their own contracts with both their group and individual

---

Box 8.2   A blueprint of responsibilities (see Proctor 1988b)

Supervisor responsibility

- To ensure a safe enough space for students to lay out practice issues in their own way.
- To help students explore and clarify thinking, feeling and fantasies which underlie their practice.
- To share experience, information and skill appropriately.
- To challenge practice which is adjudged unethical, unwise or incompetent.
- To challenge personal or professional blind spots perceived in individuals or the group.
- To be aware of the organizational contracts which the supervisor and the students have with college, employers, clients and the supervision group.

Student responsibility

- To themself.
- To identify practice issues with which they need help and to ask for time in the group to deal with these.
- To become increasingly able to share these issues freely.
- To identify what kind of responses they want.
- To become more aware of the organizational contracts they are in, in their workplace, in the college, with clients and with the supervision group.
- To be open to others' feedback.
- To monitor tendencies to justify, explain or defend.
- To develop the ability to discriminate what feedback is useful.

Responsibility to others (when in group supervision)

- To share with other members all the responsibilities of the supervisor, in such a way that safety and challenge can both be possible in the group.
- To monitor tendencies to advise or compete.

---

supervisor. They were given a blueprint, based on the current staff thinking about supervision. An example is provided in Box 8.2.

The other major issue that needs to be focused on in a course for student supervisors is hinted at in the contract blueprint (see Box 8.2) where it says: 'To be aware of the organizational contracts which the supervisor and the students have with college, employers, clients and the supervision group'. Most often the student supervisor is part of an extended triangle, with the student having two supervisors (one in the college and one in the placement) and two organizational contexts to work between. We mentioned in Chapter 7 the dynamics that are created in triangular relationships, with the tendency to create splitting, with one supervisor becoming the 'good supervisor' and the other the 'bad supervisor'. Student supervisors need to learn how to negotiate clear contracts not only with their supervisees, but also with their co-supervisor in the practice setting. They also need to learn how to carry out three-way assessment and evaluation meetings with the supervisee and the co-supervisor.

Team and group supervision course

This course is for all those who supervise in groups or teams. Such a course would also be useful for experienced team leaders and for training officers who are increasingly finding that they are called upon to provide team consultancy services as well as setting up courses.

It is important that all the people who attend such a course are already trained and experienced supervisors. If not, they should be given some basic supervision training before attending this type of course.

As in the basic course, it is useful to start by reviewing the knowledge, skills and abilities of the course members and then looking at what their learning needs are from this particular course. This process is also important as it acts as a model for the course members in how to negotiate a working contract with a group or team.

The course then needs to provide an opportunity to explore the differences between individual and group supervision and to encourage the course members to present the difficulties they have, which are specific to working with groups. Chapters 9 and 10 provide the basis for presenting some of the themes specific to supervising in groups and teams and the course also needs to include teaching on group dynamics, the developmental stages in the formation and growth of a team and some basic theory of team development.

Chapter 10 also provides the outline of some of the models and techniques we teach to team supervisors, both for them to use with the teams they supervise and also for them to explore their work while they are on the course. Course members can actively involve each other in the dynamics of their supervised teams by using the other group members as a 'sculpt' of a team they would like to explore. They then bring the sculpt to life and have other course members try out various ways of supervising the same enacted group (for a description of sculpting see Chapter 10).

Another useful strategy for teaching group supervision skills is as follows:

- Divide the group into two, A and B.
- Each group meets separately for a time, to explore their learning needs.
- Then Group A provides a consultant and a process observer for Group B. Group B does the same for Group A.

- After a designated length of time the consultants and observers return to their groups to process all three types of experience – that of the consultant, the observer and the members who received consultancy.
- The exercise can also include structured feedback from the group members to the visiting consultant.

This exercise can continue through several cycles or until every course member has had the opportunity to be in each role.

Where possible the team supervision course should also be taught as a short sandwich course, so that course members can further explore some of their new perspectives in an action learning stage, before returning to the course with more monitored experience which they can share with the other course members.

Therapeutic supervision course

This course designed for those who supervise counselling, psychotherapy and other therapeutic work, also has to ensure that its members have already acquired the skills, knowledge and techniques included in the core supervision course. If not, such teaching would need to be included in this course.

Where this course needs to go further and deeper than the basic course is in understanding the ways of working with the interlocking psychodynamic processes of the therapy relationship and the supervision relationship. We use our own model of the 'seven-eyed supervisor' (see Chapter 6) to teach this area and have developed a series of different experiential exercises to train supervisors in each of the seven modes, as well as exercises in how to integrate the modes into their own personal style (CSTD 1999).

The course also needs to address the developmental model (see Chapter 5) and how the supervision style needs to change and adapt according to the developmental stage of both supervisee and the supervision relationship.

Advanced supervision course

Such a course would either be for very senior staff within an organization (e.g. assistant chief probation officers, consultant psychiatrists, etc.) or for those who are either internal or external organizational trainers and consultants. It can also be run for those who want to further their learning to become advanced supervisor practitioners.

Once again the course members should already have the knowledge, techniques and skills equivalent to those taught on the courses already discussed. Our own experience of running an advanced supervision course, over many years, has led us to believe that the main focus should be on providing a learning space for supervisors to return to the knowledge and skills they have developed from earlier supervision training, in the light of having applied these skills in their own work setting. This means that the course is appropriately less structured and more student determined than the earlier courses, with plenty of opportunity for supervisors to present difficult situations from their own supervision practice.

We have also discovered that a series of other inputs are useful when supervisors have reached this stage. These include:

- In-depth work with video recordings of supervision practice either pre-prepared at work or filmed on the course.
- The use of interpersonal process recall techniques (Kagan 1980; CSTD 1999) to reflect on the detailed dynamics of videoed or practice sessions.
- Case study seminar on ethical dilemmas in supervision (see below).
- Workshop on developing transcultural competence (see below and Chapter 7).
- Seminar on dealing with issues concerning appraisal, evaluation and accreditation (see below).
- Reflections of case material involving inter-agency dynamics (see Chapter 11).
- Seminar on ways of developing supervision policies in organizations and also how to assist in bringing about organizational change at the levels of culture and ethos, strategy and structure (see Chapters 12 and 13).

Training in ethical dilemmas

In Chapter 4 we discussed the importance of developing your own ethical principles as well as familiarizing yourself with the codes of ethics of your professional association. We quoted Michael Carroll's four stage model of ethical decision making. Carroll (1996) also includes a very comprehensive checklist for training supervisors in ethical decision making. We provide an abbreviated version of this checklist (see Box 8.3) which we use on our courses as a framework for reviewing real ethical dilemmas, either brought by participants or supplied by ourselves from our past experience.

Training in transcultural competence

Training in this area can utilize the material included in Chapter 7. We also use our own paper 'Anti-discrimination and oppression in supervision' (CSTD 1999).

We begin the workshop by asking people to share something about their cultural background. This can be done by asking them to share the history of either their first or last name. We have developed a pair exercise on training courses to deepen an inquiry attitude to transcultural issues in a relationship:

Box 8.3   A checklist for ethical decision making in supervision training (based on Carroll 1996)

1 Creating ethical sensitivity

- Creating one's own list of moral principles.
- Reading ethical codes and related literature.
- Case vignettes on ethical and transcultural issues.
- Sharing critical incidents from members' own experience.

2 Formulating a moral course of action

- Identify the ethical problem or dilemma.
- Identify the potential issues involved.
- Review the relevant ethical guidelines.
- Ascertain who else should be consulted.
- Consider possible and probable courses of action.
- Enumerate the consequences of the various options.
- Decide on the best course of action.

3 Implementing an ethical decision

- Anticipate the potential difficulties in implementing the decision.
- Explore the internal fears and resistances to taking the action.
- Set up the necessary support and strategies for dealing with the potential difficulties and resistances.

4 Living with the ambiguities of an ethical decision

- Dealing with the anxiety and fears attending the decision.
- Confronting one's internal and anticipated external critical judgements.
- Accepting the limitations involved.
- Formulating the learning from the experience that can be applied elsewhere.

- Person A says to Person B: 'What I would like you to know about my cultural background is . . .'
- Person B says: 'What I heard was . . .'
- Person A clarifies.
- Person B says: 'I would supervise you differently on the basis of what I have heard by . . .'
- Person A gives feedback on what they would find helpful from the suggestions made by Person B.
- Steps 1–4 are carried out with A and B reversing roles.
- Having explored their differences, A and B share ways in which they may be unawarely similar.

This can be followed by using the vignettes from Chapter 7 and asking groups to answer the following three questions:

* What cultural assumptions may be in operation in the behaviour of the therapist and client?
* How might they need to change their mind sets and behaviour to work in a more transculturally competent manner?
* How would you supervise the therapist?

This in turn can be followed by role-playing a supervision session with the therapist from the vignette.

Evaluation and accreditation

Since writing the first edition of this book the whole area of supervision training and accreditation has grown and become more fixed. In the 1980s there was no formal accreditation for being a supervisor and little in the way of formal training. Most practitioners became supervisors as a result of having been in the profession long enough. While we welcome the growth in research, training and accreditation in the field of supervision we become increasingly concerned that the joy of continual learning can be overshadowed by the need to fulfil externally generated requirements, and the anxiety this evokes.

Accreditation begins with some form of appraisal. We believe that all appraisal processes should start with the individual appraising themselves and being challenged to face openly their own strengths and weaknesses. This should be followed by some form of structured 360-degree feedback, including supervisees, fellow trainee supervisors, as well as trainers and more experienced supervisors. The reason for this is to support the supervisor in taking their own authority, and lessen the degree to which they become dependent or reactive to the authority of others. Another reason is that supervisory ability is always embedded in the supervisory relationship and can never become a mechanical process. Therefore, assessment should also be within a relationship that ideally acknowledges the intersubjective and power dimensions involved (see Chapter 7).

Earlier in this chapter we offered a format for carrying out a self-appraisal. The same form can be used by supervisees to appraise their supervisor, as well as by the supervisor's supervisor. It is then possible to review the different ratings given by all three parties and for the person being appraised to reflect on how they see their proficiencies and learning needs differently from others' perceptions.

Where accreditation is carried out by some official professional body, it is important that it avoids the twin dangers of *individual autonomy* on the one hand and *institutionalized authority* on the other. The danger of *individual autonomy* is that accreditation that just rubber stamps the individual's own self- and peer-assessment abrogates the responsibility of the elders of a profession to initiate a new member into the community of practising professionals. This involves challenging their own self-perception, challenging peer collusion in their training group and ensuring that they have been exposed to training and experience that is of the necessary depth and breadth appropriate for the work they will supervise. The most important challenge is that the supervisor seeking accreditation is aware of their own shortcomings and personal biases, and can respond to feedback on these in an open and undefensive manner.

The danger of *institutionalized authority* is that the professional body becomes increasingly fixed in its professional requirements and that these become more and more based on quantifiable inputs in the training that the supervisor has undergone, rather than on the qualities and abilities the supervisor has developed through both training and experience. It is also important that the evaluation process happens within a direct form of relationship and not via the examination of paperwork by a distant and unknown committee. There is also a tendency for professional bodies constantly to increase the standards required from those being evaluated. This can be justified as a wish to improve, but it can also be driven by a socioeconomic process of professions restricting the gateway into an already crowded market niche. It can also be driven by a collective psychological process which searches for perfection rather than accepting our human ignorance and fallibility. In Chapter 1 we talked about 'good enough' supervision, and accreditation must evaluate someone as a 'good enough' supervisor, who is committed to continuing their learning and development.

It is doubly important that supervisor evaluation and accreditation is carefully managed, as the accredited supervisor will often have to combine the role of supervisor with that of providing evaluation and contributions to accreditation of their supervisees. It is important that they experience how to this can be done both effectively and sensitively, where support and challenge are combined in a healthy relationship.

Conclusion

In this chapter we have emphasized the importance of supervision training that is experiential, practical, involves action learning and is appropriate to the type of supervision that the course members give. However, supervision courses can never be a substitute for having good supervision oneself.

In teams, organizations or professions that do not have a healthy tradition and practice of supervision, it is unrealistic to try to solve this absence by randomly setting up supervisor training courses. Supervisor training will always be most effective when it is part of a strategic plan to create an organizational learning culture. How to go about creating the right sort of organization or team climate in which supervision can flourish will be explored at length in Chapters 12 and 13.

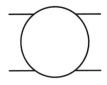

Part Three

Supervising groups, teams and networks

Group, team and peer-group supervision

Introduction

The emphasis so far in this book has been mainly on individual supervision. This is because we see it as the best context in which to address many of the key issues and processes within supervision, before approaching the same issues in the more complex setting of a group. However, many of the issues so far covered, such as contracting, modes of supervision, the importance of transcultural and anti-oppressive practice and ethics, also apply to supervision in groups.

In this chapter we will first explore the advantages and disadvantages of group supervision, before going on to look at the practical skills of setting up and managing supervision groups. We then explore the particular issues involved with team and peer supervision.

Group supervision

Advantages

There are several reasons why you might choose to supervise in a group rather than individually. The first of these reasons may be connected to economies of time, money or expertise. Clearly if there is a shortage of people who can supervise, or if their time is very limited, supervisors can probably see more supervisees by conducting supervision groups. However, ideally group supervision should come from a positive choice rather than a compromise forced upon the group and the supervisor.

The second advantage of group supervision is that unlike one-to-one supervision the group provides a supportive atmosphere of peers in which new staff or trainees can share anxieties and realize that others are facing similar issues.

The third advantage is that group supervision gains from the supervisees' receiving reflections, feedback and inputs from their colleagues as well as the group supervisor. Thus potentially this setting is less dominated by the supervisor (with the concurrent dangers of over-influence and dependency). A group can, when working well, challenge collusions between the supervisor and the supervisees.

The fourth advantage is that a group can also provide a way for the supervisor to test out their emotional or intuitive response to the material presented by checking if other group members have had the same response. This can best be illustrated by referring to the concept of paralleling mentioned in Chapter 6.

We like using the idea of paralleling in groups in particular because the variety of responses of different members can be used to good effect. One of us usually starts group supervision sessions by asking the members to entertain the possibility that we do to others what has been done to us. He introduces the terms introjection and projection, explaining that, if we swallow something without digesting it properly, we may have to vomit it up later. It is usually these cases that are brought to supervision, where some aspect of the client has not been digested. If members of the group can be aware of what they are experiencing, or have been asked to swallow, this can be an extremely useful clue for clarifying what is undigested by the supervisees and client. By using the terms introjection and projection on an easily understood level, we are inviting all the members of the group to trust their here-and-now reactions as part of the supervision work. Here is an example which illustrates the process at work:

> On a supervision course for therapeutic community members, a
> new young staff member presented a client with whom she had
> been having difficulty. After an initial enthusiasm and opening up,
> the client was either missing her session or hardly communicating.
> As soon as the worker began to present her client as facilitator,
> I found myself switching off. I just did not want to be bothered.

However, I kept going for about ten minutes asking seemingly appropriate questions until I could stand it no longer. I shared my feelings of uninterest hesitantly – they just did not seem to fit – and group members seemed to be so involved. In fact it turned out that the group was split roughly half and half. One half was very involved and the other half had totally switched off too, but like me was trying to appear involved. The presenter was astonished to see how accurately her feelings for her client of both being very involved and identifying with her, and not wanting to know about her, were being mirrored. The group really began to work well and deeply after that, because permission had been given to share apparent negativity, and its relevance was confirmed. This is one way in which the supervisor can check whether their countertransference is coming from their own psyche or is a useful reaction triggered by the material presented.

The fifth advantage is that a group can also provide a wider range of life experience and thus there is more likelihood of someone in the group being able to empathize both with the supervisee and the client. A group provides a greater empathic range not just of gender, race or age, but also of personality types.

The sixth advantage is that groups provide more opportunity to use action techniques as part of the supervision. In a group it is possible to re-enact the therapy session with a fellow group member playing the client. This can be developed through the use of sculpting and role-reversal techniques. Below are three particular techniques, the first two described by Gaie Houston (1985: 66) (see also Hawkins 1988).

The person presenting the problem, Cecil, sets up the scene he is talking about by first giving a brief outline of what is bothering him. He then goes and stands behind someone he would like to become a central character. He puts his hands on, say, Janet's shoulders, and speaks as if he is the person Janet is to play. For instance: 'I am Rebecca. I am divorced, 50 and Jewish, and lost over 40 members of my family in the holocaust. I suppose I am terribly angry. But all I let out is a sort of dominating sweetness, and I talk and talk through every group session.' Even doing this, Cecil is likely to make more empathetic connection with Rebecca than if he talked about her in the third person. He places other people to play other significant characters, in his group, or in Rebecca's life as he sees fit. Then he casts someone to be himself. 'I am Cecil. Looking at Rebecca I feel rebellious, that I won't let her take over. Then I'm guilty for what she's been through.'

The person who is being enrolled may ask information questions, using the first person. For example, 'Do I see Rebecca as anyone else in my life?' When all are briefed, Cecil watches while the group enacts next week's meeting. They do their best to stay true to what they were instructed, while the new Cecil works to bring a fresh solution.

It can prove to be an enlightening experience for the whole group, not just Cecil. It is also possible to follow this form of re-enactment by having several other members trying to handle the same situation, becoming Cecil, while the supervisee (Cecil) becomes the client (Rebecca). This second approach provides an opportunity for the supervisees to discover more about their clients through becoming them and experiencing what it is like to be on the receiving end of different approaches.

It is important that this supervision technique is given plenty of time and there is a chance for each 'therapist' to receive feedback, first from the role-played client, in terms of what was helpful and what was un-helpful or difficult, and then from the group, who must likewise give feedback which is owned, balanced and specific. It is too easy to give clever advice and damning criticism from the audience; it is quite another matter to do what you advise on stage (see Argyris 1982).

A third technique that is appropriate for groups is an 'enacted role set'. A supervisee presents a client and the rest of the group are enrolled as different parts of the client/worker network in the same way as the enrolling described above. For example, someone could be enrolled as the supervisee's boss who is putting pressure on the supervisee to sort out this difficult client. This is affecting the quality of the supervisee's work, as they do not feel fully present to the client. Someone else can play the boss's boss and explore the pressure they are putting on the boss. Someone can play the client's partner who actually is fed up with the client and subtly sabotages any improvement the client makes. The point is that all these (and many more) factors are all present in the one-to-one but are often not recognized explicitly. The supervisee sees the problem as only to do with the client and does not take into account the system to which the client belongs. What then happens is that there is a short role-play of a session and the rest of the enrolled members listen in role as if they were a fly on the wall. They then feed back their responses in role and the supervisee is astonished to find out that what they say corresponds to the positions the people take in real life. The problem can then be related to the total context, not just the interpersonal or intrapersonal one.

The final advantage of group supervision is that where possible the supervision context should reflect the therapeutic context which is being supervised. Thus, if the supervisees run groups, learning can be gained from the supervision taking place in a group with other group leaders. This provides opportunities to learn from how the supervisor runs the group and also how the dynamics of the presented groups are mirrored in the supervision group (see Chapter 6, p. 80).

Disadvantages

There are also some disadvantages to supervising in groups. Group super-vision is less likely to mirror the dynamic of individual therapy as clearly as would individual supervision.

Also, as soon as you work in a group, you have to contend with group dynamics. These can be a benefit if they are made conscious within the group and used as an adjunct to the supervisees increasing their self-awareness through their part in the group process. However, the group process can also be destructive and undermining of the supervisory process if, for example, there is a competitive spirit in the group. The dynamics of the supervisory group can also become a preoccupation. We have both been in supervision groups that have gradually become centrally concerned with their own dynamics almost to the exclusion of any interest in the clients of those present. We will discuss group dynamics more in Chapter 10.

The final disadvantage of group supervision is that there is obviously less time for each person to receive supervision. The individual might therefore only get a turn every three meetings and, if these are held fortnightly, this could in effect mean supervision directly for oneself only every six weeks.

Selection of group members

This is a very important part of group life for both members and leaders. Clarity of purpose and needs should be very carefully considered by all concerned, as should range of experience and skills. In terms of size, a supervision group needs to be three people at the very minimum, and no more than seven, otherwise members will have to fight to get enough time and attention.

The group also has to have enough similarity in the types of clients they work with, their general theoretical approach to their work, and their level of accomplishment. However, in a group that is too similar in these three areas the learning and challenge is limited and there is a danger of promoting 'consensus collusion' (Heron 1975).

In the training course that one of us has been running in Bath it has also been important to ensure a geographical mix in the supervision groups, where possible, to limit the possibilities of the group members personally knowing the clients that are presented. This can be a problem in any provincial setting.

Contracting

Once the group has been selected, the group supervisor needs to have the skills to manage the contracting. It is good to ensure clarity of purpose, as mentioned above – there is often a hidden agenda of 'getting a bit of therapy on the side', for example, and the group needs to be clear about its policy on this, checking to see that expectations are realistic. The time factor and the number of clients that can be supervised also needs to be acknowledged.

Some useful questions for the supervisor to bear in mind are:

- What should the goals of this group supervision be?
- What roles should the group supervisor adopt to permit the realization of these goals?
- What balance between didactic material, case conceptualization and interpersonal process is most productive for trainee learning?
- What is the role of evaluation in this group?

Some of the issues around contracting are similar to those mentioned in Chapter 5, but the issues around confidentiality are more complex. We have found it necessary in some groups to have a ground rule that, if you think you know the client being presented you declare this and, if necessary, leave the room for the duration of that presentation.

Setting the climate

The next task is to create a safe climate for the supervisees to open up their work to others, a process that always generates some fear and anxiety. Supervisees will often be concerned about the following:

- 'Will I be found out?'
- 'Will everyone else find flaws that I am unaware of, not only in my work but who I am as a person?'
- 'Will they think why the hell does he think he can be a therapist with those attitudes or hang-ups?'

The climate must be one that encourages a sharing of vulnerabilities and anxieties without group members being put down or turned into 'the group patient'. It is an easy escape route for group members to avoid their own insecurities by finding a group patient which allows them the chance to return to the much safer role of therapist!

Simple ground rules help to avoid destructive group processes, such as ensuring that all statements are owned and group members speak from their own experience. Avoid good advice: 'If I were you I would'; and preaching: 'Therapists ought to be warm and accepting', etc. As mentioned above, another useful ground rule is to ensure that feedback from group members is owned, balanced and specific. It is also important that the group supervisor ensures that there is a roughly equal amount of sharing between all group members, both in terms of quantity and level of self-disclosure.

Self-disclosure can feel safer if the group leader also shares some of their own insecurities, anxieties and times when they do not know, rather than always having to be the one with the answers (see Jourard 1971).

Acknowledging the group dynamic

It is essential that the group leader also ensures that group dynamics do not proceed unacknowledged and finds a way of bringing the dynamics into awareness so that they can be attended to and learned from, without taking over as the major focus of the group. Awareness of the here-and-now dynamics is an essential part of the learning process but the distinction between a supervision group and a 'T' group, encounter group, or therapy group must be maintained. (For more details see Chapter 10).

Structuring the group

For the group supervisor there are a number of choices about how to structure the group session. Which one they choose will depend on the type and size of group as well as their own style and inclination.

One of us starts group supervision sessions, which are part of a psychotherapy training, with a round of each group member stating what issues they have that they would like to bring to the group. This is followed by a negotiation between the competing requests to decide on the order and how much time each person should have.

A variant that can be used with this approach is to follow the round with an exploration of whose issue most represents the current 'core concern' of the group. This can be done by asking group members to identify which issue, other than their own, they would learn most from exploring and then working with the issue that has the most interest. This ensures that the person who is the centre of the work is not just working for him or herself, but has the energy and interest of the group.

Other colleagues of ours divide the group time equally between all those present so that they all know they will get some attention during each group session. This becomes impractical if the group is too large and/or the time too short.

The group may arrange a schedule where each group member knows in advance that he or she will be the one presenting on a particular day. This makes it possible for some outline notes on the case to be circulated in advance. This moves the session more into a group case study with a greater emphasis on learning from an overview, rather than focusing on current concerns and difficulties. This structure may entail group members having other supervision for their more immediate supervision needs.

Another option is to trust the process and to wait to see what emerges and where the interest of the group moves. You can also start by checking out what has happened to issues that were explored at the previous meeting.

Supervision style

Group members, unless they are very experienced, will mostly take their lead from the group supervisor and make interventions with a similar style and focus to that of the leader. It is thus very important that supervisors be aware of how they are modelling ways of responding to material that is shared. The supervisor needs to model or explain that there is a

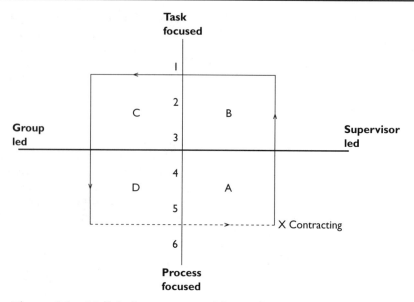

Figure 9.1   Model of group supervision styles

range of ways of listening and responding to what is shared to encourage a multi-layered approach (see Chapter 6).

In Figure 9.1 we show four quadrants, each representing a different style of group supervision. In quadrant A, the supervision group is more directively led by the group supervisor and has a strong focus on the group process. In quadrant B, the supervisor is still taking the central lead, but the focus is more on the content of the cases brought. In quadrant C, the group moves over to taking more leadership responsibility among the members, but with a focus on the cases brought. In quadrant D, the group take responsibility for focusing on their own process.

Each quadrant has its own shadow side, if the supervision group gets stuck in just this one style. Quadrant A groups can become a therapy group, attending to the personal needs of the members, but ignoring the client issues. Quadrant B groups can become a forum for the group supervisor to show off their expertise and create dependency from the group members. Supervision that becomes stuck in Quadrant C can become competitive and peer-advice giving, with group members trying to outdo each other with 'If I were you' solutions. Quadrant D supervision groups can become over-collusive peer support groups and like groups in quadrant A, inward looking and failing to attend to the task.

Good group supervision needs to be able to move flexibly through all these areas, depending on the needs of the group and the stage of group development. Most commonly a supervision group will begin in quadrant A in its forming and contracting phase, move into quadrant B, as it begins to settle to its task, and then gradually incorporate quadrants C and D, as the group becomes more mature and self-responsible. However, good

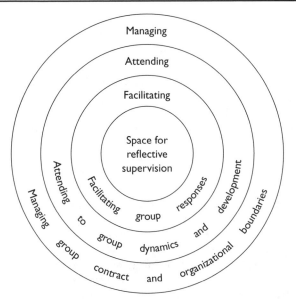

Figure 9.2   The contextual rings of the group supervision process

supervision groups, once well established will cycle through all four quadrants, and avoid getting stuck in the shadow side of any single quadrant.

A group supervisor needs to be able to manage a number of simultaneous processes, as supervision in a group is contained within a number of rings of context (see Figure 9.2) (see also Inskipp and Proctor 1995). The central skills of facilitating reflective supervision shown in the inner ring are similar to working one-to-one. However, to use the richness of the group to the full, the group supervisor must facilitate the responses of the group members and link these back to the case, shown in the second ring.

The third contextual ring involves managing the group dynamics and attending to the developmental stage and developmental needs of the group process. The outer ring involves ensuring that the supervision happens within an appropriate contract and boundaries. The group contract, as discussed above, is something that is not a one-off event, but a process that must be regularly revisited. The contract may also involve more than the group members and supervisor, as the group supervision may be happening in the context of an organization, or members may be sponsored by a number of different organizations. The boundaries and relationship with these organizations become an important context that the supervisor must attend too in order that the supervision feels appropriately contained.

Team supervision

Team supervision is different from group supervision. It involves working with a group who have not come together just for the purpose of joint supervision, but who have an interrelated work life outside the group. Thus, although many of the approaches to group supervision that we have outlined above are relevant, there are other factors that have to be managed.

There is a difference between teams that share work with the same clients (such as a mental health team in a psychiatric hospital, or the staff of a residential home) and teams which, although they work with similar approaches and in the same geographical area, have separate clients (such as a GP practice or a field social work team). A simple way of classifying the nature of teams is to use a sports analogy. In football teams all members play the same game at the same time, albeit with different special roles, and are highly interdependent. In tennis teams the team members play the same game, but do so either individually or in pairs. In athletics teams the members take part in very different sports, at different times, but occasionally work together (relays), train together, combine their scores and support each other's morale.

Casey (1985) warns of the dangers of thinking that all work must be done in teams and provides a model for deciding when teamwork is necessary. Payne and Scott (1982) also provide guidance for considering what sort of supervision is appropriate for which sorts of team.

Supervision in teams that know each other's clients has both advantages and disadvantages, as often in supervision you are attending not to the client 'out there' but to how the client has entered into the intrapsychic life of the supervisee. For example:

> In a residential home where a staff member, Jane, was exploring her profound irritation with one of the difficult boys called Robert, the other members of the team all piled in with their ways of handling Robert. The supervisor had to work very hard to reopen the space for Jane to explore what it was that Robert triggered in her, who he reminded her of, and to help her generate more options for herself. He created this space by pointing out to the team that the Robert she was struggling with could almost be thought of as a different Robert from the Roberts they were each relating to. This was true on two counts: first, Robert was a very fragmented and manipulative boy who would present quite differently to each staff member; second, every staff member was differently affected by him, depending on their own personality, history and ways of reacting.
>
> It was crucial in this case that Jane's space was protected or she would have quickly become the staff member seen as the one who couldn't cope with Robert and been covertly elected to carry the helpless aspects of Robert and of the team working with him. By letting the team flood her with good ideas for dealing with this boy, the supervision would have colluded with intensifying the split within the team and hence in Robert. Certainly after having worked with the feelings of helplessness in Jane and helping her to understand and generate more creative options for herself, it was

then possible to return to the team and explore their differing experiences and views of the boy, so that the fragmented feelings that had been scattered throughout the team could gradually be put together.

When conducting team supervision there are still issues about group selection. First, it is necessary to decide where the boundary of the team is drawn. Do you include assistant staff, clerical staff or trainees? If it is an interprofessional team, issues of inclusion and exclusion are even more highly charged. Second, good team supervision should alert the team to the danger of the tendency to fill vacancies with 'more people like us'. There is a need for teams to have some degree of homogeneity, but teams also need a balance in personality types, age, gender and skills. Belbin (1981) has carried out a classic study of the range of roles a team needs in order to be effective.

Team supervision also supposes that in addition to the team members needing supervision, another entity also requires supervision. This is the team itself. We consider the team as an entity to be more than the sum of its parts and to have a personality and intrapsychic life of its own. Some writers call this the 'team culture' or 'team dynamic'. We will discuss this further in Chapter 10. It is important to note that team supervision is different from other forms of supervision in that it inevitably involves some form of team development.

Steve Fineman (1985), in his study of a social work department, looked at five different teams. One of the teams was significantly more effective in maintaining a high morale and low levels of stress than the other four. One of the key factors in this success was the effective team supervision by the team leader: '[the] mutual trust found links with the team leader's activities in promoting support. Indeed his integrative meetings with staff on professional matters – which he took most seriously and sensitively judging from his and other reports – were probably critical ingredients in helping to set the supportive climate' (p. 106).

In Chapter 10 we will illustrate ways of exploring and improving team dynamics, and in Part 4 we will discuss how to access and change the culture of both organizations and teams.

Peer supervision

Many professionals on our courses complain that they cannot get good supervision as their immediate line senior has neither the time nor the ability to supervise them. We are often surprised that they have not even considered the possibility of setting up peer supervision for themselves. One of us was in the position of running a therapeutic community and his immediate line manager was the assistant director of a large mental health charity organization who had no direct experience of either therapeutic communities or supervision. This experience is similar to many of the situations we find with senior practitioners in various professions who are nominally supervised by senior managers with little or no clinical experience. In response to this situation Peter set up a series of peer supervisions. First, he exchanged supervision with his deputy who was more experienced than he in the work with the clients. This worked very well for receiving supervision for the work with clients, but did not solve the problem of Peter's not receiving supervision on his leadership of the staff team.

Peter's second peer supervision was with the senior trainer within the organization who had spent many years working in a variety of thera-peutic communities. Again this worked well for a time, but as both she and he were involved in the senior management meetings of the organization, mutual sharing of their struggles with the management structure became an over-dominant focus.

The third move Peter made was to use the facilities of a professional association (in this case the Association of Therapeutic Communities) to set up a peer supervision group for senior staff within therapeutic communities. He was surprised to find that many other senior practitioners in voluntary organizations, social services departments and the National Health Service shared the same shortage of and need for supervision. This proved a rich and rewarding group with the opportunity to focus on whole community problems and dynamics. This group went on existing well after Peter and the other original members had left.

One of us had his own peer supervision setting for his psychotherapy work which was a peer triad with a consultant psychiatrist/psychotherapist and a clinical psychologist/psychotherapist. At each meeting one of the three members took his turn at being supervisor. Each of the other two got 40 minutes' supervision. At the end of each person's supervision the supervisee shared with the supervisor what he found helpful and difficult and then the supervisor shared his own reflections of the session. This was followed by the third member (who has been observing) giving feedback, both positive and negative, to the supervisor. This suited the needs of those in the triad who received not only supervision on their psychotherapy but reflections and learning on how they supervised.

This piece of autobiography illustrates how peer supervision can be either individually reciprocal or be in a group of workers with similar needs, approaches and levels of expertise. It also illustrates how it is possible to look for peer supervisors not only within your immediate workplace but also in similar workplaces within your own organization or with workers from different organizations. We have been involved in helping a number of staff set up their own peer supervision systems. These include heads of children's homes giving each other reciprocal supervision in one local authority; a group of principal officers meeting regularly for peer supervision in another local authority; and an interprofession peer supervision system in a community mental health team.

One area that has actively encouraged the development of peer supervision has been humanistic psychotherapy. This is partly due to the professional commitment of the profession and bodies like the Association of

Humanistic Psychology Practitioners (AHPP) and the United Kingdom Council of Psychotherapy to continuous supervision throughout one's professional career, not only when one is in training. This is backed up by members of AHPP having to reapply for membership every five years – in their reapplication they have to state what supervision they are currently having.

Peer supervision clearly has many advantages, but there are also many pitfalls and traps. In the absence of a group leader there is a greater need for a firm and clear structure and it requires greater commitment from the group members.

Gaie Houston (1985) has written about some of the traps or games (as in transactional analysis) that we have known peer groups to fall into.

- *Measuring cocks*: Houston describes a group where the various members used phrases about their groups such as: 'Mine are so cooperative'; 'Mine say I have helped them a lot'; and 'It was such a powerful experience'. She goes on to write: 'An American consultant I know calls this activity measuring cocks. All the statements in it add up to "Mine's Better Than Yours". Everyone feels tense, knowing that if one person wins and has the biggest or best, everyone else has lost'.
- *Ain't it awful?*: in this game the peer group sits around, reinforcing each other's sense of powerlessness. One variant of the game is to spend the time sharing how you must be mad to work for this 'authority' or 'hospital'. Another variant is for therapists or counsellors to spend their time showing how clients are hateful, vicious and manipulative beings who resist your best endeavours at every attempt. This can spill over into another game called 'Get the client'.
- *We are all so wonderful*: peer-group members can avoid having their anxieties revealed about being criticized or found out by heaping fulsome praise on other peer members as an unacknowledged payment for returning the favour. This becomes a covert form of protection racket and in the long term ensures that that group is too fearful to let new members join or old members leave, as this might threaten the unearthing of what is buried. John Heron (1975) refers to this as 'consensus collusion'.
- *Who is the best supervisor?*: this is a straightforward but often undisclosed or acknowledged competition to fill the void left by not having a group supervisor. It can emerge through group members straining to make the cleverest or most helpful comments, or through distracting peripheral arguments on the efficacy of this or that approach. Peer groups often have no mechanism for dealing with their group dynamics and unfortunately group members who point out the processes that are going on may get caught up in the competition to be the 'supervisor'.
- *Hunt the patient*: groups, like families, can identify one member to be the 'patient' and the focus for the inadequate or difficult feelings to which the others do not wish to own. Having an identified patient also allows the other group members to retreat into the safe and known role of therapist and collectively to try to treat the elected patient. A

probation officer might be elected to carry all the fear of violence for the peer group. While the other members 'help' this member explore their fears, they also protect themselves from facing similar fears within themselves.

These games are not the sole prerogative of peer groups, but there is more risk of such groups falling into some of them as there is no outside facilitator (or one of them) whose job it is to watch the process. Some of these games will be explored further in Chapter 10.

How to form a peer supervision group

It is clear from the above that peer supervision has many pitfalls, but if properly organized it also has many advantages. In workshops that we have run we are often asked for advice in starting and running peer groups and we generally give the following recommendations:

- Try to form a group that has shared values but a range of approaches. It is important that you can dialogue together within a reasonably shared language and belief system but, if you all have the same training and style of working, the group can become rather collusive and lack a more distant perspective.
- The group needs to be no more than seven people. It must also ensure that it has enough time to meet the needs of all its members. It is no good having a peer supervision group of seven people, all of whom have a large number of clients for whom they want supervision, unless the group meets regularly for at least two or three hours.
- Be clear about commitment. It is not helpful for the group members to commit themselves because they think they ought to, and then fail to meet the commitment. Members must be encouraged to share their resistance to meeting for supervision and, if possible, to share how they might avoid or otherwise sabotage the supervision group. For example, one member may warn the group that he or she is likely to get too busy with more pressing engagements, while another member may say that her or his pattern is to get bad headaches.
- Make a clear contract. It needs to be clear about frequency and place of meetings, time boundaries, confidentiality, how time will be allocated and how the process is to be managed. You might need to be clear how you will handle one group member's knowing the clients that other members bring for supervision; will the person leave the group while that client is being discussed or will they be expected to get supervision on that person elsewhere?
- Be clear about the different expectations. Some members may expect a greater focus on their personal process than others are comfortable with. Some members may expect all their client work to be covered by the group, while others may also have individual supervision elsewhere.

Some members may expect a greater amount of advice on what to do next, while others may expect to use role-play or other experiential techniques. Try to discover if there are any hidden group agendas. We came across one peer group that consisted of two separate subgroups that were working out their relationships.

- Be clear about role expectations. Who is going to maintain the time boundaries or deal with any interruptions? Who is going to organize the rooms? Is there going to be one person each time who carries the main responsibility for facilitating or will this emerge out of the group process?
- Build some time into each meeting (it need only be five or ten minutes) to give feedback on how the supervision process has been for each person. This can include appreciations and any resentments.
- Plan to have a review session every three months when all the members receive feedback on their role in the group, the dynamics of the group are looked at and the contract is renegotiated. Many of the exercises and approaches that are mentioned in Chapter 10 for exploring the dynamics of teams and groups can be adopted by a peer group in its own review.

There are several other books that give useful hints on establishing peer groups for therapeutic work and, although they have a different focus they often throw up similar dynamics. We suggest that those who are interested read Ernst and Goodison (1981) and Shohet (1985, Ch. 9).

Organizing a peer supervision meeting

Many of the suggestions made above about structuring group supervision also apply to peer-group supervision:

- Set ground rules: for example, members should give direct, balanced and owned feedback; members should avoid patronizing advice; time is equally shared.
- Either start each session by discovering who has what needs or have a set rotational system for allocating time.
- Encourage all the members to be clear about what they need from the group in relation to what they are sharing: do they need just to be listened to; to be given feedback; to be facilitated in exploring their countertransference; or helped in exploring where to go next, choosing between various options, etc? It is often useful if you do not know what the person wants to ask: 'What has led you to bring this particular issue today?'; or 'What is it you need in relation to this case?'
- Decide about informal time. Often, if you have no social or informal time scheduled, the need to catch up with each other's news, to gossip, and to make personal contact can interrupt the other tasks of the group. Some peer groups schedule a short social time at the beginning and/or end of the supervision group.

Conclusion

Groups clearly have many advantages over individual supervision in the range of possible learning opportunities and different perspectives that they can provide. They also have many potential pitfalls. Those leading supervision groups need to be aware of and work with the group dynamic and this necessitates that they have some training in group leadership and dynamics. Peer groups also need to have a system for attending to their own process so that it stays healthily supporting the task of supervision rather than diverting or sabotaging it.

The mode of supervision should reflect what is being supervised, so some form of group supervision is ideally suited for those being supervised on their group work. Group supervision is also useful in expanding the range of perspectives that one draws upon in reflecting on one's individual work, but we would recommend that, in the case of in-depth individual counselling and psychotherapy, group supervision should be an adjunct to, rather than a replacement for, individual supervision. The exception to this is that peer or group supervision can be quite adequate for senior practitioners who have developed not only their own individual competence but also an integrated form of self-supervision (see Chapter 3).

Exploring the dynamics of groups, teams and peer groups

Introduction
Group stages
Group dynamics
Facilitating group or team reviews
Contracting
Giving feedback
Estrangement exercise
Exploring the group dynamics
Sculpting the group
Exploring the wider context
Conclusion

Introduction

In the previous chapter we touched on some of the dynamics that may operate in supervision groups. In this chapter we will examine these dynamics a little further and propose some structures for working with them. For whether your supervision group is led, peer or part of a working team, its effectiveness will depend to a large extent on the ability of its members to be aware of, and process, the group dynamics that prevail. We therefore believe that all those who consider supervising in groups should have some training in this field and we will outline some of the factors that we see occurring most often. Training should include understanding the basic stages that groups go through and how to facilitate the group development in the various stages.

Group stages

Margaret Rioch has written extensively on the interface between supervision and group dynamics. In *Dialogues for Therapists* (Rioch *et al.* 1976) she charts a complete series of group supervisions (which she terms seminars) with therapists in training. After each seminar she comments on the group dynamics and concludes that 'It is also clear that the group interaction was an important part of the process, sometimes furthering, sometimes interfering, with the learning'.

Most of the theories and our own experience would suggest that groups have to start by dealing with their own boundaries, membership and the group rules and expectations. Schutz (1973) calls this 'inclusion', and Tuckman (1965) calls it 'the stages of Forming and Norming'. This is the contracting stage in group supervision, where the issues of confidentiality, commitment to the group, how time will be allocated and what will be focused on (and what will be excluded) need to be decided and clarified.

Soon after this period of clarifying the basic structure of the supervision group, there is often a period of testing out power and authority within the group. This can take the form of rivalrous competitiveness: 'Who does the best work?'; 'Who most cares about their clients?'; 'Who has the most difficult cases?'; 'Who makes the most penetrating insightful comments?'; etc. Or it may take the form of testing out the authority of the supervisor by challenging their approach, trying to show that one can supervise other group members better than the supervisor can, or inappropriately applying their recommendations to show that they do not work. This is called the stage of 'fight/flight' by Bion (1961), 'authority' by Schutz (1973) and 'storming' by Tuckman (1965).

It is only when these stages have been successfully handled that the group can settle to its most productive work, with a climate of respect for each individual and without either dependency or rivalry in its relationship to the supervisor.

Group dynamics

Rioch's description of the seminars she ran shows how these stages of group development certainly cannot be ignored when supervising in a group. Understanding the theories of group development and having insight into the group dynamics are not enough. The group supervisor must also know how to confront the group process and facilitate positive group behaviour.

In *Dialogues for Therapists*, Rioch illustrates in detail the importance of confronting the issues of both competition and authority in the supervision group. After a long discussion among participants in her seminar she says: 'Could it be that the seminar is skirting around the question of who is the best therapist here? That is no doubt a hot potato, and what is even more hot is the question of who is the worst therapist' (Rioch *et al.* 1976).

Looking at the issue of competition and group process she writes:

> The issue of competition can contribute to the work of the group if everyone tries to do the best he can. It may also interfere if people

become too afraid of being rejected or envied . . . In this seminar, as in most groups, there was a strong competitive element. The instructor is trying to point out that this was going on even as people were overtly discussing other issues. Although it was not the primary task of the group to learn about its own processes, it was often desirable to observe what the group was doing, particularly when its processes interfered with the primary task of learning to be useful to clients. The problem in the seminar was to use the students' competition, resistance and transference to the instructor in the service of the task of helping clients.

(Rioch *et al.* 1976)

She also usefully points out that supervisors are also part of the process:

It may also be helpful to teachers and supervisors to remember that they are subject to the same group pressures that are influencing their students. In other words, teachers and supervisors are competitive, resistant and reluctant to expose their failures, incompetencies, and insecurities. It is important that they should model for their students, not so much perfection which is impossible, but a willingness to learn from their imperfections.

(Rioch *et al.* 1976)

Receiving authority projections and being comfortable with them are part of both the supervisor's and the helper's role:

the instructor, who was reasonably well liked on a conscious level by seminar members, readily took on the role of an old witch in the unconscious fantasies of seminar members when they felt, as they sometimes did, like abused children in a fairy tale. Hansel and Gretel were scarcely in any position to be therapeutic to their clients. Neither did they harbour warm feelings toward the old witch whom they shoved into the oven in the happy ending.

(Rioch *et al.* 1976)

After a discussion in which members of the group hint that it would be better and freer without the leader, one of the members says: 'The real problem is not how nice it would be without her, but how to live with her. And not only with her, but with all the other authorities too'. Rioch sums up some of the ambivalence that we think is very often present in a supervision group, especially of trainees, when she says: 'As mature young people engaged in serious study, the students consciously wanted to use the instructor as a teacher and resource person, not as an adversary to be overthrown or a parent to take care of them. But less consciously, as in all groups, the elements of adolescent rebellion and childish dependency were present and active' (Rioch *et al.* 1976).

Another pitfall is to engage in therapy (described in Chapter 9 as 'hunt the patient'). The problem case or member is dealt with perhaps sympathetically but certainly in a way that is subtly putting down. The purpose of this game is that the group members can allay their anxieties and inadequacies and move into the more comfortable helping role.

Finally, it is possible to look at the dynamics of supervision presentation in terms of how you might consider a dream. When Robin runs dream groups, he does not pay attention only to the actual dream, but to when in the group life it is told and how it is told. For example, if someone tells him a dream in which the dreamer is struggling to get somewhere, and is angry that no one is helping them, he holds the hypothesis that the dreamer could be feeling this way in the group as well as in the dream. The way the dream is told can also give clues. A dream in which the person could make no headway was reflected in the group as it struggled for different ways of working with the dream and was blocked with 'yes buts'. Similarly, a supervision case can be a statement to the group and a reflection of how the supervisee feels in the group expressed through the client.

An example of this occurred with a trainee who was having a very hard time staying on one of our courses. She presented a client who was near to despair and was wondering if it was too late for her to work with this client. The group offered helpful suggestions but nothing seemed to help until the supervisor suggested that maybe she was afraid that things had got too bad on the course, and that it was too late for her, the counsellor, to put things right. This was a tremendous relief, as she realized how she was trying to communicate her despair to group members via the client.

Another time there was extreme tension and lack of progress in a supervision group and someone volunteered to present a case. It seemed a trifle masochistic as the group was not in a supportive place. We suggested that she make sure that she did want to present. Despite her reassuring us that the group tension did not bother her, we decided to pay attention to group process rather than just blindly work with the material presented. It turned out that she was working in an establishment where she felt other staff members were using her to do their work. The parallels with what was happening in the group became obvious. It also transpired that she was the one in her family who always tried to sort things out, so this issue of working for others was operating on three levels: family, work and here and now in the group. By commenting on the group process we were able to make sure that she did not get stranded in the here-and-now and were able to facilitate the group as well as the individual.

Facilitating group or team reviews

In our roles as consultants and supervisors we have been called in to help groups, teams or peer groups explore their dynamics and to facilitate them in finding better ways of functioning. This has ranged from a simple one-off meeting to an in-depth three-day team development session. Whatever the length and whether it is a team, group or peer group, some of the issues we would explore and how we would explore them would be the same, as follows.

Contracting

We would begin by clearly contracting with the group members as to what they want from us as consultant or facilitator of the team. This would entail asking intentionally naive questions, such as:

- What is the purpose of your meetings?
- What do you expect from one another?
- Why have you called me in as a consultant? And why now?
- How would you know if this consultancy had been successful for you?
- What specifically would be happening differently?

Clear contracting is not only important for the success of the consultancy but it also models the way members of the team or group can contract among themselves, both about how they meet generally, but also about how each person can be proactive in negotiating with the group their supervision needs.

Giving feedback

Before looking at what the group can become, it is necessary to start by finding out more about what it already is. One way to do this is for each person to receive feedback from all the other group members on what they have appreciated and found difficult about their contribution to the group.

Then each person can say what they have most appreciated and found most difficult about the group as a whole. This provides the beginnings of three lists: what the group values and needs to build on; what it wants to change; and what is missing and needs to be introduced.

Estrangement exercise

This provides another means of getting at the issues in the team or group that need to be addressed. In this exercise each member takes on the role of a person, totally different from the role player, who might attend an international conference on supervision. This person could be from a foreign country, be a different gender, be a member of the press, etc. It is important to choose somebody who will see things very differently from you, but whose perspective you are able to take up.

When the group members have taken up their roles and given them-selves names, they are asked to close their eyes and relax. They are then led through a fantasy of arriving at the international conference, meeting people, hearing talks, etc. Then they find they are going on a visit to a supervision group to see how it operates. The group they visit happens to be the group they belong to in their everyday personas. In the fantasy they are directed to attend to what they notice when they first arrive, how they are received and by whom, how the group gets under way, who initiates, what the starting rituals are, what other roles are taken up, who is most verbal, who least verbal, what is the non-verbal behaviour and what is it indicating, what do they feel as they watch the group pro-ceed, how does it end and what happens after the ending.

Still in the fantasy they say goodbye to the group and return to the conference where there is a message awaiting them, asking them to write to the group they have just visited and give them feedback. This is requested to be in the form of:

- What do you think was most positive about the group that needed to be built on?
- What do you think was most problematic that needs to be changed?
- What is one new thing that you think the group should introduce?

Still in role, people come out of the fantasy journey and actually write their letter from their assumed role to their own group. Having signed off and de-roled, they then read either their own or each other's letters to the group and the issues are collected under the three different headings.

This can provide an agenda for exploring changes in how the group functions, leading to a re-contracting stage. But it is also possible to go deeper in exploring the unconscious dynamics.

Exploring the group dynamics

Some useful statements that can be used in exploring the deeper, uncon-scious dynamics of groups are:

- The unwritten rules of this group are . . .
- What I find it hard to admit about my work is . . .
- What I think we avoid talking about here is . . .
- What I hold back on saying about other people here is . . .
- The hidden agendas that this group carries are . . .

Sculpting the group

This is an approach taken from sociodrama which we have adapted and developed for exploring the underlying dynamics of teams and groups. It comprises the following stages:

- *Stage 1*: the group is asked to find objects or symbols that represent what is at the heart or core of the group. These are placed in the centre of the room.
- *Stage 2*: without discussing it, the group members are asked to stand up and move around until they can find a place that symbolically represents where they are in the group (i.e. how far are they from the centre? Who are they close to and who are they distant from?) Then they are asked to take up a statuesque pose that typifies how they are in the group. This often takes several minutes as each person's move is affected by the moves of the others.
- *Stage 3*: each person is invited to make a statement beginning: 'In this position in the group I feel . . .'
- *Stage 4*: all the members are given the opportunity to explore how they would like to move to a different position in the group and what such a move would entail for them and from others. For example, one person who has sculpted on the outside of the group might say that they would ideally like to be right in the middle of the group. Having verbalized this desire, they would be invited to find their own way of moving into the centre and seeing what that shift felt like for them and for the others in the middle.
- *Stage 5*: the group is asked to reframe using the following questions: If this group were a family what sort of family would it be? Who would be in what role? Who would be the identified patient? etc. Or if this group were a television programme which programme would it be? Again who would be in what role and what would be the transactions? It is also possible for groups to try out their own frames. There are countless possibilities – meals, animals, countries, modes of transport, myths, Shakespearean plays, etc.
- *Stage 6*: then a chair is introduced as the 'creative consultant's chair'. Each person is invited to go and sit in it and to make the statement: 'If I were the creative consultant to this group I would . . .' This gives the opportunity for each person to leave their own role-bound perspective and to see the whole system and make a comment from outside.

Exploring the wider context

As in individual supervision where Mode 7 focuses on the wider social and organizational context in which the work operates (see Chapter 6), it is also important to focus on the context that surrounds the boundary of the team. All teams and groups exist within a wider context which they are both affected by and affecting. Thus a social work team exists in the context of the clients it works with, the whole organization of which it is a part, the other agencies it works alongside, the ratepayers and the council that controls its activities.

A peer supervision group of psychotherapists may have a different context. The sorts of people they affect and are affected by may include their clients, their families and friends, their own therapists and any individual supervisors they also see.

This wider system can also be sculpted through what we call an 'enacted role set', as follows:

- *Stage 1*: the group or team brainstorms all the significant roles that are affected by and/or affect the group. It then selects the most important roles and relationships that need to be explored.
- *Stage 2*: one person takes on the role of each of these aspects of the wider system (e.g. one person represents all the clients, one person the partners of the group members, etc.).
- *Stage 3*: the group is symbolically placed in the middle of the room and the various roles place and sculpt themselves in relation to the group.
- *Stage 4*: each role makes three statements:
  What I offer this group is . . .
  What I expect from this group is . . .
  What I see happening in this group is . . .
- *Stage 5*: it is then possible to explore dramatically a dialogue between the group and the people and roles that it relates to.

Having completed this exercise the group can look at how it would like to change its relationship with those with whom it interrelates. Here is an example:

A community work team were exploring how they could improve their team's functioning. They did this in a two-day team development workshop. The first day they had worked on their internal dynamics, support and supervision arrangements and had given each other a lot of feedback. On the second day they wanted to explore how they could change their relationship with the wider network. They began by brainstorming to establish who were the significant others in the wider network who had a stake in how they operated. From this list they choose to explore their relationship with the following stakeholders:

- The senior management team
- The director of the community leisure department to whom they were responsible
- The community leisure committee
- The ratepayer
- The personnel department of the council
- The social work department
- The education department

All of these roles were taken on by the team members who sculpted themselves in a position in relation to the other stakeholders and to a chair that represented their community work team. Each person in role then used the three statements:

- What I offer this team is . . .
- What I expect from this team is . . .
- What I see happening in this team is . . .

There was much laughter, amusement and surprise as they found they were able to say many challenging things about their own team, when speaking from the role of the other stakeholders. They were also able to explore dramatically the relationship with some of these stakeholders by creating a dialogue in which one team member would speak for the team and another would respond in the role, for example, of the education department.

Conclusion

Whether you work in a team, or have supervision in a group or peer group, regular attention needs to be paid to the dynamics that are operating within the process. In supervision groups, as in any other group, it is important to create a balance between focusing on the task, the individuals within the group and the group maintenance activities. The task needs will centre on attending to the improvement of the work done with clients by the group members. The individual needs include the need for support, reassurance, approval, acceptance, etc. The group maintenance needs include the issues of competitiveness, rivalry, authority, inclusion/exclusion, subgrouping, etc.

Where there are good group or team supervisions, they will try to see that all three types of needs are attended to and are in some degree of alignment with each other. However, the team leader is not only someone who can attend to the dynamics, but also part of the dynamics that are operating. In addition, the team or group supervisors are inevitably limited in the amount they can be aware of in such a complex system. Thus there is a necessity to build some structures whereby the whole group is able to share in the responsibility for focusing not only on the task needs, but also on the individual and group maintenance needs.

Some structures can become a regular part of group supervision meetings, such as spending ten minutes at the end of each group, with each group member, saying 'What I have most appreciated about this session has been . . . What I have found most difficult about this session has been . . .' Other structures may take place at greater intervals, such as an agreement to have a review of how the group is functioning every three months, with structured feedback to the group facilitator and to each member.

Teams that work regularly and intensively together need also to take regular time away from the pressures of the front line work to stand back and look at how they are individually and collectively functioning, and how they relate to the wider system in which they operate. This may take the form of an away day, or a team development workshop, or sessions with an outside consultant, or it may be part of a larger organizational change and development programme.

Whichever way a team or group decides to manage their own dynamics, it is important to remember that the time to start focusing on what is happening in the process is when things are going well, not when the group or team is in a crisis. When the levels of conflict, hurt and fear rise it becomes much more difficult to see what is happening and to take the risk of making changes. However, for some teams it is only when they hit a crisis that they create the motivation to face what is happening and sometimes 'crises create the heat in which new learning can be forged' (Hawkins 1986).

Supervising networks

Introduction

In the previous chapter we advocated the need for supervision at all levels – the individual, the team, the department and the organization. We also recommend that each level is supervised as a whole entity (e.g. the department is supervised with regard to how it functions *as* a department). This supervision is essential if each level, whether it be in a social work department, health service or school, is going to provide a measure of containment, holding and understanding for what happens within it.

The bucket theory of containment and displacement

We sometimes describe the containment process in a way that one organization called 'the bucket theory'. All helping organizations are, by their very nature, importing distress, disturbance, fragmentation and need. These are usually met by individual workers, who, if they are empathically relating to the client's distress, will experience parallel distress and sometimes disturbance and fragmentation within themselves. How much of this they will be able to contain and work through will depend on the size of their emotional container (or bucket); will relate to their personality, their emotional maturity and professional development; to the amount of pressure and stress they are currently under at work and at home; and, most important, to the quality and regularity of the supervision they receive.

What is not contained at this level will lead to decreased functioning in the worker and can also lead to fragmentation in the team. This comes about because workers who are stressed most often act out this stress on their colleagues. They can get irritable with the secretary, angry with their boss and non-cooperative with their colleagues. Fights can develop about who is responsible for what, and arguments flare up over duty rotas. Team meetings begin to start later and later and become more fractious.

In Chapter 10 we talked about the need for the team to take stock of how they were functioning, individually and as a whole unit. Good team supervision increases the ability of the team to contain pressure, stress and disturbance.

What the team does not contain can once again spill further out into the department or organization. Communication channels are often the first to suffer, with projections increasing both from the team onto management and other teams, but also onto the team from other parts of the organization.

The team can become either the identified patient or the scapegoat for the organization – their problem child (see the section on the pathologizing culture in Chapter 12, p. 170). Being either the identified patient or the scapegoat means that the team has not only its own problems but can have the disturbance from elsewhere in the organization projected onto it.

The organization needs good regular supervision and time when it stands back and reflects on its own health and functioning. Particularly in times of cuts in resources this is essential, but often ignored. The result is that consultant psychiatrists or directors of services stop working cooperatively and start to fight each other for diminishing resources, while basic-grade workers retreat back into the enclaves of their own teams.

Some of this organizational supervision needs to be done by the leader within the organization. As Mao Tse-tung said, the job of a leader is to give back to the people clearly what the people give to the leader confusedly. However, few heads of caring organizations receive good training in the skills required for supervisory overview and leadership of the organizational processes. Being a leader requires different and additional skills from being a good manager.

Also, no matter how good the leadership and 'helicopter skills' of consultant psychiatrists, directors of social services or heads of schools, they will always be part of the organizational system they are also trying to support and supervise. This means that they will also be part of the problems of that system, and unconsciously trapped within the perspective of their particular organizational culture.

What the organization does not contain, process and understand, can then spill over the boundaries of the whole organization and get played out between professions and organizations. This is not only enormously costly to all the helping professions, but very hard to supervise. Even so, some form of outside consultancy supervision is nearly always necessary.

Here are three case studies of a client's process being enacted between a variety of professional agencies. We wish to explore how supervision both within and between these agencies could address the complex issues involved; how it could help the staff to work together in the interests of the client, rather than enact the client's process through interprofessional rivalries.

To avoid breaching confidence, significant details of the cases have been changed and material from more than one case has been combined. However, the cases are in essence both true and typical of inter-organizational working as we experience it, working across a large number of different agencies.

The story of Andrew and his multiple therapeutic agencies

This case illustrates the way in which clients involve a whole network of helping professionals, often with different expectations. We include it in order to illustrate how in many situations clients are involved with a number of helping professionals, each of whom has a personal investment in and perspective of the client. In such cases the supervisor cannot afford to focus only on the worker and his or her relationship with the client, but must also focus outwards on the network of professionals and how they are enacting the various aspects of the client.

> The client, whom we will call Andrew, had spent several years in a special hospital for the criminally insane for burning down supermarkets. He had been sent to a halfway-house therapeutic community, in order to be gradually rehabilitated back into the community. Any reoffence would mean his immediate recall to the special hospital.
>
> The counsellor in the therapeutic community has not only to relate to the expressed needs of the client (Andrew) but also to cope with the pressures and demands of the personal and professional network with which Andrew is involved.
>
> The hospital is anxious that the therapeutic community ensures Andrew has no opportunity to reoffend. The local probation officer, who is greatly overworked, whose team is understaffed and who is thus under a great deal of pressure, wants the community to keep Andrew 'off her back'. Andrew has taken to phoning her every time he is at all upset or lonely in the community – a bit like the way a new boy at boarding school might phone his mother.
>
> Andrew's parents want the community to help Andrew to return to their very religious and Victorian values, the deviation from which they see as the start of his problems. They insist that the local priest calls regularly.
>
> The local authority, who are paying the fees for Andrew to be at the community, want to know when he will be starting work and thus reducing their financial burden.

Andrew himself is ambivalent. Part of him wants to open up and explore himself in the groups and counselling; but part of him wants the staff by magic to remove his seething anger or to give him the early parenting that he never received. He presents as very cool and together, with no problems at all. All his anxieties and fears he feeds into the other professionals outside the community. The counsellor cannot understand why the others are all getting so worried.

The counsellor needs to be helped by their supervisor to see how Andrew's process is being acted out on a network level. The supervisor also had the responsibility to work with the network to help them understand not only how they are part of the therapeutic team, but that their behaviour is also likely to be a symptom of Andrew's process.

In any situation where there is more than one helping professional involved, it is important that the network meet and decide both who is the key worker, and whose task it is to manage and supervise the helping network (this ideally should be the supervisor of the key worker).

The story of Brenda and spreading anxiety

Brenda, a London girl in her early twenties is seeing a counsellor who is based at a GP practice. Her father died the previous year and her mother, who has always suffered from mild depression, is unable to give her much support. The girl is unable to cope at college, and the GP has given her low-grade anti-depressants and sent her on to the resident female counsellor. The counsellor works slowly and steadily with the client seeing her fortnightly for hourly sessions. The client is quite defensive and only slowly opens up. If there is a very emotional session, the client tends to miss the following appointment.

After a year's work Brenda is still having difficulty and overeating, although she has been back at college for six months. She develops low-back pain which again necessitates her missing college. The counsellor mentions an osteopath that she herself goes to see. Brenda goes to the osteopath and at first is delighted. The treatment seems to ease the pain and makes her feel a lot better about herself. Then suddenly a session with the male osteopath inadvertently awakens feelings about sexual interference by a man (unnamed) and, as a consequence, she stops seeing both the osteopath and the counsellor.

Brenda gets worse and the GP, who is now anxious, refers her to the local psychiatric outpatients department, where a young registrar decides to take her on for psychotherapy, without any prior consultation with the counsellor.

Clearly Brenda's process is being played out, not within a contained therapeutic situation, but through multiple transference onto four different professionals. The professionals are not only failing to work together to bring about some integration of the various fragments of Brenda's process, but are also enacting some of the typical interprofessional rivalries endemic within and between each of their roles.

Any situation, where splitting and multiple transference are ensuring that no one helper can work with the whole process, requires the difficult supervision process of a case conference. In this case the case conference needs to involve the GP, counsellor, osteopath and psychiatric registrar and perhaps even the tutor from the college. To make this happen would require overcoming several major hurdles:

• The client is working unconsciously to keep the various professionals apart.
• It is unlikely that all these busy professionals would be willing to give the time for this case conference concerning a client who is not in a major crisis (yet).
• The different professional trainings militate against interprofessional work. Orthodox and complementary medical practitioners mostly distrust each other and avoid working together. Some medical training teaches doctors to treat other staff as 'ancillary paramedics'.
• There would be issues of who convenes such a meeting and who would provide the supervisory overview. If no one provides this overview, there would be a distinct danger that the case conference would just enact the client's process, rather than come to a better understanding and a new way of working with it.

Clearly, supervision could have helped this situation. The place where it could have created the most change would have been in the supervision of the psychiatric registrar who needed different supervision from what he was receiving. He attended a weekly supervision group with the consultant psychiatrist where he would present a case only once every six weeks, and this would be focused on in terms of the one-to-one relationship. In this case such supervision would tend to ignore the wider social network where most of Brenda's process was being enacted.

It is probably the psychiatric consultant who could best call a case conference and, instead of the psychiatric service taking over the therapeutic work, its skills and resources could be used to relocate and help support the therapeutic work back in the community, with the front line workers.

The GP team needed supervision to explore why the GPs referred patients to the psychiatric services, often out of a somewhat panic reaction to a deterioration in a client, and before first exploring the case with their own counsellors and health visitors who were also involved. Often the GPs referred to the counsellor clients who were burdening them with their neuroses, but, if the same client later turned up at surgery in a way that was disturbed or disturbing, the GPs would tend to refer to the psychiatric hospital without first checking what was happening in the counselling. This would happen despite the fact that the counsellor was better trained therapeutically than the junior registrars who would normally see clients at the hospital.

Supervision could also increase the amount that the other involved professionals learned from this experience. The counsellor could have been better supervised in exploring her unconscious motivation in referring the client to her own male osteopath.

The osteopath also needed supervision that would help him be alert to signals from women clients who had a history of sexual abuse and also help him learn how to work with such clients in an appropriate, sensitive and therapeutic way, and when to refer on to a female colleague.

The story of Carol and sexual abuse

Carol, a sixth-form student at a boarding school in the Midlands, came to the psychiatric hospital near her home in the Home Counties. She had been anorexic for two years. She had a sister of 15 and two half-brothers who were twins aged 3. Her own father had left home when she was 12 and she still idolized him.

Carol initially confided to her schoolteacher that she had been interfered with sexually by two men – both unknown. This was shared with the hospital. Carol was first seen by the male consultant, but then referred by him to a female nurse-therapist who was part of his team, and whom he supervised. There was soon evidence of splitting and multiple transference with the teacher becoming the 'bad person' and the therapist the 'good and helpful' adult. This splitting later spread to the two involved organizations. Carol had gone to hospital at Christmas as an in-patient, rather than go home. She told the school that she wished to do so again at Easter and they told her that, if she did, she would not be allowed back at the school. Despite this she was admitted to hospital and was treated twice weekly by psychodynamic psychotherapy from the same nurse-therapist.

During the next three months, without any behavioural techniques being used, she put on over a stone in weight. As she did so, she became progressively more distressed and unhappy and required medical treatment with an anti-depressant to help her sleep and to help her feel less distressed.

It came to light in the therapy that Carol had been sexually abused by her stepfather. It was thought that this abuse was only mild, but the precaution was taken of informing the family GP in case the younger twins were at risk. The GP was confident that the twins were well and that there was no sign of abuse, physical or sexual.

It was thought that the abuse by the stepfather was not serious enough to warrant further action and the breaking of the patient's confidentiality. As a precaution the supervisor contacted the Medical Defence Union and asked under what circumstances confidentiality could be broken. He was informed that, if a serious crime had been committed by someone, then it was appropriate to break confidentiality. The local health authority regulations suggested that a wide variety of people should be informed at the slightest suggestion of a child being at risk of abuse. This included the chief medical officer, social services, the police and the GPs involved.

Carol then informed the psychotherapist that the abuse had been severe and had involved full sexual intercourse for about two years. The therapist and supervisor later discovered that she had informed the therapist the day before her sister was due to return home – i.e. that she was unconsciously protecting her sister. When asked about her sister she at first said that her sister was not at risk, but then explained that the sister was not at risk as long as she herself was at home to protect her.

After receiving the information, the supervisor arranged to contact the mother and stepfather to confront them about the situation. He felt that he was now responsible to protect the at-risk sister, but was still in a dilemma about whether or not to involve social services. His previous experience of involving social services and the police in such situations had not been good, for it had led to increased distress within the family, but rarely to any resolution of the family situation, or acceptance of responsibility by either the perpetrator or the mother.

The supervisor and therapist were also anxious about breaking confidentiality. The client had been informed that all information shared in the therapy was confidential, but that on occasions the psychotherapist would need to discuss the case with her supervisor. The therapist and supervisor were both beginning to feel distressed, anxious and angry themselves.

The supervisor rang the relevant social service team leader to discuss the situation in theory without mentioning names but, after a short discussion, made a unilateral decision to make an official warning of possible child abuse.

The supervisor explored the situation in his own supervision. What had made him change his mind, and why was he carrying all the responsibility for the patient, the patient's sister and the therapist? He explored how he felt not only totally responsible for the whole system, but also helpless and vulnerable. He also explored how he identified both with the patient (he himself had experienced a lot of distress as a boy) and with the perpetrator (being male, a father and someone whose job gave him power over people).

The case was extremely intrusive and produced distress in the supervisor and therapist, even when they were not at work. They half shared their feelings in an interdisciplinary staff meeting, but this led them to feel unsupported and as if they were receiving all the disowned anger and hostility of the other staff.

Through supervision the psychiatrist was helped gradually to express the great mixture of feelings that he was carrying in relation to this case. Only when these had been supportively listened to by his supervisor could the psychiatrist be challenged about why he was taking on board feelings and responsibilities that did not belong to him. He became aware of how he tended to use omnipotence as a defence and how this was not only a personal trait, but also something that was part of the culture of medical training.

The psychiatrist also began to explore his failure to challenge the therapist to confront the situation with the patient. Instead he had enacted once again the conflict's being taken one stage further away from the family, where it belonged, and being carried by others. First the abused daughter was forced to take the conflict which belonged to her stepfather. Then the teacher and therapist started to carry the conflict for the girl. Then the psychiatrist took away the responsibility. The psychiatrist's supervisor could have been next in line, had they not recognized the process as it was happening and started to put the responsibility firmly back where it belonged.

The nurse-therapist needed support from the psychiatrist in order to point out to Carol how she was unconsciously worried about her sister's being abused. She also needed to help Carol recognize how she was feeling responsible, while understandably not wanting to accuse her stepfather, but also secretly wanting to punish him – not only for the abuse, but for being the intruder in the family position that rightfully belonged to her real father.

By the therapist's allowing the psychiatrist to take over, she was leaving the process to become once more one between a young girl and an older man in authority, thus replicating the role of opting out and turning a blind eye that the mother had played.

Carol and the therapist needed, then, to be active participants in deciding how to manage the dilemma. Even if Carol opted out from any responsibility of confronting the situation, she needed to be constantly informed of what the therapist and the psychiatrist were doing.

Then, instead of the family's being handed over to either the social services or the police to deal with, the social services should have been brought in to meet with Carol and the therapist (with the psychiatrist as supervisor to the case conference) to work as a team on how to tackle the situation. If it became clear that the stepfather had carried out a criminal act, then the police would have to be added to this therapeutic team.

Throughout this process, it is important that the distress and vulnerability do not get separated from those carrying the responsibility and potency. The two must be kept together in order to avoid splitting and to make contained therapeutic work possible.

The story of sexual abuse in Cleveland

The Butler-Sloss Report (1988) that followed the enquiry into how cases of suspected sexual abuse were handled in Cleveland recommended much greater cooperation between the health service, social services, police and GPs. One of the difficulties in putting such an important and valid recommendation into practice is that of providing good supervision in these multidisciplinary settings. As we have illustrated in the two previous case studies, it is not enough for there to be good supervision within the respective disciplines; there must also be supervision of the whole therapeutic network.

One simple model which can assist in understanding such cases, and how they can get played out between agencies, is the triangle of persecutor, victim and rescuer. In this model not only do each of the roles get caught within the system, but the roles can suddenly shift around. Let us illustrate this from the Cleveland situation (Butler-Sloss 1988; see also Campbell 1988).

The situation began with two doctors believing they had diagnosed sexual abuse in over 100 cases. They recommended to the social services that these children be taken into care. (At this stage the triangle appears as shown in Figure 11.1.)

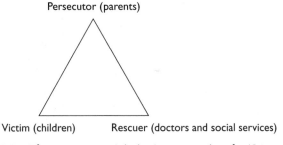

Persecutor (parents)

Victim (children)   Rescuer (doctors and social services)

Figure 11.1   The persecutor/victim/rescuer triangle (Stage 1)

There soon developed a massive outcry from the parents and disbelief from the media that sexual abuse could be so widespread. The local MP and a number of local and national papers started a crusade to rescue the victimized families. (The triangle now appears as shown in Figure 11.2.)

But, as in many such triangles, the rescuers turned on the persecutors, they called for their dismissal and painted them as villains who were evil, rather than as dedicated professionals trying to do their jobs. The female doctor involved was portrayed by some popular newspapers as almost a witch, intent on breaking up innocent families. (The triangle becomes as shown in Figure 11.3.)

Like all such processes, this could have continued for a long time. The only way to stop the process is for one of the elected

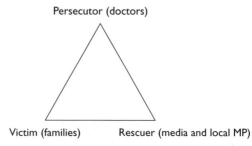

Figure 11.2   The persecutor/victim/rescuer triangle (Stage 2)

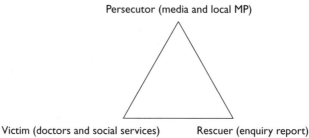

Figure 11.3   The persecutor/victim/rescuer triangle (Stage 3)

rescuers not to turn to persecuting the previous persecutors, but to understand the process as a whole. In this respect Butler-Sloss and her team produced a remarkably effective report, avoiding being drawn into the triangle with the hasty throwing of blame and instead bringing good supervisory understanding of the whole situation, in which there were not 'goodies and baddies', but in which there were well-intentioned people on all sides who had made mistakes or been misguided.

One of the key pieces of learning that we would like to see come out of the very painful and costly Cleveland situation is that all staff, even if they are senior paediatricians or social service directors need some form of regular supervision which helps them question their own work in a supportive way, so that they do not retreat into omnipotent conviction on the one hand, or turn a blind eye on the other. Let it not be forgotten that the professionals in the Cleveland case discovered incidents of child abuse that other professionals may well have ignored.

Conclusion

The Butler-Sloss Report (1988) rightly called for much better cooperation between all the helping agencies. What still has to be further developed is the need for senior staff in social work, hospitals, general practice, the police force, etc. to be trained not only in good supervision practice, but also in how to supervise complex, interdisciplinary situations.

We have argued elsewhere in this book that all first-line supervisors should receive training in supervision (see Chapter 8). We would also strongly advocate that those who supervise from more senior positions within an organization should be given the opportunity to go on an advanced supervision skills training course that particularly focuses on working with complex organizational and interprofessional situations.

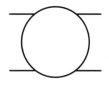

Part Four

The organizational context

Towards a learning culture

Introduction

In the seven-eyed supervisor model of supervision (see Chapter 6), Mode 7 involves focusing on the wider context in which the supervision happens. One of the core contexts is the culture of the organization in which the therapeutic work and the supervision is happening. In Chapter 3 we mentioned how the culture of the organization can not only influence and frame the supervision, but even block effective supervision from happening (see p. 27). In Chapter 7 we explored the wider societal cultures which impact on the work with both clients and supervisees.

In this chapter we will illustrate different types of culture that are prevalent in helping organizations and how these affect supervision. In Chapter 13 we will explore how to bring about change in organizations to produce a culture that is more conducive to staff learning and supervision.

What is culture?

In Chapter 7, following Herskowitz (1948), we defined culture as the different explicit and implicit assumptions and values that influence the behaviour and social artefacts of different groups.

The understanding of culture derived from anthropology has been more recently used to understand the deeper context of organizations. McLean and Marshall, in their book *Working with Cultures: A Workbook for People in Local Government* (1988), quote the definitions of various writers, including themselves, who have studied organizational cultures. Organizational culture is:

> ... how things are done around here.
>
> (Ouchi and Johnson 1978)

> ... values and expectations which organization members come to share.
>
> (Van Maanen and Schein 1979)

> ... the social glue that holds the organization together.
>
> (Baker 1980)

> ... the way of thinking, speaking and (inter)acting that characterize a certain group.
>
> (Braten 1983)

> ... the taken for granted and shared meanings that people assign to their social surroundings.
>
> (Wilkens 1983)

> ... the collection of traditions, values, policies, beliefs and attitudes that constitute a pervasive context for everything we do and think in an organization.
>
> (McLean and Marshall 1983)

McLean and Marshall (1988) go on to explore how culture is carried not only in the high-profile symbols of an organization such as logos, prestige events and training programmes, but also in the low-profile symbols: 'Essentially everything in an organization is symbolic; patterns of meaning in the culture mirrored in multiple forms of expression – in language, relationships, paperwork (or its lack), physical settings ... how meetings are called and conducted, who sits next to whom, who interrupts, what time different topics are given, what lines of reasoning prevail and so on'.

Thus the organization's culture of supervision can be seen in the high-profile symbol of its policy about supervision, but can be more accurately seen in its low-profile symbols: where supervision takes place, who supervises, how regular the sessions are, what importance is given to them and what priority they have when time pressures necessitate something being cancelled.

There can be a split between the high and low cultures which is similar to the distinction that Argyris and Schön (1978) make concerning 'espoused theory' and 'theory in action'. Some social services departments have a policy with grand phrases about the key importance of supervision and ongoing development and support of staff; yet supervision is the first thing to be cancelled when there are staff shortages.

Other writers have referred to the organizational culture as representing the unconscious of the organization, as it is embedded in the ways of experiencing what happens; thus they see culture as less to do with what is done and more to do with how it is viewed, heard and experienced.

Levels of culture

Hawkins (1994c, 1997) has built on this work as well as the writings of Geertz (1973) and Schein (1985) to develop a model of five levels of organizational culture, each level being fundamentally influenced by the levels beneath it:

- *Artefacts*: the rituals, symbols, art, buildings, mission statements, policies etc.
- *Behaviours*: the patterns of relating and behaving; the cultural norms.
- *Mind sets*: the ways of seeing the world and framing experience.
- *Emotional ground*: the patterns of feeling that shape the making of meaning.
- *Motivational roots*: the fundamental aspirations that drive choices.

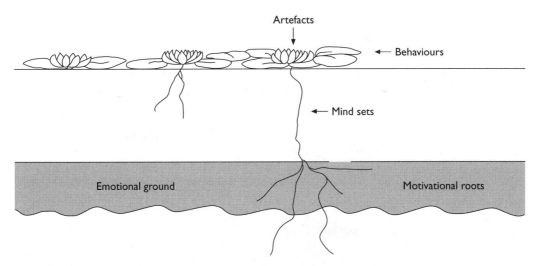

Figure 12.1 The five levels of organizational culture (after Schein 1985)

Like Schein (1985) we have utilized the water lily to illustrate this model (see Figure 12.1). The water lily illustrates that what is most noticeable about culture is the artefacts: the building, logo, mission statement, annual report, etc., which equate with the flower of the lily. Just above the surface of the water the leaves of the water lily represent the typical behaviours of the culture. If the artefacts demonstrate the espoused values of the organization, the behaviours show the values in action. Many organizations have run into difficulties when there has been a rift between their rhetoric (what they say) and the reality of what they do. Beneath the surface are the mind sets, which hold in place the belief systems of a culture. These in turn grow out of the emotional ground or climate of the organization. The motivational roots are about the alignment of individual purposes and motivations with those of the collective organization.

Cultural dynamics that lead to degenerate supervision

In working as organizational consultants to a number of health services, social work departments, probation teams, counselling and psychotherapy organizations, and voluntary organizations, we have come to recognize certain distinct and typical cultural patterns that exist across all the helping professions. We have called these 'cultural dynamics':

- Hunt the personal pathology
- Strive for bureaucratic efficiency
- Watch your back
- Driven by crisis
- The addictive organization

We do not want to create another typology or classification of organizational cultures, as there are already many in existence (Handy 1976; Harrison 1994). Rather we would see these patterns as recognizable system dynamics within the dominant organizational culture. Indeed, an organization may contain a number of these dynamics at the same time. Each of these cultural dynamics will create different motivations, emotional feelings, attitudes, behaviours and policy around supervision. Each, in time, will lead to degenerate and even perverse forms of supervision.

Hunt the personal pathology

This culture is based on seeing all problems as located in the personal pathology of individuals. It is highly influenced by psychodynamic casework theories, but has little understanding of either group dynamics or how systems function.

If there is a problem of one department not functioning, the first thing that managers with this cultural mind set do is to look for the problem *person*. This is often the head of the department. The belief is that, if we can cure the sick individual, the department will be healthy. If the sick individual does not seem to respond to treatment, then you look for a way of removing him or her.

This approach can happen at all levels of the organization and can degenerate very quickly into scapegoating. The residential home for children will report that all their troubles would be solved if only they could find a way of moving young Tommy somewhere else. However, when and if they do move Tommy to another home, then Sally becomes the problem child, and so on.

We have also worked with teams where the team has located all its problems in one member. 'If only Jack would take early retirement', they all sigh. This attitude ensures that they are impotent in addressing the collective team problems, as you cannot solve a problem that you do not first own as, in part, yours.

In one large voluntary organization, individual homes were elected one at a time to be 'the problem child' of the organization. The unspoken belief was that if *this* home could be sorted out then the whole organization would be problem free!

In this culture supervision can become problem centred and aimed at treating pathology. This can create a subtle form of paranoia in the supervisees who fear that, if they do not keep the focus on the pathology of their clients, they themselves may become 'a suitable case for treatment'. On one of our five and a half day supervision skills courses, one head of an old people's home went back to his home to introduce supervision as his mid-course project. He announced in the staff meeting that he was going to introduce supervision and that he was going to start with James. James immediately exclaimed: 'Why pick on me – what have I done wrong?'

In this culture we also find that staff will sometimes say: 'I do not need supervision this week as I do not have any problems'. Team leaders will tell us that they give supervision on an ad hoc basis 'when problems arise'. This culture creates the belief that, if you go for supervision, you must have a problem or, more perniciously, there must be something wrong with you.

This attitude is intensified by the policy of giving students the most regular supervision, the new staff the next largest amount, and senior staff no supervision at all. The message in this low-profile symbol is very clear: 'if you want to get on in this culture, demonstrate that you do not need supervision'; and 'Supervision is only for the untrained, inexperienced or needy'.

Supervision caught in this cultural pattern can degenerate into pseudo-therapy or 'let us both analyse the client'.

Strive for bureaucratic efficiency

This form of organizational culture has been extensively written about by Isobel Menzies (1970) in her classic work on nursing cultures in hospitals entitled *The Functioning of Social Systems as a Defence against Anxiety*. This form of culture is high on task orientation and low on personal relatedness. There are policies and memos to cover all eventualities and all meetings have tight agendas.

In this culture supervision is mostly concerned with checking that all the tasks have been done correctly. We have worked with team leaders who have arrived at supervision with their staff with an agenda which is like a mechanic's checklist. When they have ticked off all the items, the supervision is finished. They may say as they walk out of the door, 'Oh by the way, how are you?' but they may not stay to hear the answer.

For the supervisee the supervision is one of reporting back what they have and have not achieved. Again the culture is problem centred but this time the ethos is that of mechanics rather than sickness and treatment. There is little space for understanding in the rush for tidy answers.

Watch your back

This form of organizational culture becomes prevalent where the climate is either very politicized or highly competitive. Some departments are riven with internal power battles between subgroups. Sometimes this is on political or racial grounds, but sometimes it is more to do with cliques and who is on whose side. In this atmosphere much energy goes in ensuring that the other sides do not have all the information for fear of the possibility that they will use what they know against you. Meanwhile you make sure that you use everything you can to expose the other group.

Charles Handy (1976) in his book *Understanding Organizations* points out: 'In all organizations there are individuals and groups competing for influence or resources, there are differences of opinion and of values, conflicts of priorities and of goals. There are pressure groups and lobbies, cliques and cabals, rivalries and contests, clashes of personality and bonds of alliance'. Often in the helping professions power and rivalry are denied and then become even more powerful as shadow forces that are not recognized (see Chapter 2).

This form of culture can also develop in a very hierarchical organization where the climate is set so that those who 'keep their noses clean' will get promotion. This leads staff to ensure that they cover up any difficulties, inadequacies or problems they are having, as it would be detrimental to share these: 'I have regular meetings with my supervisor, but always steer clear of my problems in coping with my report work. Can I trust her? I need her backing for my career progress, but will she use this sort of thing as evidence against me? There are some painful areas that are never discussed but need discussing so much. It is an awful dilemma for me' (Fineman 1985: 52).

What happens to supervision in this culture depends on who your supervisor is. If you are supervised by one of your own power subgroup, it becomes conspiratorial and falls into discussing 'how awful the other sides are'. If you are supervised by someone who is 'one of them' or a manager you do not trust, then it is centred on covering up, putting a good gloss on the work you have done and making sure you are seen in a good light.

Driven by crisis

On one of our courses, where we were teaching the archetypal roles of helping (see Chapter 4), one of the course members suggested Superman as an archetypal role that some supervisors play. We were doubtful about this until, on our very next course, there was a very quiet head of a children's home who sat taking notes in the corner. He was dressed more traditionally than the other course members, with a tie and jacket. Added to this, his glasses and studiousness made him seem more like a librarian than a social worker! In the middle of the second day a message arrived for him to say that there was a problem at his home. He jumped up in the middle of the session and seemed to grow before our very eyes. 'I must *go* – there is a crisis in my home', he exclaimed loudly, as he swept out of the room. It was clear that this head of home became much more alive when there was a good crisis for him to handle, and we are sure that his clients duly obliged by producing regular crises for him to respond to.

We have visited other homes and departments where the staff never have uninterrupted time to meet, as one of them is always responding to the latest crisis. In this type of organizational culture there is never time to reflect properly on the work or the plan ahead – the focus is always on the intensity of the moment. As in the story above, clients pick up this culture and realize that, if you want to get attention around here, produce a crisis.

When we first worked in a halfway house for the adult mentally ill, cutting one's wrists seemed to be contagious. Even those who had no previous record of wrist-cutting seemed to be starting. The staff were always rushing to the local casualty department, holding hastily bandaged arms. Eventually we managed to stem the flood of crises long enough to hold a staff meeting to reflect on this. We realized that those who cut their wrists were getting far more attention than the other residents. We, as a staff group, were perpetuating this particular crisis culture. The staff made it clear to the community that in future they would not visit clients in the hospital who had overdosed or cut their wrists and would instead give more attention to the clients who avoided such behaviour. Immediately the number of crises dropped dramatically.

In other organizations staff have told us that the only way to get time with the director is to have a crisis in your section – then the director, who is always too busy to see you, sends out an urgent summons for you to see them. In another voluntary organization the assistant director would fly in by plane or helicopter and give supervision in the nearest café, pub or in the car, before flying back to 'base'.

In this culture supervision is rarely a high priority and will get cancelled regularly, always for very important reasons. When it does happen, it often creates the atmosphere of being in a tremendous rush and having to solve problems in a hurry before the next wave or onslaught bears down upon us.

The addictive organization

Since writing the first edition of this book, both of us have been involved in working with the concept of the addictive organization. In 1991 we wrote a review (Hawkins and Shohet 1991) of the book by Ann Wilson Schaef and Diane Fassel, entitled *The Addictive Organization* (1990), in which we described the four major forms of addiction in an organization as:

- Where the key person in an organization is an addict. We have known directors and chief executives who have been alcohol dependent or workaholics, who's whole life was absorbed in their professional life.
- Where there are a number of people in the organization replicating their addictive or co-dependent patterns. In another book, Schaef (1992) quotes the shocking statistic that in one study of nurses in the USA 83 per cent were found to be the eldest children of an alcoholic parent.
- Where the organization itself is an addictive substance, eliciting high degrees of dependency and workaholism from its members. This can be fuelled by the covert messages that say if you want to get on here, you do not take lunch breaks or leave until late in the evening.
- Where the organization itself is the addict. Here, the organizational system functions in a parallel way to an addictive personality. The organization becomes unable to face its own truth and confront its own difficulties, and starts to rationalize and defend dishonest and abusive behaviour.

One of the key notions in the field of addiction that is used by Schaef and Fassel (1990) is that of co-dependence. These are the partners, family or work colleagues who service, accommodate and protect the addict and their addiction. In the case of the addictive organization the entire workforce can be either acting addictively or colluding as a co-dependent.

In our article we invite the reader to reflect on an organization they either work for or supervise, and to answer the following questions:

- What are the 'family secrets' in the organization – the things that most people know about, but which cannot be talked about publicly or openly? Why are they not being commented on?
- Whose behaviour cannot be commented on or confronted?
- What are the lost ideals and motivating visions that once inspired those working in the organization?
- How many of the following rules that make up the dysfunctional family system (Subby 1984) apply to the organization?
  - It is not okay to talk about problems
  - Feelings should not be expressed openly
  - Communication is best if indirect, with one person acting as a messenger between two others
  - Be strong, good right and perfect
  - Make us proud
  - Don't be selfish

- Do as I say, not as I do
- It is not okay to play or be playful
- Don't rock the boat

If the organization has a culture of addiction, then it is important to interrupt the denial and dishonesty before attempting any other mode of development. Schaef and Fassel (1990) are sharply critical of many of the approaches to organization development that facilitate the client organization in being more skilful in staying addicted. They criticize:

- stress management programmes that provide individual managers with techniques to keep their workaholism even longer and more intensively;
- programmes in worker participation which become subtle ways of staying in control;
- mission statements that become a 'fix' – 'It reassures us that we are important and do important work'.

Shifting the cultural dynamic

The first step in shifting the cultural dynamic is to become aware of the culture. This is not as easy as it sounds, for in the words of the Chinese proverb, 'The last one to know about the sea is the fish'. Our current favourite definition of organizational culture is: 'what you stop noticing when you have worked somewhere for over three months'. Newcomers and visitors can often offer insightful feedback on your culture. There are also a number of exercises devised by the Bath Consultancy Group for accessing your own culture (Hawkins 1994c):

- looking at typical patterns of behaviour;
- collecting stories of organizational heroes, villains and fools;
- common metaphors;
- staging the unofficial induction programme;
- listing the unwritten rules, etc.

Using such exercises a group can produce a detailed description of your own organizational culture, at all the five levels previously mentioned.

Just bringing the organizational culture to the surface can lead to some degree of change. Individuals and organizations may suddenly realize that they do not have to carry on with the same beliefs and ways of working that have become institutionalized. Their new awareness leads to greater choice.

Having *surfaced an awareness* of their culture, an organization can move on to exploring how they wish this culture to shift. One way of starting this process is known as 'three-way sorting' (Hawkins 1994c). The team or organization may have generated a great amount of data about their culture from carrying out the above exercises – they are then asked to create three new lists:

- What lies at the heart of the organization? What are the core values, the root metaphors, etc.? What needs to be safeguarded and nurtured as the organization moves on?
- What can be discarded, is no longer appropriate and has outlived its usefulness? What is the excess baggage that is slowing down change?
- What needs to be incorporated, acquired, done differently – how does the change represent a time of possibility and opportunity?

This exercise represents the first step towards creating a cultural shift. To really change the culture in a sustainable way is a much longer and more difficult process which is beyond the focus of this particular book. We have written about this elsewhere (Hawkins 1994c, 1997). However, we propose that all helping professions need to move away from the above forms of dysfunction and towards a more embedded learning and developmental culture.

Creating a learning developmental culture

Supervision best flourishes in a learning developmental culture. Such a culture is built on a belief system that a great deal of the work in all helping professions is about creating the environment and relationships in which clients learn about themselves and their environment, in a way that leaves them with more options than they arrived with. Further, it believes that helping professionals are best able to facilitate others to learn if they are supported in constantly learning and developing themselves. An organization that is learning and developing right from the top of the organization to the bottom is far more likely to be meeting the needs of its clients, because it is also meeting the needs of its staff. One of the authors has written extensively about the learning culture elsewhere (Hawkins 1979, 1980, 1986, 1991, 1994a, b), but we will summarize here the key attributes of such a culture and how they affect supervision.

- Learning and development are seen as continuous lifelong processes. Thus in a learning culture the most experienced and the most senior staff ensure that they have ongoing supervision or consultancy and do not see supervision as just for the untrained and inexperienced. The actions of the senior managers speak louder than their policy statements and it is important that they conspicuously exemplify the learning culture by, among other things, having supervision themselves.
- A learning culture emphasizes the potential that all the different work situations have for learning, both individually and collectively. Learning

is not just something that happens in the classroom or on a training programme, but is built into the very fabric of work.

- Problems and crises are seen as important opportunities for learning and development, both individually and organizationally. Major crises are seen as growth points and the culture is one where it is safe to take risks, as failures are seen as events to be learned from, not as evidence for the prosecution of individuals.

- Good practice emerges neither from an action culture that is always dealing with the latest problems and crises, nor from a theorizing culture that is withdrawing from the real issues to draw up theoretical policy papers. Good practice comes from staff, teams and departments that are well balanced in all parts of the learning cycle, which goes from *action*, to *reflection*, to *new thinking*, to *planning* and then back to *action* (see Kolb *et al.* 1971; Juch 1983).

- This means that supervision needs to avoid rushing for quick solutions, but also needs to avoid getting lost in abstract theorizing. Rather, it must start with reflecting on the concrete experience and try to make sense of this in a way that allows the experience to challenge one's own way of seeing and thinking about the world. But supervision must not stay at the point of new insight, but rather use this new insight to generate new options, evaluate these options and choose what new strategy to put into operation. This new action then needs to be reviewed in the following supervision so that the learning cycle does not become a one-circuit process.

- Learning becomes an important value in its own right. Supervisors carry the attitude 'How can I help these supervisees to maximize their learning in this situation so that they can help the client learn too?', rather than the attitude 'How can I ensure that the supervisees make no mistakes and do it the way I think is right?'

- Individuals and teams take time out to reflect on their effectiveness, learning and development. In a learning culture there are team development sessions or 'away days' (see Brown 1984 and Chapter 10). There are also 360-degree staff appraisals that go well beyond the senior grading the staff member on performance. They should involve a cooperative process of the staff members' appraising their own development, their own strengths and weaknesses and then receiving feedback on and refinement of their own appraisal from both their peers and their senior.

- A good appraisal system will focus, not just on performance, but also what the staff member has learned, how they have developed and how their learning and development can best proceed and be nurtured in the forthcoming period.

- There should be a high level of ongoing feedback, both from peers and between levels within the organization. Also, feedback would be encouraged from those with whom the work team or organization relate: customers, other helping organizations, professional networks, politicians, etc.

- Time and attention will be given to the transition of individuals: how new staff are welcomed and inducted into the team and organization;

how they are helped to go through leaving and changes in status within the organization. Time would be given to this in both team and individual supervision.

- Roles will be regularly reviewed and negotiated. They will be allocated not just on the basis of efficiency, but also on the potential that each role provides as a learning opportunity for its incumbent. This would include the role of supervisor which would not just be allocated to the automatic person in the hierarchy.
- In such a culture the learning does not reside just in individuals, who may up and leave. Rather, it is ensured that the learning happens at the team and organizational levels and is both recorded and lived in the developing culture.

Supervision, the learning organization and the learning profession

Where organizations have confronted the cultural dynamic that leads to degenerate supervision and have developed a healthier learning and developmental culture, there is likely to be effective individual learning and development. However, this is not enough, for there is still a danger that despite the learning of all the individuals, the organization itself will have stopped learning and developing.

Supervision can also be the place where a living profession breathes and learns. For too long we have reduced the concept of supervision to a cultural socialization process where the elders of the professional community shape the practice, behaviours, understanding, perceptions, feelings and motivations of the apprentices and noviciates.

All the approaches discussed in the cultural patterns above have learning flowing from the supervisor to the supervisee. The learning is about conforming to the pre-formed professional norms and precepts – the culture's written and unwritten rules. Certainly, both quality control and inducting newcomers into the professional collective wisdom are important aspects of supervision, but if supervision is reduced to just these two aspects, as is often the case, we create a self-reinforcing profession which ceases to learn and develop. Eventually the profession becomes ossified, operating more and more within well-worn grooves of practice.

David Bohm (1989: 73), who was an outstanding professor of nuclear physics and an eloquent follower of the spiritual teacher Krishnamurti, spoke about the challenge of creating self-renewing cultures, in organizations, professions and societies:

Therefore the key question is: is it possible to have a constantly creative culture? As soon as you set up a culture its meanings become repetitive and they begin to get in the way. Nevertheless we need a culture.

Nobody has solved the problem of how the vision can be constantly renewed. It becomes more static, more of a habit. The thing becomes

... a disposition which gradually gets fixed. It gets transmitted from one generation to the other as a disposition, and the people who pick it up don't understand it in the same way as the people who had it, because they are merely imitating the disposition and not understanding the meaning from which it came. They may understand part of it, but not as well as those who came before. Each time it is made a little weaker.

It's this repetition through generations which reinforces the habit to go along with the old ways of thinking and all the old social relationships and the old culture. Especially now this problem has to be solved if the civilizations are to survive. In the old days you could say 'well, a civilization could die and another one start up' but now with modern technology we may destroy the whole thing. The problem has become more urgent.

Supervision has a key challenge to move beyond the three central roles as defined by Kadushin (1976):

- Managerial (quality control)
- Educative (development of the supervisee)
- Supportive (ensuring the supervisee is able to process their experience, rather than be overwhelmed by it)

If we are to create learning professions that constantly renew their cultures, then supervision needs to become the learning lungs that assist the professional body in its learning, development and cultural evolution. This entails not only focusing on both supervisee and supervisor learning, but providing a dialogical container in which new learning can emerge in the space between the supervisor and supervisee. Supervision needs to be practised in a way that allows learning to emerge in the interaction between the three unique areas of experience that are brought into relationship with one another:

- The client situation and context
- The supervisee's experience and understanding
- The supervisor's experience and understanding

Too often we have seen supervision reduced to the exchange of pre-existent 'thoughts' and knowledge. The supervisee tells their supervisor what they have already thought and know about their client, and the supervisor shares their pre-existent knowledge about similar clients or processes.

One useful test to review whether a supervision session has provided new generative learning is to ask four questions at the end of the session:

- What have we learned that neither of us knew before we came into supervision?
- What have we learned that neither of us could have arrived at alone?

- What new capability have we generated in this session?
- What new resolve have we each created?

The answers to these four questions will show the possible outputs of the dialogical learning that is generated in the space of our thinking and feeling together, rather than what has transpired from the exchange of pre-existent 'thoughts' and 'felts'. David Bohm, at a seminar in 1990, defined the difference between thoughts and thinking as follows:

> Thinking implies the present tense – some activity going on which may include critical sensitivity to what can go wrong. Also there may be new ideas, and perhaps occasionally perception of some kind inside. 'Thought' is the past participle of that. We have the idea that after we have been thinking something it just evaporates. But thinking doesn't disappear. It goes somehow into the brain and leaves something – a trace – which becomes thought ... thought is the response from memory – from the past, from what has been done.
>
> (Bohm 1989: 73)

For a learning profession it is not enough to shift supervision from an exchange of thoughts to dialogical and generative thinking. We also have to consider how the learning that emerges from these supervisory dialogues can flow into the learning and cultural evolution of the wider profession. How do the learning lungs provide the necessary oxygen to the lifeblood of the organization?

We believe that any organization or profession working in the helping professions needs to create learning pathways, which can be used for harvesting emergent learning from supervision sessions, and for taking this learning into new collective practice and standards. Such learning pathways can include:

- supervision case reviews and action learning sets;
- supervisor seminars for the exchange of learning;
- conferences on new practice;
- new papers, articles and guidelines on professional practice using case material, appropriately disguised, from supervision.

Conclusion

In this chapter we have tried to show how supervision is not just an event, but an ongoing process which should permeate the culture of any effective helping organization. Nearly all organizational cultures have a mix of several of the organizational dysfunctions that we have illustrated and caricatured. We have yet to meet an organization that fully lives up to the ideals of the learning developmental culture. This said, some organizations do go a long way along the road to creating such an environment.

One example, which alas no longer functions in the same way, is Dingleton Hospital in Scotland. How it functioned and gradually became more of a learning culture can be read in Jones (1982).

In the next chapter we will explore how you can go about developing supervision in your own or another's organization. Developing supervision policy and practice should include attending to the organizational culture and helping it to evolve away from some of the patterns illustrated in this chapter, towards being a learning developmental culture. In such a culture, learning and development are an intrinsic part of every aspect of the workplace. Ultimately we believe that clients of all helping professions learn, develop and heal best in places where the staff are continuously learning.

Developing supervision policy and practice in organizations

Introduction

In the last chapter we explored the different types of organizational culture in the helping professions and advocated the need to move to a learning developmental culture. We believe that supervision is at the core of such an organizational culture. At many training courses and conferences we have been asked by dedicated staff from many different professions, 'How do I go about developing supervision practice in my organization?' This has never been an easy question to answer for several reasons:

- Every organization is different and has different needs.
- It depends on where you are starting from.
- Organizational change is a complex process and it is dangerous to follow (or preach) a simple recipe, or buy somebody else's solution.

However, having worked with a great variety of organizations who have been attempting to develop their supervision policy and practice, and listened to and read about many more, we have been able to discern a pattern or map of managing such development. Hopefully this map will avoid the 'simple recipe' and will point out several of the traps and pitfalls along the way. It is important to remember the maxim that the 'map is not the territory'.

We suggest that there are seven stages in the organizational development process for introducing or upgrading the supervision policy and practice. These are:

1 Create an appreciative inquiry into what supervision is already happening
2 Awaken the interest in developing supervision practice and policy
3 Initiate some experiments
4 Deal with resistance to change
5 Develop supervision policies
6 Develop ongoing learning and development processes for supervisors and supervisees
7 Have an ongoing audit and review process

These stages are not just a linear process, but also a continuous cycle of development.

Step 1: create an appreciative inquiry into what supervision is already happening

Many efforts to initiate change create unnecessary resistance by starting with the attitude that what is already happening is inadequate and hence change must be imported from outside. This approach fails to honour the dedicated efforts of those who are already working at providing supervision in the organization.

When we first worked in this field nearly 30 years ago, it was possible to come across organizations where supervision was an unheard of concept. This is no longer the case in most professions and most countries. Change needs to start by appreciating what is already happening and what individuals and teams have already achieved. These pioneers can then become partners and collaborators in developing the supervision practice of the organization.

Step 2: awaken the interest in developing supervision practice and policy

We mentioned earlier in the book the maxim that you cannot solve a problem that you do not own, and in organizational change it is no good trying to change an organization, department or team that does not recognize it needs to change. The impetus for change must come from within. If staff do not own the problem, they are not going to own the solution. External agents, be they more senior managers, supervisors or external consultants, can help the organization or department to bring to the surface its own perceived strengths and problems, its unutilized capacities and resources and the environmental changes that are acting upon it and its dissatisfaction with the status quo. What they cannot do is create the commitment to change that must come from within.

The two most effective ways of getting commitment to the need for supervision are to demonstrate the cost of *not* having supervision, and to create a vision that demonstrates the benefits of good supervision.

The costs of lack of supervision can be found in a number of diverse sources:

- Poor or outdated practice
- Client complaints
- Staff morale
- Staff attitude surveys
- Staff turnover rates
- Practice audits
- Comparisons with best practice in the field

It is also necessary to get commitment to the change process from those who have power or authority in relation to the department or organization which wants to change. Change in one part of an organization has an effect on the other parts of the organization and can create in those above or to the side resistance which may lead to the change effort being sabotaged. It is important before embarking on any change programme to map out all the interested parties (those who will be affected by the change process) and consider how they can be brought on board.

Bob Garratt (1987), who works with global organizations, suggests asking three questions to ensure that you maximize the political support for your change effort from the wider network:

- *Who knows?* Who has the information about the problem? Not opinions, views, half-truths or official policies, but hard facts which will determine the dimensions of the problem.
- *Who cares?* Who has the emotional investment in getting change made? Again, this is not who talks about the problem but who is involved in and committed to the outcome. These are often the people directly involved in and committed to the outcome.
- *Who can?* Who has the power to reorder resources so that changes occur? Who, when faced with facts, commitment and energy, has the power to say 'Yes'?

When working with organizations to develop their supervision practice we have often been asked whether it is better to have 'top-down' or 'bottom-up' change. Our answer is both, and in addition you need 'middle-out' change!

The fastest change happens when:

- those at the top create the climate and framework in which others can get on and make the change happen;

- those at the bottom move from moaning about the absence of, to professionally articulating the need for, supervision;
- those in middle management take on the responsibility to orchestrate the change process.

Step 3: initiate some experiments

In most organizations you can find not only pockets of good practice (see Step 1) but also small groups of people who have the desire and commitment to take things forward. Rather than drive change from the centre or top of the organization it is often more effective to support and build on the creative energy of those in the middle of the organization. Finding one unit or division that wants to go ahead and try out new practice or have its seniors undertake an external training programme can often generate interest well beyond its own boundaries.

There is a danger of one unit becoming too élitist and special which can lead to them being both envied and discounted. This can be avoided by having two or three units each engaging with their own experiments into supervision approaches, or ensuring that a single unit is constantly including others in its experiment and inquiry process.

Step 4: deal with resistance to change

However, even in an organization that achieved a large amount of the above preconditions, change would still create resistance. The difference is that in such an organization the resistance to the change would have a much better chance of being successfully worked through.

Resistance to change and unwillingness to engage in new behaviour are fuelled by a number of factors (Plant 1987):

- Fear of the unknown
- Lack of information
- Misinformation
- Historical factors
- Threat to core skills and competence
- Threat to status
- Threat to power base
- No perceived benefits
- Low trust in the organization
- Poor relationships
- Fear of failure
- Fear of looking stupid

- Reluctance to experiment
- Custom bound
- Reluctance to let go
- Strong peer-group norms

Kurt Lewin (1952) adapted from physics into the field of human relations the law that says *'Every force creates its equal and opposite force'*. He developed the concept of forcefield analysis: the more you push for change the more resistance you create. This is clearly seen in the following example taken from an intergroup negotiation:

> Group A bring three arguments to support their case. Group B bring three arguments to support theirs. Group A, instead of looking for common ground, make the mistake of adding three more reasons why they are right. Group B immediately double the number of reasons for their viewpoint and at the same time raise their voices. Group A raise their decibel level by almost the same amount and start ridiculing the case of group B who, surprise, surprise, reply in kind.

When you try to create any form of change (be it in an individual worker or a whole organization) and you meet resistance, pushing harder for the change just creates more resistance. Lewin suggests that, instead, you stop and attend to what is creating the impasse. You draw a line down the page and on one side you put all the forces that are supporting the change. On the other side you show all the forces that are resisting the change. Then in order to shift the status quo, you find ways of attending to the resistances in a way that would meet the underlying needs that are fuelling them. If you can honour and redirect the resistances, the change will happen without having to use greater effort.

Figure 13.1 gives an example of a forcefield analysis of a situation in which a new team leader is trying to introduce supervision into a team where it has previously not existed. In this situation an increase in the enthusiasm of the team leader about supervision or even their trying to convince team members about how good it would be for them would tend only to increase their paranoia about what the team leader was trying to get them to do. Alternatively it might give them the sense that they really must be in a bad way for the team leader to be so insistent that they need supervision. The wise team leader would instead look at ways of honouring and redirecting their resistances. Perhaps they would give their team time to talk about their previous bad experiences of supervision, or would engage them in planning the best and most time-efficient supervision system for that particular team.

In dealing with resistance it is also useful to realize that resistance often changes over time and can go through various stages. Fink *et al.* (1971) postulate four phases through which groups or organizations will pass in response to change:

Figure 13.1 Introducing individual supervision into a team

- Shock
- Defensive retreat
- Acknowledgement
- Adaption and change

In *shock*, interpersonal relations become fragmented, decision making becomes paralysed and communication confused. This leads to *defensive retreat*: individuals become self-protective, teams retreat into their own enclaves and become inward looking, decision making becomes more autocratic and communication more ritualized. In the *acknowledgement* phase individuals and teams begin to admit that there are things that need changing and more support and confrontation are present. When the fourth stage of *adaption and change* is reached, relations become more interdependent, there is more communication between individuals and across team boundaries, there is more willingness to explore and experiment with other ways of operating, and communication becomes more direct and open.

Thus it can be counter-productive to give people your marvellous scenarios for their future. They need to be involved in the thinking through and planning of the changes so that they have the opportunity to react, then understand the need for change, and then adapt to the future necessities. It is very easy to think that because you have worked through the issues and come up with a good solution, other people need only to accept the rightness of the solution and do not need to go through the thinking process.

Step 5: develop supervision policies

All organizations need a clear statement of policy on supervision. Kemshall (1995) suggests that such a policy needs to state clearly:

- Purpose and function of supervision
- How supervision contributes to the agency's overall aims
- Minimum standards for the content and conduct of supervision
- Minimum requirements for supervision contracts, to include frequency and agenda setting
- Anti-discriminatory practice
- How supervision will be recorded and status of supervision notes
- The relationship between supervision and appraisal
- Rights and responsibilities of both supervisee and supervisor
- Methods for resolving disagreements and/or breakdowns in the process
- The type of confidentiality expected and guaranteed
- How 'poor performance' will be dealt with and 'good performance' acknowledged

To these we would add:

- What supervision should focus on
- What priority supervision should be given in relation to other tasks

A colleague of ours, Liz Pitman, has developed this approach in helping a number of organizations develop their own supervision policy in a way that matches good practice to the reality of local resources and conditions. Organizational policies on supervision can then be used as the basis for a formal contract between the supervisor and supervisee. A sample contract is provided by Tony Morrison (1993).

Step 6: develop ongoing learning and development processes for supervisors and supervisees

In Chapter 8 we outlined the general broad curriculum that we believe is necessary for supervision training. However, we would also warn against the mind set that separates learning and doing – that sees learning as happening off-the-job on training courses and practice happening at work. While we believe every helping organization should establish an ongoing training programme for supervisors along the lines outlined, we also believe that the best learning on how to supervise emerges from actual supervision.

The first step to becoming a skilled supervisor is to receive good supervision. Without this fundamental step the supervisor lacks both a good role model and also a solid inner experience of how beneficial supervision can be in one's professional life. The second step is to have supervision from more than one supervisor, so that one develops a range of role models, from which one can develop one's own style.

This fundamental learning is difficult in an organization that has not yet established a tradition of good supervision practice with experienced supervisors. Therefore in the early stages of developing better practice a number of strategies can be utilized:

- using external supervision for senior practitioners;
- specifically recruiting new staff from agencies where supervision has been more established;
- arranging peer supervision between those staff who first undertake the supervision training.

To receive good supervision also entails learning the skills of being a good proactive supervisee. It is a mistake to believe that supervision training should only be focused on the supervisor. Workshops and conferences on how to get what you need from supervision can also provide an impetus in raising the level of supervision practice.

The final trap in planning supervision training is to believe that there is a programme that you can finish and then 'tick off' that aspect of your development as completed. Supervision learning is continuous and needs updating, as do books on supervision! The nature of the training changes and senior supervision practitioners need less structured input and more space to reflect on what is emerging in their supervision practice and explore new emergent challenges. These may include supervising people from different cultures (see Chapter 7), different professions or different orientations, as well as new ethical issues encountered or changes in professional practice.

It is also important to build into the organization mechanisms whereby the organization can learn from what emerges in supervision. In Chapter 12 we listed a number of processes that can be embedded in an organization to create learning pathways, from the front-line experience shared in supervision to collective knowledge and wisdom, both about supervision and effective practice.

Step 7: have an ongoing audit and review process

In the same way that an individual supervisor's development is a continuous process, so is the development of supervision practice and policy in both organizations and professions. Each year an organization should undertake some form of review of its supervision practice. A full review every year may not be possible, in which case a full review can be untertaken every three years with an interim review every year as part of the organization planning and review process.

The review and audit should include:

- Where and what and how much supervision is happening
- Staff satisfaction with the quality of supervision
- An assessment of the impact of supervision on practice
- The number of supervisors that have undertaken training, and to what level
- Illustrations of best practice within the organization

- Comparison to best practice in the profession
- An anti-oppressive audit

An audit is only as good as the change in practice that it produces. A full audit and review should produce changes to policy, training, practice guidelines and actual practice. As far as possible supervision needs to be built into the ongoing fabric of the organization through such mechanisms as:

- Induction programmes
- Recruitment and promotion criteria
- Staff appraisals
- Job descriptions
- Staff competence frameworks
- General audits
- Reviews of practice

Conclusion

Introducing supervision into an organization can easily falter after the initial enthusiasm. We have had several experiences of successfully running supervision trainings with high commitment from those attending, only to see their enthusiasm turn to frustration as others in the organization have not responded in the way they expected or hoped.

Supervision is likely to be established in a more sustainable way if the whole organizational process is carefully designed and monitored. This needs to include anticipating the potential personal, cultural and organizational resistances that are likely to be encountered and finding ways of engaging the needs behind the opposition.

The seven-stage cycle of developing supervision practice and policies is relevant for any organizational change process and can inform the supervision of any staff who are responsible for initiating a change process.

14 Conclusion: the wounded helper

> Until recently there was a GP in Glasgow whose patients would queue up for over three hours to see any other doctor but him. His lack of caring and sensitivity and his boredom with patients he had 'looked after' for years, eventually alienated them. Until, that is, his grandson was found to have leukaemia and slowly, through his own hurt and pain and anger, he was able to touch his patients again. Why is it that often, the very people we expect to understand the anguish of pain, illness and maybe death, often turn their professional, and for that matter human, backs until perhaps such time as they themselves have similar traumas?
>
> (*Guardian* 1986)

In many helping professions, from social workers to alternative health practitioners, from doctors to teachers, and from nurses to marriage guidance counsellors, the hardest work, and yet also the simplest, is to meet the clients in their pain and helplessness. Some professionals, like the doctor mentioned in the *Guardian* quotation above, are in flight from their own pain and therefore have to construct enormous barriers between themselves and the pain of their clients. Other professionals take care of their own distress by projecting it into their clients and needing to make their clients better.

When the client gets too close, the doctor may reach for his prescription pad, the social worker may give advice, the probation officer plan a contract, and each in his or her own way is trying to take the pain away. Sometimes this is necessary as the pain and hurt in the client have become unmanageable for them and they need temporary relief before returning to face that wound within themselves. However, professionals can reach too quickly for ways of making it better, for their own needs – for it is they rather than the clients who cannot bear to sit with the pain and distress. We often remind supervisees that their clients have lived with this pain for many, many years and the clients' ability to tolerate the pain is probably much greater than theirs. There are many therapists who have shown the way to 'stay with' what is happening. Winnicott (1971) writes: 'If only we [therapists] can wait [and resist a personal need to interpret] the patient arrives at understanding creatively'.

There is so much pain and hurt in the world that, if we get caught into believing we have to make it all better heroically, we are setting ourselves up to be overwhelmed and to burn out quickly. However, if we react to this reality with professional defensiveness, we may treat the symptoms, but we fail to meet and support the human beings who are communicating through these symptoms. The middle ground entails being on the path of facing our own shadow, our own fear, hurt, distress and helplessness, and taking responsibility for ensuring that we practise what we preach. This means managing our own support system, finding friends and colleagues who will not just reassure us but also challenge our defences, and finding a supervisor or supervision group who will not collude in trying to see who can be most potent with ways of curing the client, but will attend to how we are stuck in relating to the full truth of those with whom we work.

Often we have had the experience of working in supervision with a supervisee who is very stuck in knowing what to do next with the client. In the supervision, supervisees may start by looking for better answers and techniques for managing the client out there, but the real shift comes when they start to look at their *own* responses to the client. They might find that they are frightened of the aspect of themselves that the client represents; that the client reminds them of someone in their own lives, restimulates a past distress within them, or produces a strong counter-reaction to their problems.

When this has been explored, supervisees will often report at their next session, with some surprise, that they did not need to use any of the new strategies for managing the client, for 'It was as if the client had heard the supervision and had arrived at the next session much freer'. Some people may term this 'absent healing', but at a much simpler level we believe that the client very quickly responds to an awareness that the helper is now ready to hear what the client needs to share.

Jampolsky (1979) tells a story where his own readiness through self-supervision made a direct and immediate impact on a client:

> The episode took place in 1951 at Stanford Lane Hospital, which was then located in San Francisco.
>
> The situation was one in which I felt trapped and immobilized by fear. I was feeling emotional pain, and thought I was threatened with potential physical pain. The past was certainly colouring my perception of the present . . .
>
> I was called in at 2 a.m. one Sunday morning to see a patient on the locked psychiatric ward who had suddenly gone berserk. The patient, whom I had not seen before, had been admitted the previous afternoon with a diagnosis of acute schizophrenia. About ten minutes before I saw him, he had removed the wooden moulding from around the door. I looked through the small window in the door, and saw a man six feet four inches tall weighing 280 pounds. He was running around the room nude, carrying this large piece of wood with nails sticking out, and talking gibberish. I really didn't

know what to do. There were two male nurses, both of whom seemed scarcely five feet tall, who said, 'We will be right behind you, Doc.' I didn't find that reassuring.

As I continued to look through the window, I began to recognize how scared the patient was, and then it began to trickle into my consciousness how scared I was. All of a sudden it occurred to me that he and I had a common bond that might allow for unity – namely, that we were both scared.

Not knowing what else to do, I yelled through the thick door, 'My name is Dr Jampolsky and I want to come in and help you, but I'm scared. I'm scared that I might get hurt, and I'm scared you might get hurt, and I can't help wondering if you aren't scared too.' With this, he stopped his gibberish, turned around and said, 'You're goddam right I'm scared.'

I continued yelling to him, telling him how scared I was, and he was yelling back how scared he was. In a sense we became therapists to each other. As we talked our fear disappeared and our voices calmed down. He then allowed me to walk in alone, talk with him and give him some oral medication and leave.

Jampolsky has more recently written a book on the importance of forgiveness of both self and other, in all therapeutic work (Jampolsky 1999).

In this book we began by examining motives for wanting to help others. We see this as the beginning of self-supervision – the ability and the desire to question one's practice. In the first instance we concentrated on some of the less straightforward motives – not because we believe that people are fundamentally devious, but because a thorough examination of motives can help us to be more honest with ourselves and therefore our clients.

From this examination of motives and the need for commitment to continual emotional growth we explored, in Chapter 3, ways of taking charge of our own needs for support and supervision. We emphasized that there were skills that could be learned in being an effective supervisee that formed part of being an effective supervisor.

In Part 2 we introduced many of the issues involved in being a supervisor: the maps and models that are available in understanding the process and framework of supervision; the boundaries of the relationship; some of the skills needed for effective supervision and ways of establishing training courses for different types of supervisor. Throughout this exploration we did not confined ourselves to one approach, but rather presented the various choices and issues that each supervisor needs to consider in the process of establishing a personal style of supervising. The style chosen needs to be appropriate to the profession, the organization within which the supervision takes place, the level of development, the culture and the needs of the supervisee, and also the personality of the supervisor.

In Part 3 we explored supervision in groups, peer groups and work teams. We examined the advantages and disadvantages of these forms of supervision and also ways of working with group dynamics and team development.

However, supervision does not take place in isolation and we devoted the fourth part of the book to looking at the organizational context in which supervision takes place. We outlined ways of looking at the 'culture' of organizations and some of the typical cultural dysfunctions that prevail within helping organizations. We looked at the importance of establishing a learning culture to provide the climate that supports and sustains supervision, not just in formal sessions, but also as an integral part of the working context.

In writing this book we have stressed the need to integrate the emotional and the rational, the personal and the organizational, the educative, supportive and managerial aspects of supervision. This integration inevitably provides a creative tension that has to be constantly understood and worked with.

Our ways of working have followed and developed the process-centred approach to supervision which was first suggested by Ekstein and Wallerstein (1972), in which the emphasis is on the interaction between client, worker and supervisor. In this approach we avoid the polarization of focusing solely on the client or the supervisee; instead we focus on how the relationship between the worker and the client emerges in the supervision session, both in the content brought by the worker and in the process that emerges between worker and supervisor.

Throughout the book we are aware that we have been acting on the assumption that supervision is worthwhile. We have occasionally cited evidence that job satisfaction is related to receiving good supervision, quoted cases where shifts have occurred through supervision, and included both theory and personal accounts. But ultimately, as Rioch *et al.* (1976) suggest:

> There is no way to escape the fact that in helping others we are not really able to count the cost or measure the results . . . The truth is that we are performing an act of faith – faith in our clients, and the workers we supervise. It does not really matter that this is occasionally misplaced or that we fail more than once in spite of experience or skill. Like other kinds of faith, this one persists although it is based on things unseen and unheard. Essentially, it is faith in the value of truth, not so much truth with a capital 'T' that would reveal to us the nature of ultimate reality, but truth as the opposite of the small daily self deceptions or the large paranoid delusions that destroy people's respect for themselves and each other.

This commitment to truth, we believe, is more important than any technique or theoretical approach. Eventually the time comes when we have to act from some deep place within ourselves – perhaps induced by a crisis or a client who tests us out or who is very similar to us. At these times it may be that the right course of action is something which goes against all our previous convictions:

There were rules in the monastery, but the master always warned against the tyranny of the law. 'Obedience keeps the rules', he would say, 'but Love knows when to break them'.

(De Mello 1985)

Good supervision, like love, we believe, cannot be taught. The understanding, maps and techniques that we provide in this book cannot and, perhaps should not, protect supervisee and supervisor alike from times of self-questioning and doubt. At these times it is the quality of the relationship that has already been established between them that contains the supervisee in times of crisis and doubt. How we personally relate to our supervisors and supervisees is far more important than mere skills, for all techniques need to be embedded in a good relationship. We agree with Hunt (1986) when she says: 'It seems that whatever approach or method is used, in the end it is the quality of the relationship between supervisor and supervisee that determines whether supervision is effective or not'. This relationship provides the container for the helper and forms part of the therapeutic triad we referred to in Chapter 1. It is a relationship that, like any other, will have its difficulties. But without it we believe the work with clients is incomplete.

As Dr Margaret Tonnesmann (1979) emphasized in her lecture at the fourth annual conference to commemorate the work of Donald Winnicott:

The human encounter in the helping profession is inherently stressful. The stress aroused can be accommodated and used for the understanding of our patients and clients. But our emotional responsiveness will wither if the human encounter cannot be contained within the institutions in which we work. Defensive manoeuvres will then become operative and these will prevent healing, even if cure can be maintained by scientific methods, technical skills and organizational competence. By contrast, if we can maintain contact with the emotional reality of our clients and ourselves then the human encounter can facilitate not only a healing experience, but also an enriching experience for them and for us.

A good supervisory relationship is the best way we know to ensure that we stay open to ourselves and our clients.

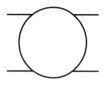

Appendix 1: BAC Code of Ethics and Practice

For Supervisors of Counsellors

1   Status of the Code

1.1   In response to the experience of members of BAC, this Code is a revision of the 1988 Code of Ethics & Practice for the Supervision of Counsellors.

2   Introduction

2.1   The purpose of the Code is to establish and maintain standards for supervisors who are members of BAC and to inform and protect counsellors seeking supervision. Throughout this Code the terms Counsellor and Counselling are used in accordance with the definition of counselling in the Code of Ethics & Practice for Counsellors.

2.2   All members of this Association are required to abide by existing Codes appropriate to them. They thereby accept a common frame of reference within which to manage their responsibilities to supervisees and their clients, colleagues, members of this Association and the wider community. Whilst this Code cannot resolve all ethical and practice related issues, it aims to provide a framework for addressing ethical issues and to encourage optimum levels of practice. Supervisors and supervisees (counsellors) will need to judge which parts of this Code apply to particular situations and they may have to decide between conflicting responsibilities.

2.3   Counselling Supervision is a formal and mutually agreed arrangement for counsellors to discuss their work regularly with someone who is normally an experienced and competent counsellor and familiar with the process of counselling supervision. The task is to work together to ensure and develop the efficacy of the supervisee's counselling practice.

Counselling Supervision is the term that will be used throughout this Code. It is also known as supervision, consultative support, clinical supervision or non-managerial supervision. It is an essential part of good practice for counselling. It is different from training, personal development and line management accountability.

2.4   This Association has a Complaints Procedure which can lead to the expulsion of members for breaches of its Codes of Ethics & Practice.

3   Nature of Counselling Supervision

3.1   Counselling supervision provides supervisees with the opportunity on a regular basis to discuss and monitor their work with clients.

It should take account of the setting in which supervisees practise. Counselling supervision is intended to ensure that the needs of the clients are being addressed and to monitor the effectiveness of the therapeutic interventions.

3.2 Counselling supervision may contain some elements of training, personal development or Line-management, but counselling supervision is not primarily intended for these purposes and appropriate management of these issues should be observed.

3.3 Counselling supervision is a formal collaborative process intended to help supervisees maintain ethical and professional standards of practice and to enhance creativity.

3.4 It is essential that counsellor and supervisor are able to work together constructively and that counselling supervision includes supportive and challenging elements.

3.5 There are several modes of counselling supervision (see 5), which vary in appropriateness according to the needs of supervisees. More than one mode of counselling supervision may be used concurrently. This Code applies to all counselling supervision arrangements.

3.6 The frequency of counselling supervision will vary according to the volume of counselling, the experience of supervisees and their work setting.

4   Anti-discriminatory Practice in Counselling Supervision

4.1 Anti-discriminatory practice underpins the basic values of counselling and counselling supervision as stated in this document and in the Code of Ethics & Practice for Counsellors. It also addresses the issue of the client's social context, B.2.7.3 of that Code (1996).

4.2 Supervisors have a responsibility to be aware of their own issues of prejudice and stereotyping, and particularly to consider ways in which this may be affecting the supervisory relationship. Discussion of this is part of the counselling supervision process.

4.3 Supervisors need to be alert to any prejudices and assumptions that counsellors reveal in their work with clients and to raise awareness of these so that the needs of clients may be met with more sensitivity. One purpose of counselling supervision is to enable supervisees to recognise and value difference. Supervisors have a responsibility to challenge the appropriateness of the work of a supervisee whose own belief system interferes with the acceptance of clients.

4.4 Attitudes, assumptions and prejudices can be identified by the language used, and by paying attention to the selectivity of material brought to counselling supervision.

5   Modes of Counselling Supervision

There are different modes of counselling supervision. The particular features of some of these modes are outlined below.

Some counsellors use combinations of these for their counselling supervision.

5.1 One to One, Supervisor–Supervisee

This involves a supervisor providing counselling supervision on an individual basis for an individual counsellor who is usually less experienced than the supervisor. This is the most widely used mode of counselling supervision.

5.2 Group Counselling Supervision with Identified Counselling Supervisor(s)

There are several ways of providing this form of counselling supervision. In one approach the supervisor acts as the leader, takes responsibility for organising the time equally between the supervisees, and concentrates on the work of each individual in turn. Using another approach the supervisees allocate counselling supervision time between themselves with the supervisor as a technical resource.

5.3 One to one peer Counselling Supervision

This involves two participants providing counselling supervision for each other by alternating the roles of supervisor and supervisee. Typically, the time available for counselling supervision is divided equally between them. This mode on its own is not suitable for all practitioners.

5.4   Peer Group Counselling Supervision

This takes place when three or more counsellors share the responsibility for providing each other's counselling supervision within the group. Typically, they will consider themselves to be of broadly equal status, training and/or experience. This mode on its own is unsuitable for inexperienced practitioners.

5.5   Particular issues of competence for each mode are detailed in the Code of Practice B.2.6.

6   The Structure of this Code

6.1   This Code has two sections. Section A, the Code of Ethics, outlines the fundamental values of counselling supervision and a number of general principles arising from these. Section B, the Code of Practice, applies these principles to counselling supervision.

A   CODE OF ETHICS

A.1   Counselling supervision is a non-exploitative activity. Its basic values are integrity, responsibility, impartiality and respect. Supervisors must take the same degree of care to work ethically whether they are paid or work voluntarily and irrespective of the mode of counselling supervision used.

A.2   Confidentiality

The content of counselling supervision is highly confidential. Supervisors must clarify their limits of confidentiality.

A.3   Safety

All reasonable steps must be taken to ensure the safety of supervisees and their clients during their work together.

A.4   Effectiveness

All reasonable steps must be taken by supervisors to encourage optimum levels of practice by supervisees.

A.5   Contracts

The terms and conditions on which counselling supervision is offered must be made clear to supervisees at the outset. Subsequent revisions of these terms must be agreed in advance of any change.

A.6   Competence

Supervisors must take all reasonable steps to monitor and develop their own competence and to work within the limits of that competence. This includes having supervision of their supervision work.

B   CODE OF PRACTICE

B.1   Issues of Responsibility

B.1.1   Supervisors are responsible for ensuring that an individual contract is worked out with their supervisees which will allow them to present and explore their work as honestly as possible.

B.1.2   Within this contract supervisors are responsible for helping supervisees to reflect critically upon their work, while at the same time acknowledging that clinical responsibility remains with the counsellor.

B.1.3   Supervisors are responsible, together with their supervisees, for ensuring that the best use is made of counselling supervision time, in order to address the needs of clients.

B.1.4   Supervisors are responsible for setting and maintaining the boundaries between the counselling supervision relationship and other professional relationships, e.g. training and management.

B.1.5   Supervisors and supervisees should take all reasonable steps to ensure that any personal or social contact between them does not adversely influence the effectiveness of the counselling supervision.

B.1.6   A supervisor must not have a counselling supervision and a personal counselling contract with the same supervisee over the same period of time.

B.1.7   Supervisors must not exploit their supervisees financially, sexually, emotionally or in any other way. It is unethical for supervisors to engage in sexual activity with their supervisee.

B.1.8   Supervisors have a responsibility to enquire about any other relationships which may exist between supervisees and their clients as these may impair the objectivity and professional judgement of supervisees.

B.1.9   Supervisors must recognise, and work in ways that respects the value and dignity of supervisees and their clients with due regard to issues such as origin, status, race, gender, age, beliefs, sexual orientation and disability. This must include raising awareness of any discriminatory practices that may exist between supervisees and their clients, or between supervisor and supervisee.

B.1.10   Supervisors must ensure that together with their supervisees they consider their respective legal liabilities to each other, to the employing or training organisation, if any, and to clients.

B.1.11   Supervisors are responsible for taking action if they are aware that their supervisees' practice is not in accordance with BAC's Codes of Ethics & Practice for Counsellors.

B.1.12   Supervisors are responsible for helping their supervisees recognise when their functioning as counsellors is impaired due to personal or emotional difficulties, any condition that affects judgement, illness, the influence of alcohol or drugs, or for any other reason, and for ensuring that appropriate action is taken.

B.1.13   Supervisors must conduct themselves in their supervision-related activities in ways which do not undermine public confidence in either their role as a supervisor or in the work of other supervisors.

B.1.14   If a supervisor is aware of possible misconduct by another supervisor which cannot be resolved or remedied after discussion with the supervisor concerned, they should implement the Complaints Procedure, doing so within the boundaries of confidentiality required by the Complaints Procedure.

B.1.15   Supervisors are responsible for ensuring that their emotional needs are met outside the counselling supervision work and are not solely dependent on their relationship with supervisees.

B.1.16   Supervisors are responsible for consulting with their own supervisor before former clients are taken on as supervisees or former supervisees are taken on as clients.

B.2   Issues of Competence

B.2.1   Under all of the modes of counselling supervision listed above, supervisors should normally be practising and experienced counsellors.

B.2.2   Supervisors are responsible for seeking ways to further their own professional development.

B.2.3   Supervisors are responsible for making arrangements for their own supervision in order to support their counselling supervision work and to help them to evaluate their competence.

B.2.4   Supervisors are responsible for monitoring and working within the limits of their competence.

B.2.5   Supervisors are responsible for withdrawing from counselling supervision work either temporarily or permanently when their functioning is impaired due to personal or emotional difficulties, illness, the influence of alcohol or drugs, or for any other reason.

B.2.6   Some modes require extra consideration and these are detailed in this section.

	A	B	C	D	E	F	G	H
One to one supervisor – supervisee	X							
Group counselling supervision with identified and more experienced supervisor	X	X		X	X			
One to one peer counselling supervision	X	X	X	X			X	X
Peer group counselling supervision	X	X	X	X		X	X	X

A All points contained elsewhere within the Code of Practice should be considered.

B Sufficient time must be allocated to each counsellor to ensure adequate supervision of their counselling work.

C This method on its own is particularly unsuitable for trainees, recently trained or inexperienced counsellors.

D Care needs to be taken to develop an atmosphere conducive to sharing, questioning and challenging each other's practice in a constructive and supportive way.

E As well as having a background in counselling work, supervisors should have appropriate groupwork experience in order to facilitate this kind of group.

F All participants should have sufficient groupwork experience to be able to engage the group process in ways which facilitate effective counselling supervision.

G Explicit consideration should be given to deciding who is responsible for providing the counselling supervision, and how the task of counselling supervision will be carried out.

H It is good practice to have an independent consultant to visit regularly to observe and monitor the process and quality of the counselling supervision.

B.3   Management of Work

B.3.1   The Counselling Supervision Contract

3.1.1   Where supervisors and supervisees work for the same agency or organisation the supervisor is responsible for clarifying all contractual obligations.

3.1.2   Supervisors must inform their supervisee, as appropriate, about their own training, philosophy and theoretical position, qualifications, approach to anti-discriminatory practice and the methods of counselling supervision they use.

3.1.3   Supervisors must be explicit regarding practical arrangements for counselling supervision, paying particular regard to the length of contact time, the frequency of contact, policy and practice regarding record keeping, and the privacy of the venue.

3.1.4   Fees and fee increases must be arranged and agreed in advance.

3.1.5   Supervisors and supervisees must make explicit the expectations and requirements they have of each other. This should include the manner in which any formal assessment of the supervisee's work will be conducted. Each party should assess the value of working with the other, and review this regularly.

3.1.6   Supervisors must discuss their policy regarding giving references and any fees that may be charged for this or for any other work done outside counselling supervision time.

3.1.7   Before formalising a counselling supervision contract supervisors must ascertain what personal counselling the supervisee has or has had. This is in order to take into account any effect this may have on the supervisee's counselling work.

3.1.8   Supervisors working with trainee counsellors must clarify the boundaries of their responsibility and their accountability to their supervisee and to the training course and any agency/placement involved. This should include any formal assessment required.

B.3.2   Confidentiality

3.2.1   As a general principle, supervisors must not reveal confidential material concerning the supervisee or their clients to any other person without the express consent of all parties concerned. Exceptions to this general principle are contained within this Code.

3.2.2   When initial contracts are being made, agreements about the people to whom supervisors may speak about their supervisees' work must include those on whom the supervisors rely for support, supervision or consultancy. There must also be clarity at this stage about the boundaries of confidentiality having regard for the supervisor's own framework of accountability. This is particularly relevant when providing counselling supervision to a trainee counsellor.

3.2.3   Supervisors should take all reasonable steps to encourage supervisees to present their work in ways which protect the personal identity of clients, or to get their client's informed consent to present information which could lead to personal identification.

3.2.4   Supervisors must not reveal confidential information concerning supervisees or their clients to any person or through any public medium except:

(a) When it is clearly stated in the counselling supervision contract and it is in accordance with all BAC Codes of Ethics & Practice.

(b) When the supervisor considers it necessary to prevent serious emotional or physical damage to the client, the supervisee or a third party. In such circumstances the supervisee's consent to a change in the agreement about confidentiality should be sought, unless there are good grounds for believing that the supervisee is no longer able to take responsibility for his/her own actions. Whenever possible, the decision to break confidentiality in any circumstances should be made after consultation with another experienced supervisor.

3.2.5   The disclosure of confidential information relating to supervisees is permissible when relevant to the following situations:

(a) Recommendations concerning supervisees for professional purposes e.g. references and assessments.

(b) Pursuit of disciplinary action involving supervisees in matters pertaining to standards of ethics and practice.

    In the latter instance, any breaking of confidentiality should be minimised by conveying only information pertinent to the immediate situation on a need-to-know basis. The ethical considerations needing to be taken into account are:

(i)   Maintaining the best interests of the supervisee
(ii) Enabling the supervisee to take responsibility for their actions
(iii) Taking full account of the supervisor's responsibility to the client and to the wider community

3.2.6   Information about work with a supervisee may be used for publication or in meetings only with the supervisee's permission and with anonymity preserved.

3.2.7   On occasions when it is necessary to consult with professional colleagues, supervisors ensure that their discussion is purposeful and not trivialising.

B.3.3   The Management of Counselling Supervision

3.3.1   Supervisors must encourage the supervisee to belong to an association or organisation with a Code of Ethics & Practice and a Complaints Procedure. This provides additional safeguards for the supervisor, supervisee and client in the event of a complaint.

3.3.2   If, in the course of counselling supervision, it appears that personal counselling may be necessary for the supervisee to be able to continue working effectively, the supervisor should raise this issue with the supervisee.

3.3.3   Supervisors must monitor regularly how their supervisees engage in self-assessment and the self-evaluation of their work.

3.3.4   Supervisors must ensure that their supervisees acknowledge their individual responsibility for ongoing professional development and for participating in further training programmes.

3.3.5   Supervisors must ensure that their supervisees are aware of the distinction between counselling, accountability to management, counselling supervision and training.

3.3.6   Supervisors must ensure with a supervisee who works in an organisation or agency that the lines of accountability and responsibility are clearly defined: supervisee/client; supervisor/supervisee; supervisor/client; organisation/supervisor; organisation/supervisee; organisation/client. There is a distinction between line management supervision and counselling supervision.

3.3.7   Best practice is that the same person should not act as both line manager and counselling supervisor to the same supervisee. However, where the counselling supervisor is also the line manager, the supervisee should have access to independent counselling supervision.

3.3.8   Supervisors who become aware of a conflict between an obligation to a supervisee and an obligation to an employing agency must make explicit to the supervisee the nature of the loyalties and responsibilities involved.

3.3.9   Supervisors who have concerns about a supervisee's work with clients must be clear how they will pursue this if discussion in counselling supervision fails to resolve the situation.

3.3.10   Where disagreements cannot be resolved by discussions between supervisor and supervisee, the supervisor should consult with a fellow professional and, if appropriate, recommend that the supervisee be referred to another supervisor.

3.3.11   Supervisors must discuss with supervisees the need to have arrangements in place to take care of the immediate needs of clients in the event of a sudden and unplanned ending to the counselling relationship. It is good practice for the supervisor to be informed about these arrangements.

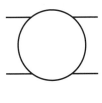

Appendix 2: Criteria for BAC counselling supervisor accreditation

Introduction

Candidates can be Accredited as a Counselling Supervisor for Individuals OR Groups OR both.

Criteria

The criteria for Accreditation of Counselling Supervisors require that:

The Candidate:

Has current individual BAC membership.

Abides by all the BAC Codes of Ethics and Practice and demonstrates a working knowledge of the Codes of Ethics and Practice for Counsellors and Supervisors of Counsellors.

Counselling Experience:

Is a BAC Accredited Counsellor or equivalent (as defined from time to time by the BAC Management Committee).

Has undertaken not less than 600 contact hours over three years with clients.

Has demonstrated in counselling supervision a capacity for safe and effective counselling practice.

Can show evidence of continuing professional development.

Supervisor Experience:

EITHER
Has satisfactorily completed a substantial structured training programme in supervision.
  OR
Can demonstrate an awareness of the values, beliefs and assumptions which underpin his/her work.
  Can provide evidence of a capacity for self regulation.
  Can show evidence that a programme of learning has been followed with a supervisor which ensures that the Code of Ethics and Practice for Supervisors of Counsellors is applied in his/her practice.
  OR
Has achieved a normally recognised standard of competence in counselling supervision.
  Is currently practising as a counselling supervisor.
  Has had a minimum of two years' practice as a counselling supervisor.
  Has had regular supervision of their work in counselling from an experienced counselling supervisor.
  Has completed a minimum of 180 contact hours with supervisees over a maximum of three years immediately prior to application.
  Can provide evidence of a range of experience ie. work with trainees and experienced counsellors; counselling supervisory relationships begun, maintained and ended.
  Can provide evidence of the way in which he/she uses his/her authority as a counselling supervisor to promote the safety of the client.
  Can provide evidence of an identified theoretical framework in his/her practice.

Experienced Counselling Supervisor Route

(To be available for two years from the relaunch of the scheme and then to be reviewed)

Criteria

The criteria for Accreditation of Counselling Supervisors through the 'Experienced Route' require that:

The Candidate:

Has current individual BAC membership.
  Abides by all the BAC Codes of Ethics and Practice and demonstrates a working knowledge of the Codes of Ethics and Practice for Counsellors and Supervisors of Counsellors.

Counselling Experience:

Has undertaken not less than 600 contact hours of counselling practice with clients.

Has demonstrated in counselling supervision a capacity for safe and effective practice.

Is in supervised practice as a counsellor at a minimum of 50 counselling hours per year.

Is or has been either: a BAC Accredited Counsellor or can produce evidence to demonstrate previous eligibility for BAC Counsellor Accreditation; a BAC Approved Member; a BAC Fellow; a COSCA Accredited Counsellor; a United Kingdom Council for Psychotherapy Registrant; a British Psychological Society Chartered Counselling Psychologist or a British Confederation of Psychotherapists Registrant.

Supervisor Experience:

Has worked for seven years as a counselling supervisor.

Is currently practising as a counselling supervisor.

Has completed a minimum of 180 contact hours with supervisees over a maximum of three years.

Can provide evidence of a range of experience ie. work with trainees and experienced counsellors; counselling supervisory relationships begun, maintained and ended.

Can provide evidence of the way in which he/she uses his/her authority as a counselling supervisor to promote the safety of the client.

Can provide evidence of an identified theoretical framework in his/her practice.

Can demonstrate an awareness of the values, beliefs and assumptions which underpin his/her work.

Can provide evidence of a capacity for self regulation.

Please note that the experienced Route to Counselling Supervisor Accreditation is to remain available for the foreseeable future.

Key terms

action learning A form of learning in which the learning is deliberately based on learning from experience and not just theories. Action learning sets, first used by Reg Revans, involve staff working in small groups to explore real work problems, issues and challenges.

anti-discrimination practices These draw attention to and work against discriminatory behaviour and policies towards minority groups.

anti-oppressive practices These encourage behaviour which attends to addressing past and current oppressive experiences based on race, gender, sexual orientation, age, disability, etc.

appraisal A meeting of a senior with a junior staff member to systematically evaluate their work and plan future developments. 360-degree appraisal involves feedback from clients, peers and subordinates.

behaviourist A school of psychology and psychotherapy which seeks to understand human behaviour. Behaviour therapists work to help change unwanted patterns of behaviour usually by trying to change conditioned responses.

burnout The psychological state reached by an individual in the undertaking of their work in which they are unable to continue through stress, illness and fatigue. Typically an individual who is 'burnt out' is suffering an imbalance between what they give out to others and what they receive for themselves.

co-counselling A type of reciprocal counselling invented by Harvey Jackins in which two people undertake to take it in turns to be client and counsellor. Emotional expression and discharge are understood to be helpful and techniques to encourage this are learned by those who undertake this method.

congruence A state of being in which the emotional, bodily and verbal response are in alignment with each other and therefore not contradictory. A congruent response is therefore felt to be authentic.

contract An agreement made between supervisor and supervisee concerning the boundaries of their work together (see Chapter 5).

countertransference The responses of the counsellor or psychotherapist to their patient/client, both conscious and unconscious. A fuller description of different types of countertransference can be found in Chapter 6 (Mode 4).

culture The different explicit and implicit assumptions and values that influence the behaviour and social artefacts of different groups (Herskovitz 1948). *Organizational culture* is the specific culture embedded in an organization.

dramatherapy A type of therapy which involves dramatic enactment and active exercises designed to explore and express conflicts and issues experienced by participants.

dynamics The tendency towards a certain movement of patterned behaviour or mood states within the psyche (which is referred to in the term *psychodynamics*) or between people, as in *group dynamics*.

empathy An understanding (usually a felt understanding) of the other from the other's point of view.

ethnic A cultural construct which describes different geographical or 'racial' groupings.

ethnocentric Having a world view confined by one's own cultural frame of reference.

ethnorelative Having a world view which takes into account and can adapt to different cultural perspectives.

forcefield analysis The analysis of the patterned behaviour within a given situation or 'field' to show the balance of changing and resisting forces. First used by Kurt Lewin (1952).

game A habitual and patterned way of relating in which two individuals play mutually relating roles. First used in *transactional analysis* (Berne 1964).

guided fantasy An exercise in which a facilitator encourages others to imaginatively immerse themselves in a situation, following it in their minds as it unfolds.

humanistic psychology This was invented to become a 'third way' (not psychoanalytic or behavioural) within psychology, having human values at its core. In therapeutic work the client's potential is uncovered during a process which stays close to the client's direct experience. A coming together of mind, body and spirit is valued.

intergroup That which happens dynamically between groups.

interpretation A term coined by Freud to describe an intervention made by an analyst to a patient which typically brings into consciousness unconscious material.

intrapsychic That which is found within the internal world of the individual.

introjection A psychic mechanism in which an experience with another is taken into the self but not properly integrated into the psyche.

libido This word was coined by Freud to describe energy (usually sexual in nature) within the psyche of an individual.

maximize Facilitate the greatest potential of any given situation.

metavision A view taken from outside the frame of reference of any given situation so as to understand it within its wider context.

multicultural A situation in which many cultures are represented.

nursing triad The mother and baby who 'nurse' are joined by the father, or other adult, who watches over and protects the two.

Oedipus theory A theory developed by Freud and named after the Greek myth. It describes a desire experienced by children at the age of about 5 within their relationship to their parents. In fantasy, and usually unconsciously, the child wishes, like Oedipus in the myth, to kill his father and marry his mother. This may be regressively re-experienced in later life.

organizational learning Learning evidenced by changes in organizations. This involves not just the sum of learning by individuals within the organization but learning which leads to changes within the whole culture.

parallel process A process which happens in one situation or relationship and is repeated in another.

personal construct theory A theory which explores the way in which experience is organized between interrelating opposites.

phenomenology A philosophical theory which is concerned with experienced phenomena.

process The developing and unfolding dynamic within an individual or group.

projection A term used to describe a state in which an individual denies or cuts off from a (usually painful or unacceptable) emotional response and seems to find it within someone else.

psyche The Latin word for 'mind', usually used to mean the whole of the self including emotional, spiritual and unconscious aspects as well as the conscious, thinking mind.

psychoanalysis A school of psychotherapy which originates in the work of Sigmund Freud. A central tenet of psychoanalysis is that the psychoanalyst or psychotherapist works to understand and uncover unconscious material which is typically discovered within the transference and countertransference relationship.

psychodynamic All forms of psychological and psychotherapeutic approaches which are informed by psychoanalytic thought.

race A cultural concept used to describe apparently different groups based on body types, colour of skin, facial features etc. which tend to occur in different geographical areas.

racism A phenomenon in which prejudiced attitudes are carried by the dominant culture of 'race' to other cultures or 'races'. *Institutionalized racism* occurs when an organization or society is imbued with racist assumptions.

restimulation A bodily and/or emotionally felt memory of past events (often but not necessarily unconscious) brought about by a similar event happening in the present.

Rogerian Ways of understanding or behaving which are guided by the theories of Carl Rogers. He advocated a *client centred* approach which privileged the client's experience in guiding the therapist in understanding and working with them.

role-play An improvised enactment of a situation by taking on roles and trying them out.

scapegoat Originally a 'scapegoat' was literally a goat which stood in for a person as a sacrifice to the gods or God as if they carried the negative characteristics which made the sacrifice necessary. Similarly within the dynamics of a group an individual may symbolically carry certain negative traits or experiences for the group and be cast out or vilified by them as a defensive way of denying these traits in themselves.

sculpting A technique first used in psychodrama in which a situation or dynamic is explored pictorially by placing members of the group to make a symbolic representation.

shadow A term coined by Jung to denote the part of the personality that is denied and/or split off. The shadow is understood to be an inevitable part of the personality and a corresponding counterpart to 'positive' aspects. In psychotherapy it is generally acknowledged that the shadow needs to be understood and come to terms with rather than cast out, so that it does not have an unconscious influence and appear in the guise of destructive patterns.

sociodrama A form of group work in which societal issues are largely explored through dramatic enactment and other action techniques. First used by Moreno.

splitting A defence mechanism first described by Melanie Klein in which the psyche is split in such a way that one part is unaware of the other.

stress A state of fatigue, ill health and (often) depression caused by distressing, strenuous and emotionally overwhelming pursuits. Typically the individual is out of balance between what is given out and what is restorative and recreational for themselves.

supervision 'A quintessential interpersonal interaction with the general goal that one person, the supervisor, meets with another, the supervisee, in an effort to make the latter more effective in helping people' (Hess 1980). *Group supervision* happens within a group with a supervisor present. *Team supervision* is supervision of a whole team working together. *Peer supervision* happens within a group between peers who supervise each other in a reciprocal way. *Unconscious supervision* is an unconscious communication from patient/client to therapist which corrects or affirms what is happening within the work.

symbiotic   A psychological state in which two people become emotionally merged as if they were the same person.

therapeutic community   An intentional community which exists to enhance the mental and emotional health of those who live within it, particularly patients/clients who have come there for that specific purpose.

therapeutic triad   The client, therapist and supervisor. A reference is made in this term to the nursing triad (see above). The supervisor is therefore in the role of the father.

transactional analysis   A psychotherapeutic theory and method founded by Eric Berne in which the psyche is understood to be divided into the three ego states of parent, adult and child and in which interactions are analysed, understood and changed to be more positive and life-enhancing.

transcultural competence   The ability to work effectively across cultural differences.

transference   Seeing a present situation/relationship through the emotional lens of a past situation/relationship. It is often used particularly to describe the relationship that is developed by patients/clients in relation to their therapist, especially within psychoanalytic and psychodynamic schools. *Multiple transference* occurs in groups when a group member relates to several group members with different transferences.

unconscious   A state of mind which is not available to conscious thought. Unconscious communication is therefore that which is not mediated through thought and thus often non-verbal.

Resources

National organizations for supervision

British Association for Supervision Practice and Research, 132 Princess Avenue, London W3 8LT.

National organizations for counselling and psychotherapy

British Association for Counselling, 1 Regent's Place, Rugby, Coventry, CV21 2PJ.
United Kingdom Council for Psychotherapy, 167–9 Great Portland Street, London, W1N 5FB.

Organizations that offer training in supervision of counsellors and psychotherapists

(*For a fuller list see Gilbert and Evans, forthcoming*)

Centre for Staff Team Development, c/o Bath Consultancy Group, 24 Gay Street, Bath, BA1 2PD.
Cascade Training Associates (Brigid Proctor and Francesca Inskip), 4 Ducks Walk, Twickenham, Middlesex, TW1 2DD.
Metanoia, 13 North Common Road, Ealing, London, W5 2QB.
Minster Centre, 1 Drakes Court Yard, 291 Kilburn High Road, London, NW6 7JR.
Northern Guild of Psychotherapy and Counselling, 77 Acklam Road, Thornaby on Tees, Cleveland, TS17 7BD.
Roehampton Institute, Department of Psychology, Digby Stuart College, Roehampton Vale, Roehampton, London, SWI5 5PU.
The Sherwood Psychotherapy Training Institute, Thiskney House, 2 St James Terrace, Nottingham, NG1 6FW.
Spectrum, 7 Endymion Road, Finsbury Park, London, N4 1EE.
The Tavistock Clinic, 120 Belsize Lane, London, NW3 SBA.
University of Leicester, Department of Adult Education, Vaughan College, St Nicholas Circle, Leicester, LE1 4LB.
The Westminster Pastoral Foundation, 23 Kensington Square, London, W8 5HN.

In-house supervision training in the helping professions

Centre for Staff Team Development, c/o Bath Consultancy Group, 24 Gay Street, Bath, BA1 2PD.

The Centre for Crisis Management and Education, Roselyn House, 93 Old Newtown Road, Newbury, Berkshire, RG14 7DE (provide specific training in how to respond to crisis and disaster situations).

GO education – The Group and Education Consultancy, 7 Cheverton Road, London, N19 3BB.

Impact Training and Consultation, 115, Long Ashton Road, Long Ashton, Bristol, BS41 9JE.

For training in supervision for the other helping professions, contact the appropriate professional organization:

British Association of Occupational Therapists, 106/1144 Borough High Street, London, SE1.

British Association of Social Workers, 16 Kent Street, Birmingham, B5 6RD.

British Psychological Society, St Andrews House, 48 Princess Road East, Leicester, LE1 7DR.

Central Council for Education and Training in Social Work, Derbyshire House, Chad's Street, London, WC1 8AD.

College of Speech Therapists, 7 Bath Place, London, EC2.

Council for Education and Training in Youth and Community Work (CETYCW), 17–23 Albion Street, Leicester, LE1 6GD.

National Association of Probation Officers, 3/4 Chivalry Road, Battersea, London, SW11 1HT.

Royal College of Nursing, 20 Cavendish Square, London, W1M OAB.

Royal College of Psychiatrists, 17 Belgrave Square, London SW1X SPG.

Note: This is only a partial list of selected institutions. For a full list please contact the British Association for Counselling or the United Kingdom Council for Psychotherapy.

Training tapes on supervision

Audiotapes
Two audiotapes by Francesca Inskipp and Brigid Proctor:
'Skills For Supervisees'
'Skills For Supervisors'

Videotapes
'Supervision: A Working Alliance', Brigid Proctor and David Willow.
All tapes are available from Alexia Publications c/o Brigid Proctor, 4 Ducks Walk, Twickenham, Middlesex, TW1 2DD.

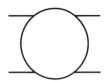

Bibliography

Ahmad, B. (1990) *Advanced Award for Supervisors: Implications for Black Supervisors.* London: CCETSW.

Albott, W. (1984) Supervisory characteristics and other sources of supervision variance. *The Clinical Supervisor,* 2: 27–41.

Aldridge, L. (1982) 'Construction of a scale for the rating of supervisors of psychology', unpublished Masters thesis. Auburn University, USA.

American Association for Counseling and Development (1989) *Standards for Counseling Supervisors.* Alexandria, VA: AACD.

Argyris, C. (1982) *Reasoning, Learning and Action.* San Francisco: Jossey Bass.

Argyris, C. and Schön, D. (1978) *Organizational Learning.* Reading, MA: Addison-Wesley.

Arundale, J. (1993) 'Psychotherapy supervision: impact, practice and expectations', PhD thesis. University of London.

Association for Counselor Education and Supervision (ACES) (1989) *Standards for Counseling Supervisors.* Alexandria, VA: ACES.

Association for Counselor Education and Supervision (ACES) (1993) *Ethical Guidelines for Counseling Supervisors.* Alexandria, VA: ACES.

Atwood, G.E. and Stolorow, R.D. (1984) *Structures of Subjectivity.* New York: The Analytic Press.

Badaines, J. (1985) Supervision: methods and issues. *Self and Society: European Journal of Humanistic Psychology,* XIII(2): 77–81.

Bartell, P.A. and Rubin, L.J. (1990) Dangerous liaisons: sexual intimacies in supervision. *Professional Psychology: Research and Practice,* 21(6): 442–50.

Belbin, M. (1981) *Management Teams: Why they Succeed or Fail.* London: Heinemann.

Bennett, M.J. (1993) Towards ethnorelatativism: a developmental model of intercultural sensitivity, in R.M. Paige (ed.) *Education for the Intercultural Experience,* 2nd edn. Yarmouth, ME: Intercultural Press.

Bennis, W. and Nanus, B. (1985) *Leaders: The Strategies for Taking Charge.* New York: Harper & Row.

Bernard, J.M. (1979) Supervisory training: a discrimination model. *Counsellor Education and Supervision,* 27: 500–9.

Bernard, J.M. (1994a) Multicultural supervision: a reaction to Leong and Wagner, Cook, Priest and Fukuyama. *Counselor Education and Supervision,* 34: 159–71.

Bernard, J.M. (1994b) Ethical and legal dimensions of supervision, in L.D. Borders (ed.) *Supervision: Exploring the Effective Components,* ERIC/CASS Digest Series. Greensboro, NC: University of North Carolina.

Bernard, J.M. and Goodyear, R. (1992) *Fundamentals of Clinical Supervision.* Boston, MA: Allyn & Bacon.

Berne, E. (1964) *Games People Play*. New York: Grove Press.

Bion, W. (1961) *Experiences in Groups*. London: Tavistock.

Bion, W. (1974) *Brazilian Lectures 1*. Rio de Janeiro: Imago Editora.

Bohm, D. (1987a) *Unfolding Meaning*. London: Routledge & Kegan Paul.

Bohm, D. (1987b) *Wholeness and the Implicate Order*. London: Routledge & Kegan Paul.

Bohm, D. (1989) Meaning and information, in P. Pylkkanen (ed.) *The Search for Meaning*. Northampton: Crucible/Thorsons.

Bohm, D. (1994) *Thought as System*. London: Routledge.

Blake, R. and Mouton, J. (1966) *Corporate Darwinism*. Houston, TX: Gulf Publishing.

Bond, M. and Holland, S. (1998) *Skills of Clinical Supervision for Nurses*. Buckingham: Open University Press.

Bond, T. (1993) *Standards and Ethics for Counselling*. London: Sage.

Borders, L.D. (ed.) (1994) *Supervision: Exploring the Effective Components*, ERIC/CASS Digest Series. Greensboro, NC: University of North Carolina.

Borders, L.D. and Leddick, G.R. (1987) *Handbook of Counseling Supervision*. Alexandria, VA: ACES.

Boyd, J. (1978) *Counsellor Supervision: Approaches, Preparation, Practices*. Muncie, IN: Accelerated Development.

Bramley, W. (1996) *The Supervisory Couple in Broad-Spectrum Psychotherapy*. London: Free Assocation Books.

Brinkmann, U. and Weerdenburg, O.V. (1999) *The Intercultural Development Inventory: A New Tool for Improving Intercultural Training?* Trieste, Italy: Sietar Europe Conference Proceedings 1999.

British Association for Counselling (1987) *How Much Supervision Should You Have?* Rugby: BAC.

British Association for Counselling (BAC) (1990) *Information Sheet No. 8: Supervision*. Rugby: BAC.

British Association for Counselling (BAC) (1996) *Code of Ethics and Practice for Supervisors of Counsellors*. Rugby: BAC.

Brown, A. (1984) *Consultation: An Aid to Effective Social Work*. London: Heinemann.

Brown, A. and Bourne, I. (1996) *The Social Work Supervisor*. Buckingham: Open University Press.

Butler-Sloss, E. (1988) *Report of the Inquiry in Child Abuse in Cleveland 1987*, Cm 412. London: HMSO.

Butterworth, C.A. and Faugier, J. (eds) (1992) *Clinical Supervision and Mentorship in Nursing*. London: Chapman & Hall.

Campbell, B. (1988) *Unofficial Secrets, Child Sexual Abuse: The Cleveland Case*. London: Virago.

Capewell, E. (1996) Staff care, in B. Lindsay and J. Tindall (eds) *Working with Children in Grief and Loss*. Newbury: Centre for Crisis Management and Education.

Capewell, E. (1997) *Handouts on Working with Trauma*. Newbury: Centre for Crisis Management and Education.

Caplan, G. (1970) *The Theory and Practice of Mental Health Consultation*. London: Tavistock.

Carifio, M.S. and Hess, A.K. (1987) Who is the ideal supervisor? *Professional Psychology: Research and Practice*, 18: 244–50.

Carroll, M. (1987) Privately circulated paper. Roehampton Institute, University of Surrey.

Carroll, M. (1994) Counselling supervision: international perspectives, in L.D. Borders (ed.) *Supervision: Exploring the Effective Components*, ERIC/CASS Digest Series. Greensboro, NC: University of North Carolina.

Carroll, M. (1995) The stresses of supervising counsellors, in W. Dryden (ed.) *The Stresses of Counselling in Action*. London: Sage.

Carroll, M. (1996) *Counselling Supervision: Theory, Skills and Practice*. London: Cassells.

Carroll, M. and Holloway, E. (eds) (1999) *Counselling Supervision in Context*. London: Sage.

Casement, P. (1985) *On Learning From the Patient*. London: Tavistock.

Casey, D. (1985) When is a team not a team? *Personnel Management*, January: 26–9.

Cherniss, C. (1980) *Staff Burnout*. Beverly Hills, CA: Sage.

Cherniss, C. and Egnatios, E. (1978) Clinical supervision in community mental health. *Social Work*, 23(2): 219–23.

Claxton, G. (1984) *Live and Learn*. London: Harper & Row.

Coche, E. (1977) Training of group therapists, in F.W. Kaslow (ed.) *Supervision, Consultation and Staff Training in the Helping Professions*. San Francisco: Jossey Bass.

Coleman, H.L.K. (1999) Training for multicultural supervision, in E. Holloway and M. Caroll (eds) *Training Counselling Supervisors*. London: Sage.

Conn, J.D. (1993) Delicate liaisons: the impact of gender differences on the supervisory relationship within social services. *Journal of Social Work Practice*, 1: 41–53.

Cook, D.A. (1994) Racial identity in supervision. *Counselor Education and Supervision*, 34: 132–9.

Cook, D.A. and Helms, J.E. (1988) Visible racial/ethnic group supervisees' satisfaction with cross-cultural supervision as predicted by relationship characteristics. *Journal of Counseling Psychology*, 35(3): 268–74.

Covey, S.R. (1990) *Principle-centered Leadership*. New York: Simon & Schuster.

CSTD (Centre for Staff Team Development) (1999) *Supervision Resource Book*. Bath: CSTD.

Davies, H. (1987) Interview with Robin Shohet.

De Mello, A. (1985) *One Minute Wisdom*. Anand, India: Guiarat Sahitya Prakash.

Dearnley, B. (1985) A plain man's guide to supervision. *Journal of Social Work Practice*, November: 52–65.

Disney, M.J. and Stephens, A.M. (1994) *Legal Issues in Clinical Supervision*. Alexandria, VA: American Counseling Association.

Doehrman, M.J.G. (1976) Parallel processes in supervision and psychotherapy. *Bulletin of the Menninger Clinic*, 40: pt 1.

Dryden, W. and Norcross, J.C. (1990) *Electicism and Integration in Counselling and Psychotherapy*. Loughton: Gale Centre Publications.

Dryden, W. and Thorne, B. (eds) (1991) *Training and Supervision for Counselling in Action*. London: Sage.

Edelwich, J. and Brodsky, A. (1980) *Burn-Out*. New York: Human Sciences.

Ekstein, R. (1969) Concerning the teaching and learning of psychoanalysis. *Journal of the American Psychoanalytic Association*, 17(2): 312–32.

Ekstein, R. and Wallerstein, R.W. (1972) *The Teaching and Learning of Psychotherapy*. New York: International Universities Press.

Eleftheriadou, Z. (1994) *Transcultural Counselling*. London: Central Book Publishing Ltd.

Ellis, M.V. and Dell, D.M. (1986) Dimensionality of supervisor roles: supervisor perception of supervision. *Journal of Counseling Psychology*, 33(3): 282–91.

Ernst, S. and Goddison, L. (1981) *In Our Own Hands: A Book of Self-Help Therapy*. London: Heinemann.

Feltham, C. and Dryden, W. (1994) *Developing Counsellor Supervision*. London: Sage.

Fineman, S. (1985) *Social Work Stress and Intervention*. Aldershot: Gower.

Fink, S.C., Beak, J. and Taddeo, K. (1971) Organizational crisis and change. *Journal of Applied Behavioural Science*, 17(1): 14–37.

Fisher, D. and Torbert, W.R. (1995) *Personal and Organizational Transformations*. London: McGraw-Hill.

Frankham, H. (1987) 'Aspects of supervision', MSc dissertation. Roehampton Institute, University of Surrey.

Freeman, E. (1985) The importance of feedback in clinical supervision: implications for direct practice. *The Clinical Supervisor*, 3(1): 5–26.

French, J.R.P. and Raven, B. (1967) The bases of social power, in D. Cartwright (ed.) *Studies in Social Power*. Ann Arbor, MI: Institute of Social Research.

Freud, S. (1927) *The Future of Illusion*, standard edition 21. London: Hogarth Press.

Friedlander, M.L. and Ward, L.G. (1984) Development and validation of the supervisory styles inventory. *Journal of Counseling Psychology*, 31(4): 541–57.

Friedlander, M.L., Siegal, S. and Brenock, K. (1989) Parallel processes in counseling and supervision: a case study. *Journal of Counseling Psychology*, 36: 149–57.

Fukuyama, M.A. (1994) Critical incidents in multicultural counseling supervision: phenomenological approach to supervision research. *Counselor Education and Supervision*, 134: 142–51.

Galassi, J.P. and Trent, P.J. (1987) A conceptual framework for evaluating supervision effectiveness. *Counselor Education and Supervision*, June: 260–9.

Gardener, L.H. (1980) Racial, ethnic and social class considerations in psychotherapy supervision, in A.K. Hess (ed.) *Psychotherapy Supervision: Theory, Research and Practice*. New York: Wiley.

Garratt, B. (1987) *The Learning Organization*. London: Fontana.

Geertz, C. (1973) *The Interpretation of Cultures*. New York: Basic Books.

Gilbert, M. and Evans, K. (forthcoming) *Psychotherapy Supervision: An Integrative Relational Approach*. Buckingham: Open University Press.

Gittermann, A. and Miller, I. (1977) Supervisors as educators, in F.W. Kaslow (ed.) *Supervision, Consultation and Staff Training in the Helping Professions*. San Francisco: Jossey Bass.

Goldberg, C. (1981) The peer supervision group: an examination of its purpose and process. *Group*, 5: 27–40.

Golembiewski, R.T. (1976) *Learning and Change in Groups*. London: Penguin.

Grant, P. (1999) Supervision and racial issues, in M. Carroll and E. Holloway (eds) *Counselling Supervision in Context*. London: Sage.

Guardian (1986) Society tomorrow, 1 October.

Guggenbühl-Craig, A. (1971) *Power in the Helping Professions*. Dallas, TX: Spring.

Hale, K.K. and Stoltenberg, C.D. (1988) The effects of self-awareness and evaluation apprehension on counselor trainee anxiety. *The Clinical Supervisor*, 6: 46–69.

Hammer, M.R. (1998) A measure of intercultural sensitivity: the intercultural development inventory, in S.M. Fowler and M.G. Mumford (eds) *The Intercultural Sourcebook: Cross-cultural Training Methods*, Vol. 2. Yarmouth, ME: The Intercultural Press.

Handy, C. (1976) *Understanding Organizations*. London: Penguin.

Harrison, R. (1994) *The Collected Papers of Roger Harrison*. London: McGraw-Hill.

Hawkins, P. (1979) Staff learning in therapeutic communities, in R. Hinshelwood and N. Manning (eds) *Therapeutic Communities, Reflections and Progress*. London: Routledge & Kegan Paul.

Hawkins, P. (1980) Between Scylla and Charybdis, in E. Jansen (ed.) *The Therapeutic Community Outside of the Hospital*. London: Croom Helm.

Hawkins, P. (1982) Mapping it out. *Community Care*, 22 July: 17–19.

Hawkins, P. (1985) Humanistic psychotherapy supervision: a conceptual framework. *Self and Society: European Journal of Humanistic Psychology*, 13(2): 69–79.

Hawkins, P. (1986) 'Living the Learning', PhD thesis. University of Bath.

Hawkins, P. (1988) A phenomenological psychodrama workshop, in P. Reason (ed.) *Human Inquiry in Action.* London: Sage.

Hawkins, P. (1989) The social learning approach to day and residential centres, in A. Brown and R. Clough (eds) *Groups and Groupings: Life and Work in Day and Residential Settings.* London: Tavistock.

Hawkins, P. (1991) The spiritual dimension of the learning organization. *Management Education and Development,* 22(3): 166–81.

Hawkins, P. (1993) *Shadow Consultancy,* working paper. Bath: Bath Consultancy Group.

Hawkins, P. (1994a) The changing view of learning, in J. Burgoyne (ed.) *Towards the Learning Company.* London: McGraw-Hill.

Hawkins, P. (1994b) Taking stock: facing the challenge. *Management Learning Journal,* 25(1): 71–82.

Hawkins, P. (1994c) *Organizational Culture: Evolution and Revolution.* Bath: Bath Consultancy Group.

Hawkins, P. (1995a) *Action Learning Guidebook.* Bath: Bath Consultancy Group.

Hawkins, P. (1995b) Supervision, in M. Jacobs (ed.) *The Care Guide.* London: Mowbrays.

Hawkins, P. (1997) Organizational culture: sailing between evangelism and complexity. *Human Relations,* 50(4): 417–40.

Hawkins, P. and Miller, E. (1994) Psychotherapy in and with organizations, in M. Pokorny and P. Clarkson (eds) *Handbook of Psychotherapy.* London: Routledge & Kegan Paul.

Hawkins, P. and Shohet, R. (1991) Approaches to the supervision of counsellors, in W. Dryden and B. Thorne (eds) *Training and Supervision for Counselling in Action.* London: Sage.

Hawkins, P. and Shohet, R. (1993) A review of the *Addictive Organization* by Schaef and Fassel. *Management Education and Development,* 24(2): 293–6.

Hawthorne, L. (1975) *Games supervisors play. Social Work,* 20 May: 179–83.

Herman, N. (1987) *Why Psychotherapy?* London: Free Association Books.

Heron, J. (1974) *Reciprocal Counselling.* Guildford: University of Surrey Human Potential Research Project.

Heron, J. (1975) *Six-Category Intervention Analysis.* Guildford: University of Surrey Human Potential Research Project.

Herskowitz, M.J. (1948) *Man and His Works.* New York: Knopf.

Hess, A.K. (ed.) (1980) *Psychotherapy Supervision: Theory, Research and Practice.* New York: Wiley.

Hess, A.K. (1987) Psychotherapy supervision: stages, Buber and a theory of relationship. *Professional Psychology: Research and Practice,* 18(3): 251–9.

Hickman, C.R. and Silva, M.A. (1985) *Creating Excellence.* London: Allen & Unwin.

Hillman, J. (1979) *Insearch: Psychology and Religion.* Dallas, TX: Spring.

Hinshelwood, R. and Manning, N. (1979) *Therapeutic Communities: Reflections and Progress.* London: Routledge & Kegan Paul.

Hofstede, G. (1980) *Cultures Consequences: International Differences in Work Related Values.* Beverley Hills, CA: Sage.

Hogan, R.A. (1964) Issues and approaches in supervision. *Psychotherapy: Theory, Research and Practice,* 1: 139–41.

Holloway, E. (1984) Outcome evaluation in supervision research. *The Counseling Psychologist,* 12(3): 167–74.

Holloway, E. (1987) Developmental models of supervision: is it development? *Professional Psychology: Research and Practice,* 18(3): 209–16.

Holloway, E. (1995) *Clinical Supervision: A Systems Approach.* Beverly Hills, CA: Sage.

Holloway, E. and Allsetter Neufeldt, S. (1995) Supervision: its contributions to treatment efficacy. *Journal of Consulting and Clinical Psychology*, 63(2): 207–13.

Holloway, E. and Carroll, M. (eds) (1999) *Training Counselling Supervisors*. London: Sage.

Holloway, E. and Gonzalez-Doupe, P. (in press) The learning alliance of supervision research to practice, in G.S. Tyron (ed.) *Counselling Based on Process Research*. Needham Heights, MA: Allyn & Bacon.

Holloway, E. and Johnston, R. (1985) Group supervision: widely practised but poorly understood. *Counselor Education and Supervision*, 24: 332–40.

Houston, G. (1985) Group supervision of groupwork. *Self and Society: European Journal of Humanistic Psychology*, XIII(2): 64–6.

Houston, G. (1990) *Supervision and Counselling*. London: Rochester Foundation.

Hunt, P. (1986) Supervision. *Marriage Guidance*, Spring: 15–22.

Illich, I. (1973) *Deschooling Society*. London: Penguin.

Inskipp, F. and Proctor, B. (1993) *The Art, Craft & Tasks of Counselling Supervision. Part 1: Making the Most of Supervision*. Twickenham: Cascade Publications.

Inskipp, F. and Proctor, B. (1995) *The Art, Craft & Tasks of Counselling Supervision. Part 2: Becoming a Supervisor*. Twickenham: Cascade Publications.

Jacobs, M. (1996) *In Search of Supervision*. Buckingham: Open University Press.

Jamplosky, G. (1979) *Love is Letting Go of Fear*. Berkeley, CA: Celestial Arts.

Jampolsky, G. (1999) *Forgiveness: The Greatest Healer of All*. Hillsboro, OR: Beyond Words Publishing.

Jones, M. (1982) *The Process of Change*. London: Routledge & Kegan Paul.

Jourard, S. (1971) *The Transparent Self*. New York: Van Nostrand.

Juch, B. (1983) *Personal Development*. Chichester: Wiley.

Kaberry, S.E. (1995) 'Abuse in Supervision', MEd thesis. University of Birmingham.

Kadushin, A. (1968) Games people play in supervision. *Social Work*, 13: 23–32.

Kadushin, A. (1976) *Supervision in Social Work*. New York: Columbia University Press.

Kadushin, A. (1977) *Consultation in Social Work*. New York: Columbia University Press.

Kadushin, A. (1992) *Supervision in Social Work*, 3rd edn. New York: Columbia University Press.

Kagan, N. (1980) Influencing human interaction: eighteen years with IPR, in A.K. Hess (ed.) *Psychotherapy Supervision: Theory, Research and Practice*. New York: Wiley.

Kahn, M.A. (1991) Counselling phychology in a multicultural society. *Counselling Psychology Review*, 6(3): 11–13.

Kareem, J. and Littlewood, R. (1992) *Intercultural Therapy: Themes, Interpretations and Practice*. Oxford: Blackwell.

Karpman, S. (1968) Fairy tales and script drama analysis, *Transactional Analysis Bulletin*, selected articles from volumes 1–9: 51–6.

Kaslow, F.W. (ed.) (1977) *Supervision, Consultation and Staff Training in the Helping Professions*. San Francisco: Jossey Bass.

Kelly, G.A. (1955) *The Psychology of Personal Constructs*, vols 1 and 2. New York: Norton.

Kemshall, A. (1995) Supervision and appraisal in the probation service, in J. Pritchard (ed.) *Good Practice in Supervision*. London: Jessica Kingsley.

Kevlin, F. (1987) Interview with Robin Shohet.

Kevlin, F. (1988) ' "Peervision": a comparison of hierarchical supervision of counsellors with consultation amongst peers', MSc dissertation. University of Surrey/ Roehampton Institute.

Kluckholn, F.R. and Stodtbeck, F.L. (1961) *Variations in Value Orientation.* New York: Row & Peterson.

Kolb, D.A., Rubin, I.M. and McIntyre, J.M. (1971) *Organizational Psychology: An Experiential Approach.* New York: Prentice Hall.

Krause, Inga-Britt (1998) *Therapy Across Culture.* London: Sage.

Lago, C. and Thompson, J. (1996) *Race, Culture and Counselling.* Buckingham: Open University Press.

Lambert, M.J. and Arnold, R.C. (1987) Research and the supervisory process. *Professional Psychology: Research and Practice*, 18(3): 217–24.

Langs, R. (1978) *The Listening Process.* New York: Jason Aronson.

Langs, R. (1983) *The Supervisory Experience.* New York: Jason Aronson.

Langs, R. (1985) *Workbook for Psychotherapists.* Emerson, NJ: Newconcept Press.

Langs, R. (1994) *Doing Supervision and Being Supervised.* London: Karnac Books.

Leddick, R.L. and Dye, H.A. (1987) Counselor supervision: effective supervision as portrayed by trainee expectation and performance. *Counsellor Education and Supervision*, 127: 139–54.

Leong, F.T.L. and Wagner, N.S. (1994) Supervision: what do we know? What do we need to know? *Counselor Education and Supervision*, 34: 117–31.

Lewin, K. (1952) Defining the field at a given time, in D. Cartwright (ed.) *Field Theory in Social Sciences.* London: Tavistock.

Liddle, B.J. (1986) Resistance to supervision: a response to perceived threat. *Counselor Education and Supervision*, December: 117–27.

Lievegoed, B.C.J. (1973) *The Developing Organization.* London: Tavistock.

Lindsay, G. and Clarkson, P. (1999) Ethical dilemmas of psychotherapists. *The Psychologist*, 12(4): 182–5.

Liss, J. (1985) Using mime and re-enactment to supervise body orientated therapy. *Self and Society: European Journal of Humanistic Psychology*, XIII(2): 82–5.

Loganbill, C., Hardy, E. and Delworth, U. (1982) Supervision, a conceptual model. *The Counseling Psychologist*, 10(1): 3–42.

McBride, M.C. and Martin, G.E. (1986) Dual-focus supervision: a non-apprenticeship approach. *Counselor Education and Supervision*, March: 175–82.

McLean, A. (1986) *Accessing Organization Cultures*, working paper. Bath: University of Bath.

McLean, A. and Marshall, J. (1988) *Working with Cultures: A Workbook for People in Local Government.* Luton: Local Government Training Board.

Marken, M. and Payne, M. (eds) (1988) *Enabling and Ensuring.* Leicester: Leicester National Youth Bureau and Council for Education and Training in Youth and Community Work.

Marshall, J. (1982) Job stressors: recent research in a variety of occupations. Paper presented to the 20th International Congress of Applied Psychology, Edinburgh.

Martin, J.S., Goodyear, R.K. and Newton, F.B. (1987) Clinical supervision: an intensive case study. *Professional Psychology: Research and Practice*, 18(3): 225–35.

Martindale, B., Morner, M., Rodriquez, M.E.C. and Vidit, J. (1997) *Supervision and its Vicissitudes.* London: Karnac Books.

Maslach, C. (1982) Understanding burnout: definitional issues in analysing a complex phenomenon, in W.S. Poine (ed.) *Job Stress and Burnout.* Beverley Hills, CA: Sage.

Mattinson, J. (1975) *The Reflection Process in Casework Supervision.* London: Institute of Marital Studies.

Mearns, D. (1991) On being a supervisor, in W. Dryden and B. Thorne (eds) *Training and Supervision for Counselling in Action.* London: Sage.

Menzies, I. (1970) *The Functioning of Social Systems as a Defence Against Anxiety.* London: Tavistock Institute of Human Relations.

Mintz, E. (1983) Gestalt approaches to supervision. *Gestalt Journal* 6(1): 17–27.

Morrison, T. (1993) *Staff Supervision in Social Care.* London: Longman.

Munson, C.E. (1987) Sex roles and power relationships in supervision. *Professional Psychology: Research and Practice,* 18(3): 236–43.

Nelson, M.L. and Holloway, E.L. (1990) Relation of gender to power and involvement in supervision. *Journal of Counseling Psychology,* 37: 473–81.

O'Toole, L. (1987) 'Counselling skills and self-awareness training: their effect on mental well being and job satisfaction in student nurses', MSc dissertation. Roehampton Institute, University of Surrey.

Page, S. (1999) Shadow and the Counsellor. London: Routledge.

Page, S. and Wosket, V. (1994) *Supervising the Counsellor: A Cyclical Model.* London: Routledge.

Parker, M. (1990) 'Supervision constructs and supervisory style as related to theoretical orientation', MSc thesis. University of Surrey.

Payne, C. and Scott, T. (1982) *Developing Supervision of Teams in Field and Residential Social Work,* Paper no. 12. London: National Institute of Social Work.

Pederson, B.P. (1997) *Culture-Centred Counselling Interventions.* London: Sage.

Pederson, B.P. (ed.) (1987) *Handbook of Cross-Cultural Counselling and Therapy.* London: Praegger.

Peters, T.J. and Waterman, R.H. (1982) *In Search of Excellence.* New York: Harper & Row.

Peterson, F.K. (1991) *Race and Ethnicity.* New York: Haworth.

Philipson, J. (1992) *Practising Equality: Women, Men and Social Work.* London: CCETSW.

Pines, A.M., Aronson, E. and Kafry, D. (1981) *Burnout: From Tedium to Growth.* New York: The Free Press.

Plant, R. (1987) *Managing Change and Making it Stick.* London: Fontana.

Ponterotto, J.G. and Zander, T.A. (1984) A multimodal approach to counsellor supervision. *Counsellor Education and Supervision,* 24: 40–50.

Pope, R.S. and Vasquez, M.J.T. (1991) *Ethics in Psychotherapy and Counselling: A Practical Guide for Psychologists.* San Francisco: Jossey Bass.

Pritchard, J. (ed.) (1995) *Good Practice in Supervision.* London: Jessica Kingsley.

Proctor, B. (1988a) Supervision: a co-operative exercise in accountability, in M. Marken and M. Payne (eds) *Enabling and Ensuring.* Leicester: Leicester National Youth Bureau and Council for Education and Training in Youth and Community Work.

Proctor, B. (1988b) *Supervision a Working Alliance* (videotape training manual). St Leonards-on-sea: Alexia Publications.

Proctor, B. (1997) Contracting in supervision, in C. Sills (ed.) *Contracts in Counselling.* London: Sage.

Ram Dass and Gorman, P. (1985) *How Can I help?* London: Rider.

Reason, P. (1988) *Human Inquiry in Action.* London: Sage.

Reason, P. (1994) *Participation in Human Inquiry.* London: Sage.

Revans, R.W. (1982) *The Origins and Growth of Action Learning.* London: Chartwell-Bratt, Bromley & Lund.

Richards, M., Payne, C. and Sheppard, A. (1990) *Staff Supervision in Child Protection Work.* London: National Institute for Social Work.

Ridley, C.R. (1995) *Overcoming Unintentional Racism in Counselling and Therapy: A Practitioners Guide to Intentional Intervention.* London: Sage.

Rioch, M.J., Coulter, W.R. and Weinberger, D.M. (1976) *Dialogues for Therapists.* San Francisco: Jossey Bass.

Rogers, C.R. (1957) The necessary and sufficient conditions of therapeutic personality change. *Journal of Counseling Psychology,* 21: 95–103.

Rowan, J. (1983) *Reality Game: A Guide to Humanistic Counselling and Therapy.* London: Routledge & Kegan Paul.

Ryde, J. (1997) *A Step Towards Understanding Culture in Relation to Psychotherapy*, working paper. Bath: Bath Centre for Psychotherapy and Counselling.

Sansbury, D.L. (1982) Developmental supervision from a skills perspective. *The Counseling Psychologist*, 10(1): 53–7.

Savickas, M.L., Marquart, C.D. and Supinski, C.R. (1986) Effective supervision in groups. *The Counseling Psychologist*, September: 17–25.

Schaef, A.W. (1992) *When Society Becomes an Addict.* Wellingborough: Thorsons.

Schaef, A.W. and Fassel, D. (1990) *The Addictive Organization.* San Francisco: Harper.

Schein, E.H. (1985) *Organizational Culture and Leadership.* San Francisco: Jossey Bass.

Schön, D. (1983) *The Reflective Practioner.* New York: Basic Books.

Schutz, W.C. (1973) *Elements of Encounter.* Big Sur, CA: Joy Press.

Searles, H.F. (1955) The informational value of the supervisor's emotional experience, in *Collected Papers on Schizophrenia and Related Subjects.* London: Hogarth Press.

Searles, H.F. (1975) The patient as therapist to the analyst, in R. Langs (ed.) *Classics in Psychoanalytic Technique.* New York: Jason Aronson.

Senge, P. (1990) *The Fifth Discipline: The Art and Practice of The Learning Organization.* New York: Doubleday.

Shainberg, D. (1983) Teaching therapists how to be with their clients, in J. Westwood (ed.) *Awakening the Heart.* Boulder, CO: Shambhala.

Sharpe, M. (ed.) (1995) *The Third Eye: Supervision of Analytic Groups.* London: Routledge.

Shearer, A. (1983) Who saves the social workers? *Guardian*, 6 July.

Shipton, G. (1997) *Supervision of Psychotherapy and Counselling: Making a Place to Think.* Buckingham: Open University Press.

Shohet, R. (1985) *Dreamsharing.* Wellingborough: Turnstone Press.

Shohet, R. and Wilmot, J. (1991) The key issue in the supervision of counsellors, in W. Dryden and B. Thorne (eds) *Training and Supervision for Counselling in Action.* London: Sage.

Shulman, L. (1993) *Interactional Supervision.* Washington, DC: NASW Press.

Skovholt, T.M. and Ronnestad, M.H. (1995) *The Evolving Professional Self: Stages and Themes in Therapist and Counsellor Development.* Chichester: Wiley.

Smith, D. (1985) The client as supervisor: the approach of Robert Langs. *Self and Society: European Journal of Humanistic Psychology*, XIII(2): 92–5.

Spice Jr, C.G. and Spice, W.H. (1976) A triadic method of supervision in the training of counselors and counseling supervisors. *Counselor Education and Supervision*, 15: 251–8.

Stevens, A. (1991) *Disability Issues: Developing Anti-discriminatory Practice.* London: CCETSW.

Stolorow, R.D. and Atwood, G.E. (1992) *Contexts of Being.* New York: The Analytic Press.

Stolorow, R.D., Brandschaft, B. and Atwood, G.E. (1987) *Treatment: An Intersubjective Approach.* New York: The Analytic Press.

Stoltenberg, C.D. and Delworth, U. (1987) *Supervising Counselors and Therapists.* San Francisco: Jossey Bass.

Subby, R. (1984) *Inside the Chemically Dependent Marriage: Denial and Manipulation in Co-dependence: An Emerging Issue.* Hollywood Beach, FL: Health Communications.

Sue, D.W. and Sue, D. (1990) *Counselling the Culturally Different.* New York: Wiley.

Symington, N. (1986) *The Analytic Experience.* London: Free Association Books.

Teitelbaum, S.H. (1990) Supertransference: the role of the supervisor's blind spots. *Psychoanalytic Psychology*, 7(2): 243–58.

Thompson, J. (1991) 'Issues of race and culture in counseling supervision training courses', MSc thesis. Polytechnic of East London.

Thompson, N. (1993) *Anti-Discriminatory Practice.* London: BASW/Macmillan.

Tichy, N.M. (1997) *The Leadership Engine: How Winning Companies Build Leadership at Every Level.* New York: HarperCollins.

Tonnesmann, M. (1979) The human encounter in the helping professions. Fourth Winnicott Conference, London, March.

Trompenaars, A. (1994) *Riding the Waves of Culture.* Burr Ridge, IL: Irwin.

Tuckman, B.W. (1965) Developmental sequences in small groups. *Psychological Bulletin,* 63(6): 384–99.

Tyler, F.B., Brome, D.R. and Williams, J.E. (1991) *Ethnic Validity, Ecology and Psychotherapy: A Psychosocial Competence Model.* New York: Plenum Press.

Weerdenburg, O. (1996) Thinking values through and through, in efdm: *Training the Fire Brigade: Preparing for the Unimaginable.* Brussels: efdm.

Wilmot, J. and Shohet, R. (1985) Paralleling in the supervision process. *Self and Society: European Journal of Humanistic Psychology,* XIII(2): 86–92.

Winnicott, D.W. (1965) *Maturational Processes and the Facilitating Environment.* London: Hogarth Press.

Winnicott, D.W. (1971) *Playing and Reality.* London: Tavistock.

Worthington, E.L. (1987) Changes in supervision as counselors and supervisors gain experience: a review. *Professional Psychology: Research and Practice,* 18(3): 189–208.

Index

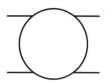

Feedback request

We would welcome any feedback on this book and any suggestions or contributions for further editions or future publications. These should be sent to:

Peter Hawkins and Robin Shohet
Centre for Staff Team Development
c/o Bath Consultancy Group,
24 Gay Street,
Bath, BA1 2PD

Tel: 0(044) 1225 333737
Fax: 0(044) 1225 333738

IN SEARCH OF SUPERVISION

Michael Jacobs (ed.)

Following the success of *In Search of a Therapist*, this final book in the series provides a unique window into the supervisory process. It takes a session, with background information, from the editor's own work with a long-term client, Ruth, and presents the dilemmas faced by the therapist to five supervisors – each one from very different therapeutic traditions:

- communicative psychotherapy
- self-psychology
- person-centred psychotherapy
- cognitive-behavioural therapy
- family therapy

In Search of Supervision offers the first real insight into the process of supervision of an actual session and enables counsellors and therapists to see how different orientations or schools of therapy and counselling react to and understand the same client and therapist. This fascinating book ends with a final chapter in which the therapist and client comment on the impact of the five supervisors on the work of their therapy together.

In Search of Supervision will be of interest to a wide range of counsellors and therapists, not only those working as or training as supervisors, but all those who experience supervision.

Contents
Michael Jacobs: in search of a supervisor – Ruth and Michael Jacobs: the session for supervision – The reader's response – Alan Cartwright: psychoanalytic self psychology – Prue Conradi: person-centred therapy – Melanie Fennell: cognitive-behaviour therapy – David Livingstone Smith: communicative psychotherapy – Sue Walrond-Skinner: family therapy – Michael Jacobs and Ruth: review and response.

Contributors
Alan Cartwright, Prue Conradi, Melanie Fennell, David Livingstone Smith, Sue Walrond-Skinner.

192pp   0 335 19258 0 (Paperback)

SUPERVISION OF PSYCHOTHERAPY AND COUNSELLING
MAKING A PLACE TO THINK

Geraldine Shipton (ed.)

- What do we really know about the supervision of therapy and counselling?
- What kind of things make it easier, and what gets in the way?
- How do therapy and supervision resemble one another, and in what ways do they differ?

In an effort to address these pressing questions, this volume brings together authors from a variety of different perspectives and orientations to comment on supervision. Although strongly influenced by psychoanalytic ideas, the book also offers humanistic insights into good supervision practices. It is recommended reading for all experienced therapists and counsellors, and will be particularly useful to those undertaking advanced courses on supervision.

Contents

176pp   0 335 19512 1 (Paperback)   0 335 19513 X (Hardback)

SKILLS OF CLINICAL SUPERVISION FOR NURSES
A PRACTICAL GUIDE FOR SUPERVISEES, CLINICAL SUPERVISORS
AND MANAGERS

Meg Bond and Stevie Holland

This is the first practical book on clinical supervision for nurses. It offers
ways of understanding the context of clinical supervision in nursing –
especially why it has taken so long to be seen as important – and pinpoints
organizational and personal pitfalls that can sabotage its effectiveness.
The book provides practical guidance for supervisees, emphasizing self-
empowerment and developing the reflective skills necessary to make full
use of clinical supervision. It offers clinical supervisors an in-depth look
at their one-to-one and group facilitation skills and shows how to develop
them. It gives guidance to managers on how to sponsor and coordinate
systems of clinical supervision.

While this book draws on theoretical literature on the subject of clinical
supervision in nursing and allied professions, readers will also benefit from
the authors' direct experience in participation, observation, training and
consultancy in clinical supervision.

Contents
*Introduction – Part 1: The context of clinical supervision in nursing – The surface
picture: the development and value of clinical supervision – The hidden picture:
resistance to clinical supervision and implications for the clinical supervision relationship – Part 2: Specific skills of clinical supervision – The clinical supervision relationship: a working alliance – Reflective skills of the supervisee – Support and catalytic
skills of the clinical supervisor – Informative and challenging skills of the clinical
supervisor – Skills of group clinical supervision – Part 3: Organising clinical supervision systems – Setting up clinical supervision – References – Index.*

256pp   0 335 19660 8 (Paperback)   0 335 19661 6 (Hardback)

THE SOCIAL WORK SUPERVISOR
SUPERVISION IN COMMUNITY, DAY CARE AND RESIDENTIAL SETTINGS

Allan Brown and Iain Bourne

The Social Work Supervisor is the first comprehensive British text on supervision of staff in social work, community care and social welfare settings. It examines the changing social work scene of the 1990s, and breaks new ground in areas such as:

- anti-oppressive supervision
- supervision of post-traumatic stress
- group supervision.

The Social Work Supervisor is a comprehensive text for the social work supervisor, and for all supervisors in social welfare and community care settings. It includes new material not found in other books on supervision. The authors emphasize the importance of the supervisory relationship, regular skilled supervision and a clear value base in the provision of good quality services.

This book provides a clear theoretical framework, bringing theory and practice together through numerous practical examples of supervision in action. One major chapter examines a range of typical supervision situations, and provides suggestions for possible supervisor responses.

The Social Work Supervisor will be invaluable reading for new and experienced supervisors; practice-teachers supervising students; trainers of supervisors; and social work managers.

Contents
Introduction – Setting the scene – The making of a supervisor – Supervision and power: an anti-oppressive perspective – Getting started: contracts and boundaries – A model for practice – The supervision relationship – Stress and trauma: the supervisor's response – Supervision and the team – Group supervision – Training and development – Core themes in a time of change – References – Index.

208pp   0 335 19458 3 (Paperback)   0 335 19459 1 (Hardback)